THE FILMS OF
JEAN-LUC GODARD

THE SUNY SERIES

CULTURAL STUDIES IN CINEMA / VIDEO

Wheeler Winston Dixon, editor

THE FILMS OF JEAN-LUC GODARD

WHEELER
WINSTON
DIXON

STATE UNIVERSITY OF NEW YORK PRESS

Published by
State University of New York Press, Albany

For information, address State University of New York Press,
State University Plaza, Albany, N.Y., 12246

Production by Marilyn P. Semerad
Marketing by Theresa Abad Swierzowski

Library of Congress Cataloging-in-Publication Data

Dixon, Wheeler, W., 1950-
    The films of Jean-Luc Godard / by Wheeler Winston Dixon.
      p.   cm. — (SUNY series, cultural studies in cinema/video)
    Filmography: p.
    Includes bibliographical references and index.
    ISBN 0-7914-3285-8 (hardcover : alk. paper). — ISBN 0-7914-3286-6
(pbk. : alk. paper)
    1. Godard, Jean Luc, 1930-   —Criticism and interpretation.
I. Title. II. Series.
PN1998.3.G63D55 1997
791.43'0233'092—dc20   96-26612
                                                                 CIP

10 9 8 7 6 5 4 3 2 1

For Gwendolyn

CONTENTS

LIST OF
ILLUSTRATIONS

ACKNOWLEDGMENTS

———————————— ◉ ————————————

The creation of any book is an arduous task, particularly when the subjects of the volume are as prolific as Jean-Luc Godard and his two principal collaborators, Jean-Pierre Gorin and Anne-Marie Miéville. For this book, I would like to thank the following people who have directly or indirectly contributed to the completion of this work; it could not have been fully realized without them. Stuart Kaufman, Jane Klain, and Gwendolyn Audrey Foster provided valuable research materials; Dana Miller typed and proofed the manuscript; Akira Lippit assisted with translations from the French; Ron Magliozzi, Charles Silver, and Sally Berger of the Museum of Modern Art helped with information for the filmography. The photographs in this volume from various films by Godard, Gorin, and Miéville appear through the courtesy of New Yorker Films, Noon Pictures, Electronic Arts Intermix, the Jerry Ohlinger Archives, Budget Films, and Cinema Parallel.

Above all other considerations, I have tried to make this volume both compact and comprehensive, covering all of Godard's work on film and video through 1995, so that the finished text might serve as a useful overview of Godard's career in its entirety. Yet at the same time, I wanted to briefly consider the numerous social, political, sexual, racial, class and economic taxonomies addressed by Godard, Gorin, and Miéville in their films and videos. Godard, it seems to me, has always functioned best within the context of a collaborative enterprise, and another critical project of this volume was the acknowledgment of the considerable input both Anne-Marie Miéville and Jean-Pierre

Gorin have had in Godard's works. Godard may sign the films and videos he makes, or he may not; but during his Dziga Vertov period with Gorin, and from 1972 to the present with Miéville, Godard's vision has been assisted and facilitated by these two key associates, whose efforts are often subsumed into Godard's *oeuvre* as a whole.

Finally, I wished to discuss the concept of "the end of cinema" as it relates to the work of Godard, Gorin, and Miéville. Godard has been stating since the closing titles of *Le Week-end* (and perhaps before) that the cinema is officially a "dead" art, like Renaissance painting or the eighteenth-century novel. Numerous factors have contributed to the "death of the cinema": these include television itself, CD-ROM technology, the Internet, the World Wide Web, home videotape, laserdiscs, cable and satellite dish transmission, to name but a few competing systems of imagistic discourse. Yet I will argue here that Godard, Gorin, and Miéville, throughout all their works, have embarked upon nothing less than a project to purposefully *exhaust* the apparatus of cinema/video, to hasten the end of film's domain over the collectively perceived consciousness of the real. If the collapse of cinema is imminent, then it may be argued that Godard and his co-workers seek to hasten its demise. Thus, this text seeks to be both brief and, to a certain degree, revisionary. The birth of cinema may now be seen to have prefigured the death of cinema, whether one dates cinema's reign from the first projection by the Lumières in 1895, or Augustin Le Prince's experimental work in England in 1888 (Rawlence, 218–19).

Cinema has thus passed into the sarcophagus of memory, as it was designed to do from its inception, and the hypertaxonomic structures of narrative, characterization, semantic syntax, and "instant read" iconographic glyphs which once informed the grammar of cinema have been rendered impotent through ceaseless repetition. Godard, Gorin, and Miéville recognized this *exhaustion* of the cinema/video apparatus long ago. The first centenary of the cinema may well be, in fact, its last. Other mediums of imagistic exchange are now powerful competitors for the public's attention. Although the spectacle of the cinema continues, the narrative structures and imagistic conceits which once thrilled audiences now bore them; it is this collapse of the narrative cinema, and the concomitant questions this collapse inevitably raises, which most fascinates Godard and his collaborators in their work as cinema/video artists. I hope, then, to begin the work of exploring this issue of the "end of cinema" in this volume, particularly as it pertains to Godard's late work.

While writing this volume, I had conversations with a number of scholars whose insights were of great value in writing this text, and I would particularly like to thank Larry Kardish, Dana Polan, David Desser, Michael Walsh, Marcia Landy, Lester Friedman and Arthur Nolletti in this regard. In addition, I owe a debt to those scholars who have written on Godard from the late 1950s onward, and I direct the reader to the "Works Cited" section of this text for a select group of interviews and critical essays on the works of Godard, Gorin, and Miéville. The credits for the films discussed in this volume have been compiled from a variety of sources, and information presented often conflicted. In such cases, I relied upon the actual credits within the films themselves as the final authority. And, of course, my thanks must go to Jean-Luc Godard, Jean-Pierre Gorin, and Anne-Marie Miéville for their creation of the films and videos discussed in this volume, works that continue to excite our imagination, and challenge our expectations of that which we call "the cinema."

CHAPTER ONE

○

The Theory of Production

Although the mainstream cinema continues to proliferate, and blockbuster films like *The Rock* (1996) and *Twister* (1996) capture huge theatrical audiences, the cinema itself is going through a period of radical change at the end of its first century, coexisting with CD-ROM interactive "movies," video cassette and laserdisc distribution, cable television, satellite television, video games, and a host of competing sound/image constructs. While such recent films as *Virtuosity* (1995) demonstrate the limitations of interactive video systems rather than heralding a seemingly limitless figurative horizon, the 1995 production of *Mortal Kombat* is a spin-off of a wildly popular video game, and owes whatever temporal popularity it achieved as an ancillary manifestation of its source material. The *Wayne's World* films are spin-offs from the television comedy showcase *Saturday Night Live*; *Super Mario Brothers* (1995) is yet another non-interactive version of an interactive original. Low-budget films such as *The Brothers McMullen* (1995), *Clerks* (1994), *Go Fish* (1994) and other fringe enterprises may momentarily capture the public's fancy, but in every case, these productions are now seen as stepping-stones to larger-scale Hollywood films rather than individual achievements in and of themselves. The exponentially rising cost of film production (not to mention distribution and publicity) helps to ensure the hegemony of the dominant industrial vision in the

1

middle-American marketplace, and the super-conglomeration of existing production, distribution and exhibition entities further assures the primacy of the readily marketable, pre-sold film, as opposed to a more quirky, individualistic vision.

Theatrical distribution, the mainstay of motion picture distribution for more than a century, is obsolete. Target audiences are increasingly younger, and these viewers perceive the experience of seeing a film primarily as an escape from the mundanity of their prepackaged existences, as witness the popularity of such lowest-common-denominator films as *Clueless* (1995), *Dumb and Dumber* (1995), *Forrest Gump* (1994), *Operation Dumbo Drop* (1995), and others too numerous to mention. European films are no longer distributed in America; they are remade in Hollywood, in English, with American stars—and then distributed overseas in this revisionist format. The few foreign films that attain moderately wide release in the United States are lavish costume spectacles.

As we approach the millennium, it is apparent that people today go to the movies *not* to think, *not* to be challenged, but rather to be tranquilized and coddled. Sequels are safe bets for exploitation, provided that the original film performs well at the box office; it is for this reason alone that nearly every mainstream film today is designed with an "open" ending, allowing the film to be franchised if the parent of the series captures the public's fancy. Television has become a wilderness of talk shows and infomercials, with time so precious that even the end credits of series episodes are shown on a split-screen with teasers from the upcoming program, to dissuade viewers from channel-surfing, which is nevertheless rampant.

Psychic hot lines offer spurious counsel at $3.99 a minute, shopping channels commodify the images we see into discrete, marketable units, "no money down" real estate brokers hope to dazzle us with their varying formulae for success. The cable movie channels run only current fare, or thoroughly canonical classics, avoiding subtitling and black and white imagery (with rare exceptions) at all costs. Revival houses screen films in only a few major cities, particularly Paris and New York. And indeed, it seems very much as if the first century of cinema will now be left to the ministrations of museum curators and home video/laserdisc collectors, rather than remaining a part of our shared collective cultural heritage.

With films so banal, is is any wonder that more adventurous viewers/auditors are turning to the internet, e-mail, the nascent world of cyberspace, in search of not only a cheap medium of expression, but also human contact? For this last is what the cinema inherently denies us; sealed in a can, projected on a screen, we watch it, and it surveills us, but the connection between viewer and viewed is gossamer thin. CD-ROM and cartridge games offer a more concrete, though still synthetic connection to the spectacle witnessed by the viewer/participant—an illusion, in fact, of control and interactivity.

The limits of this insular spectacle are striking, and the technology at present is clumsy and expensive. But the experiential horizon is there, and the strip of film that runs through a conventional 35mm projector is an archaic *aide de mémoire* of an era of puppet shows and magic lanterns. To satisfy us, the spectacle must engulf us, threaten us, sweep us up from the first. The "plots" of most interactive games are primarily simple—kill or be killed. These games achieve (at home and in the arcade) a wide currency among viewers bored by the lack of verisimilitude offered by the conventional cinema. And because of this lack, the cinema, to put it bluntly, is dying.

Would the career of a *cinéaste* like Jean-Luc Godard have been possible in our present marketplace of imagistic constructs? Denied theatrical release, relegated to the "Hot Singles" section of Blockbuster, how could any of Godard's cheap and transcendent early films ever have achieved a global audience? The exigencies of 1960s theatrical film distribution constituted a series of paradoxically liberating strictures; for a film to make a profit at all, it *had* to appear in a theater. Other markets, with the exception of television (which ran only older films) did not exist. Thus distributors were forced to seek the widest possible theatrical release pattern for even the most marginal of films, and it is this way that Jean-Luc Godard achieved and consolidated his initial reputation in the late 1950s and early 1960s. Such a project would be impossible today. Godard's budgets of the early period of his career—an average of $100,000 for a 35mm B/W feature film—are also astonishing today.

Yet what is most remarkable about Jean-Luc Godard's career in the cinema may be the fact that he has gone on making "small,

FIGURE 1. Jean-Luc Godard during editing of *Les Carabiniers* (1963). Courtesy New Yorker Films.

personal" films, films created entirely to suit himself and his collaborators, when the rest of the industry is desperately scrambling to please the widest possible audience. Godard did away with narrative after his first dozen films; now his films and videos are visual/aural essays, meditations, created in a world removed from ordinary commerce. Yet Godard still finds backers for his films, even when the results don't always please his sponsors, and seems more dedicated to his lonely, individual vision at the age of sixty-five than he was in his twenties. Jean-Luc Godard may joke in his videos and films from time to time, but he is not an entertainer. Godard is a moralist—perhaps the last moralist that the medium of cinema will ever possess.

Indeed, Jean-Luc Godard is arguably the consummate essayist and aesthetician of postnarrative cinema/video. With his first feature, *À bout de souffle* (*Breathless*), made in 1959, Godard created a visual style of radical jump cuts *within* a scene that startled both audiences and critics; in 1994, working with international Euro-star Gérard Depardieu, Godard directed *Hélas pour moi* (1994), a semi-autobiographical meditation on his life and work of such personal intensity that Depardieu, unable to stand the strain of collaborating with Godard, walked off the picture after three weeks of shooting on a six-week schedule. Typically, Godard was unfazed by Depardieu's departure: he completed the film, using all of Depardieu's material that he could salvage, and later publicly complained that he got along with the famed actor "not at all. He was supposed to work six weeks. He walked out after three. The extras did more acting than he did, but without him there would have been no money" (Sarris 1994, 89). The same thing happened in 1987 when Godard created his highly idiosyncratic version of *King Lear* with Molly Ringwald, Woody Allen, Burgess Meredith, and theatrical director Peter Sellars. Originally, Norman Mailer and his daughter, Kate, were to have appeared in the roles taken over by Ringwald and Meredith; when Mailer bailed out on the production on the first day of filming, Godard used every frame of footage he had on the Mailers in the final film (repeating one scene twice by using alternative "takes"), and incorporating the story of the Mailers' defection into a whispered voiceover on the film's soundtrack.

Godard called for the colorization of his early black and white films when others were still outraged by the process; he also directed a series of controversial advertisements for Girbaud blue jeans in 1988, to support his work as a filmmaker. During the late 1960s and early 1970s, Godard fervently declared himself a Marxist filmmaker on any number of occasions; now he flatly states that "I never read Marx" (Sarris 1994, 89). He has made only the films that pleased him, in the way that he wished to make them, using commercial stars like Brigitte Bardot (in *Le Mépris* [*Contempt*], 1963) to obtain financing when necessary, but never compromising his individuality as an artist. Indeed, this book will demonstrate that Godard is incapable of creating a conventional film, with the possible exception of *Opération béton* (1954), a documentary of the building of a dam that is Godard's first recorded cinematic effort.

Most recently, Godard has completed an autobiographical meditation on his life and work in the cinema entitled *JLG/JLG—autoportrait de décembre* (1994), produced by the French cinema distribution giant Gaumont; in 1995, Godard and Anne-Marie Miéville co-directed a sponsored video which perversely heralds the death of French cinema while purporting to celebrate its first centenary, *2 x 50 ans de cinéma français*, much to the surprise of the video's producers. For Godard, the cinema may be dead, but he continues to create work in a medium he knows to be sealed off in the past, combining a vast swirl of existing images in his ongoing personal series *Histoire(s) du cinéma* (1989–   ), and even creating an industrial film for the French telephone company Télécom (*Puissance de la parole*, 1988), which ridicules the telephone as a worthless means of false communication. No matter who his producer is, Godard does exactly as he pleases, creating work that is simultaneously caustic and idiosyncratic. With difficult yet simultaneously resonant films such as *Allemagne année 90 neuf zéro* (*Germany Year 90 Nine Zero*), made in 1991 but not released theatrically in the United States until January 1995, Godard has moved further and further away from the typical concerns of mainstream cinema: narrative, continuity, even theatrical or video distribution on a modest scale. At present, Godard seems intent upon *production* above all else—the creation of new work with a minimum of exploitation fuss. Godard's early black and white films, such as *Le Petit Soldat* (*The Little Soldier*), made in 1960, or *Les Carabiniers* (1963), touched off storms of controversy upon their initial release, and were beloved and reviled in equal measure by Godard's partisans and critics. The early films cost between $100,000 and $150,000 each, a figure that is risible today, and yet each of these early films barely recouped the combined costs of production and distribution because of their unconventional visual and narrative structure.

Then as now, Godard's films caused extreme reactions in those who viewed them. Such now-classic films as *Alphaville, une étrange aventure de Lemmy Caution* (*Alphaville*), made in 1965, and *Masculin Féminin* (*Masculine Feminine*), made in 1966, were dismissed by many contemporary reviewers when first released as amateurish, obscure, and didactic to the point of boredom. Now, *King Lear* (1987), *Passion* (1982), *Prénom: Carmen* (*First Name: Carmen*) (1983), *Détective* (1985), and *Grandeur et décadence d'un petit commerce de cinéma* (*The Grandeur and Decadence of the Smalltime Filmmaker*), completed in 1986, elicit similarly polar responses from those lucky enough to see them in a theater, or more likely on videocassette. Yet all these films really seek is an audience at once sophisticated and innocent enough to appreciate Godard's (and Gorin and Miéville's) bracingly apocalyptic vision of the cinema/video image/sound construct. Godard and his collaborators have created a cinema of resistance, a domain of hypertextual imagery that is both reflexive and peculiarly seductive. In thirty years, perhaps, one may be able to judge more accurately the scope and breadth of Godard's accomplishments.

For the present, it seems to me that all valuational judgments of Godard/Gorin/Miéville's work are both premature and ill-informed. The contextual subtext of Godard's work is not only the domain of cinema, but also literature, painting, music, and the related plastic arts. Godard and his associates represent something rare in twentieth-century culture: the filmmaker as philosopher. Nietzche's later works fell dead from the press upon their initial publication; F. Scott Fitzgerald's novels and short stories were all out of print when he died in 1940. Today, both Fitzgerald and Nietzche, and a host of other misinterpreted and prescient artists, are recognized for the visionaries they were; I would argue that the same is true of Godard. As of this writing, in late 1997, Godard continues to produce new films and videos with ever-increasing prodigiousness, without bothering with theatrical, or even home-video release in a number of cases. Godard today is intent, above all other considerations, on the creation of new work, whether or not it reaches an audience.

Jean-Luc Godard was born on December 3, 1930, in Paris, the second of four children. Godard's grandfather was a person of considerable wealth, and his parents, Paul-Jean Godard, a physician, and Odile Monod, the daughter of an extremely rich family, made sure that the young Jean-Luc's childhood was both luxurious and secure. Jean-Luc Godard had one older sibling, Rachel Godard, and many years later his parents would have two other children, Claude and Véronique. Paul-Jean Godard was from all accounts a highly distinguished practitioner, and obtained a license to practice medicine in both France and Great Britain. Odile Monod, daughter of Julien Monod, founder of the Banque de Paris et des Pays-Bas, met Paul-Jean Godard during the course of their joint medical studies at university, but Odile dropped out of school to marry Paul-Jean Godard and start a family. Godard recalls his childhood as one of idyllic peace and safety, and certainly, from a child's perspective, he is entirely correct in this perception. He spent much of his time at the home of Julien Monod, Odile's father, who owned an enormous tract of land in France near Lake Geneva. As Colin MacCabe notes, "Godard's memories of his childhood are of a paradise full of affection and wealth. Everything centered on Julien Monod and his large estate on the French side of Lake Geneva, the site of endless family gatherings, as the pious Protestant banker commemorated the feasts of the year with his numerous children and grandchildren" (MacCabe 1992, 14). Indeed, Godard would emotionally if not literally "revisit" this haunted site of childhood in his later film *Nouvelle vague* (1990), a meditation on the forces that helped to shape his intellectual outlook as an adult.

But Jean-Luc Godard also retained strong ties to his Swiss heritage, inasmuch as his father, Paul-Jean, decided almost immediately after Jean-Luc's birth to move his family to Nyon, Switzerland, where he set up a successful medical practice. His parents lived their lives with a considerable degree of domestic friction. Odile attempted to return to medical school after the birth of Claude, but soon gave up this ambition; Paul-Jean's medical practice was profitable, but scarcely of the same financial dimensions as the world of banking inhabited by the Monods. The young Jean-Luc thus travelled back and forth constantly between the serene geography of the Swiss countryside, and the palatial grounds of his grandfather's estate.

Thus there was a conflict between these two enormously talented people that seems never to have been satisfactorily resolved, and inevitably, some of this conflict spilled over into Jean-Luc's upbringing. It seems Jean-Luc Godard got along well with his mother, but was often at odds with his father, who, as Godard entered adolescence, considered his son both impractical and impulsive. After early schooling, Godard found himself in Paris in 1940 when the Nazis marched into France, and was taken to school in Brittany, and thence to Nyon, where he attended the Collège de Nyon until the end of World War II. During this period of global upheaval, then, Godard managed to absent himself from the turmoil that gripped the rest of the world almost entirely. In 1940, the Godards saw to it that Jean-Luc became a naturalized Swiss citizen, and he holds this dual French/Swiss citizenship to this day. Jean-Luc enjoyed sports, going to the movies, and other typical teenage pastimes. So until 1945, we see that Jean-Luc is privileged, perhaps slightly spoiled, but in most respects a rather average adolescent, without any real clue as to his future direction in life.

In 1945, Godard moved back to a liberated Paris immediately after the conclusion of the war, and attended the Lyceé Buffon, resuming his studies toward a baccalaureate. Godard lived with the members of his mother's family, the Monods, often staying with his mother's twin sister, and it was during this period that he grew closer to his mother at the seeming expense of his relationship with his father. Jean-Luc was becoming an increasingly troubled youth, who finished his baccalaureate only with the help of some ancillary study in Switzerland, and he was vacillating wildly as to his chosen profession. Originally, Jean-Luc registered as an anthropology major, but then drifted into mathematics, and then art. A brief flirtation with fiction writing ensued, and then cinema attracted the young man's interest. It was about this time that Godard's parents, finally acknowledging the growing gulf between their aspirations and backgrounds, decided to divorce. Thus, as Godard began his apprenticeship in the cinema, the world of domestic shelter which had nurtured him for so long was finally shattered, and Jean-Luc Godard began to seriously confront the uncertain responsibilities of adulthood.

As with François Truffaut and numerous other cinéastes who would later make up the ranks of *la Nouvelle Vague* (the New Wave) of French filmmaking that exploded on the world in 1959 after simmering in a number of short films and critical writings in *Cahiers du Cinéma* for nearly a decade, Godard began his study of the cinema *in* the cinema—watching movies. Godard has always been at great pains to credit the late director of the Cinémathèque Française, Henri Langlois, for providing, through the Cinémathèque, the young Godard with a history of the cinema when this was unavailable elsewhere. Godard attended daily screenings at the Cinémathèque with such future filmmakers as Jacques Rivette and Eric Rohmer (both of whom he met in 1948), and the critic André Bazin and future director François Truffaut (whom he first became acquainted with in 1949). In addition to his film viewing at the Cinémathèque, Godard became a regular in 1948 at Travail et Culture, a "ciné club" that regularly screened 16mm prints of classic movies, and the Ciné Club du Quartier Matin, where Eric Rohmer regularly introduced the films being screened.

In addition to Rivette, Rohmer, Bazin, and Truffaut, Godard met future filmmakers Claude Chabrol and Alain Resnais during this period, and supported himself through acts of petty thievery committed against his relatives. Godard's associate, François Truffaut, was even more of a "wild child," regularly tangling with the Parisian juvenile court system over a variety of minor offenses. It seemed that nothing but the cinema mattered to the members of this small, select band; the cinema of dreams and myths, of reality and calculated fantasy, a world that only came alive when the lights of the external world were extinguished. In 1949, Godard began attending the Sorbonne, where he would eventually receive a diploma in Ethnology in 1952; he also kept up his "cinema studies" at the Cinémathèque. The cinema was slowly, inexorably beginning to become the ruling passion of Jean-Luc Godard's existence.

In 1950, Jean-Luc Godard appeared as an actor in Jacques Rivette's *Quadrille*; he also began to write film criticism for the journal *La Gazette du Cinéma*. In 1951, Godard acted in Eric Rohmer's early film *Présentation ou Charlotte et son steak*. In March of that year, through his relationship with André Bazin, editor of the journal, he began writing for *Cahiers du Cinéma*, which was to become one of the most influential magazines in the history of cinema (a distinction it retains to this day), often writing under the pseudonym of Hans Lucas. However, in 1952, all of this activity was interrupted when Godard's father, Paul-Jean, became alarmed at the increasing political tensions in Europe, and impulsively packed up and moved to Jamaica to practice medicine. Jean-Luc followed him, although his father soon gave up on the idea and decamped to Switzerland.

Jean-Luc, however, stayed on, and for the next year and a half visited Brazil, Chile, Peru, Bolivia, and Argentina (MacCabe 1992, 14), obtaining lodging from relatives on his father's side as he went along. This nomadic existence allowed Godard to take advantage of his Swiss citizenship and avoid French military service in the rapidly expanding conflict in what is now known as Vietnam, for Godard was unwilling to undertake any sort of military obligations. This exhausted his father's patience altogether. Cut off from Paul-Jean Godard's financial support, Jean-Luc Godard drifted back to Paris, and soon found himself back in the circle of ciné clubs and *Cahiers du Cinéma*, where things were beginning to heat up. More and more of his compatriots were beginning to make their own films, but Godard held back. His critical writings appeared regularly in *Cahiers*, but Godard seemed content for the moment to be an observer, nothing more.

In 1952, Godard's mother got her son a job with the Swiss television national network (MacCabe 1992, 16). Godard's thefts of small amounts of money from his mother, his father and other relatives were becoming increasingly unattractive, and in 1953, despite his employment with the Swiss television network, Godard again became involved in the theft of some money. This time, the theft was not "in the family." Godard was jailed briefly in Zurich, then released through the efforts of his father, who nevertheless now pronounced himself exasperated with Jean-Luc's conduct, and had the twenty-three-year-old sent to a mental clinic for observation, which seems to have been a turning point in Godard's career (MacCabe 1992, 16). For the first time, Jean-Luc Godard found himself in serious trouble, confined and unproductive, unable to see films, committing petty acts of thievery to support his dreams, and cut off from the world of wealth and luxury he had known since childhood. It was during this period that Godard made up his mind to apply himself to the craft of cinema with greater seriousness than he had ever attempted before. Something had to be done. Godard, in the final months of 1953, was facing the crossroads of his life, and trying to meet the challenge of personal responsibility for his own actions.

In early 1954, Godard's mother Odile again found Jean-Luc work, this time as a construction laborer, working with a crew creating a dam in Switzerland. Godard used his wages to support the production of his first film, a seventeen-minute industrial short chronicling the making of the dam, titled *Opération béton* (1954). Godard served as producer, director, editor, and scenarist for the project, which was photographed by Adrien Porchet. Godard scored the film with music by Bach and Handel, and significantly saw that it was shot in 35mm, albeit without synchronous sound, whereas several of his *Cahiers* colleagues were content to work in the more amateur medium of 16mm film. The professionalism of the finished short prompted the construction company to buy the completed film to publicize their accomplishment, and Godard parlayed the profits into the production of his next short film, *Une Femme coquette* (1955), and returned to Paris to write again for *Cahiers* and a competitive journal, *Arts*. Godard produced *Une Femme coquette* independently, and this time he took on all the key production duties. For the film, Godard served as the "production company" ("Jean-Luc Godard Productions"), the producer and director (under his own name), and the scenarist, director of photography, and film editor (under the pseudonym of Hans Lucas which, as James Monaco points out, is "Jean-Luc in German") (Monaco, 392). Based on a short story by Guy de Maupassant, *Une Femme coquette* featured Marie Lysandre, Roland Tolma, and Godard as cast members, was shot in 16mm, and lasted all of ten minutes, with music appropriated from Bach.

However, this nascent success was overshadowed by a tragic event in Godard's personal life, when Godard's mother, Odile, was killed on April 25, 1954, in a motorcycle accident near Lausanne. Yet Godard pressed on, dedicating himself to a life within the cinema. In 1957, while keeping up his work as a critic for *Cahiers du Cinéma* and *Arts*, Godard made his first short film produced as a professional project, *Tous les garçons s'appellent Patrick (Charlotte et Véronique)*, released in English as *All Boys Are Called Patrick*. The film was shot in 35mm again, with a professional cast, including Jean-Claude Brialy, Anne Colette, and Nicole Berger. Produced by Pierre Braunberger's firm Les Films de la Pléïade, the film was directed by Godard from a screenplay by Eric Rohmer, and photographed by Michel Latouche. Godard also began working in the publicity department of the Paris branch office of Twentieth Century Fox, and produced two additional short films: *Une histoire d'eau* (1958), a bizarre "comedy" about the then-recent flooding of Paris which was "co-authored" with François Truffaut; and *Charlotte et son Jules* (1959). *Une Histoire d'eau* is little more than a bad joke extended arbitrarily to an eighteen-minute running time, with Godard serving as narrator: the title itself is a pun on *The Story of O*, a famously scandalous pornographic novel of the period. *Charlotte et son Jules* is slightly more ambitious, and features a young Jean-Paul Belmondo in a key role (although his voice is dubbed in the film by Godard himself). Thus, by early 1959, Godard had one industrial film and four fiction shorts to his name, when an opportunity came knocking that would permanently alter the course of Godard's life, and change the face of cinema forever, not only in France and the United States, but throughout the entire international cinema community.

By 1958, *Cahiers du Cinéma's* attacks on the then-moribund French cinema were becoming overwhelmingly vitriolic. One has only to read some of the early reviews published in *Cahiers* and *Arts* to realize the depth of Truffaut and Godard's scorn for the "classic" French and American film and their appreciation for all that was then new and vital in the cinema. Into this artistic vacuum stepped the young director Roger Vadim. Although his place in cinema history has been largely forgotten today, Roger Vadim's *Et Dieu créa la femme (And God Created*

Woman] was first screened in Paris on November 28, 1956, at the Cinéma Normandie, and was an immediate commercial success. Truffaut was enormously taken with Vadim's film, although it was almost universally attacked elsewhere, and wrote a long review for *Cahiers* praising the work. Vadim thus became a model for this new generation of filmmakers-to-be. Truffaut and Godard saw in Vadim's freewheeling visual and narrative structure a new vision of the cinema, completely removed from the works of the older, more respected directors then lionized in France and America. Vadim's work was fresh, original, more interested in mood than plot, more sensuous than self-consciously constructed. For Godard and Truffaut, Vadim represented an early clue to a new direction: the movement that would explode in 1959 as the New Wave.

Truffaut went so far in his attacks on French cinema of the period that he was banned from attending the 1958 Cannes Film Festival on grounds of critical apostasy, a position made even more uncomfortable because of Truffaut's marriage to Madeleine Morgenstern, who was the daughter of one of the most important film producers in France. At length, disgusted with Truffaut's attacks on the official entries for the Cannes festival, Morgenstern offered to back Truffaut's first feature film *Les 400 coups* [*The 400 Blows*] in 1959, and Truffaut (who had directed only two short films earlier in his career, *Une Visite* [*A Visit*] in 1954 and *Les Mistons* [*The Brats*] in 1957) rose to the occasion with the surprise hit of 1959, starring a young Jean-Pierre Léaud in a semi-autobiographical account of Truffaut's own highly troubled youth and early adolescence.

None of Truffaut's success was lost on the highly competitive Godard, who now yearned to make a feature film of his own. Nevertheless, the origins of this debut feature, *À bout de souffle*, are shrouded in a good deal of mystery. Roger Vadim claims that he met Godard shortly before shooting on *À bout de souffle* began, and that the film's scenario, credited in the film to François Truffaut, consisted of nothing more than a few brief phrases scrawled on a matchbox. According to Vadim, Godard cornered him one day on the set of a film Vadim was directing, announced "I'm a genius," and thrust a box of matches at the surprised director. Vadim writes: "I could make out a few words:

'He's a hooligan. Obsessed by heroes of American films. She has an accent. She sells the *New York Herald Tribune*. It's not really love, it's the illusion of love. It ends badly. Well, no. Finally it ends well. Or it ends badly'" (Vadim, 140). James Monaco, however, insists that the film "was closely based on a fifteen-page scenario by Truffaut" (Monaco, 393), which was subsequently published in *Avant-Scène du Cinéma* 79 in 1968 (Marie, 214). According to Michel Marie (202–3), Beauregard had already "turned down an earlier proposal from Godard: *Une Femme est une femme*" (202), which Beauregard and Ponti would ultimately co-produce with Godard directing. In his essay "It Really Makes You Sick!: Jean-Luc Godard's *À bout de souffle*," Marie offers substantial documentary evidence of Truffaut's significant involvement with the project. In light of all this, Vadim's claim seems fanciful.

There are also apocryphal stories that Godard was so jealous of Truffaut's success in obtaining financing for a feature film that he raided the *Cahiers du Cinéma* treasury to start production of *À bout de souffle*, and was jailed for his efforts, only to be bailed out by François Truffaut. Truffaut, according to this account, arranged with producer Georges de Beauregard to provide more conventional financing for *À bout de souffle*. There may be some truth to this highly romantic account of the film's genesis, although it seems unlikely. Nevertheless, shooting of the film began in the summer of 1959, with Godard pushing his cameraman, Raoul Coutard, around in a wheelchair on the set, while Coutard shot the film with a silent 35mm Arriflex (Godard would add the sound later). The stars were Jean Seberg and Jean-Paul Belmondo. Shooting took place in apartments, and in the streets of Paris. Natural light was used whenever possible.

Producer Beauregard was terrified by the seemingly haphazard way the film was being shot, but Truffaut and director Jean-Pierre Melville (an older filmmaker, who was nevertheless lionized by the *Cahiers* crowd for his work with the great French filmmaker Jean Cocteau on *Les Enfants terribles* [1950]) kept the financier at bay, and filming moved along at a steady if impoverished pace. Michel Marie notes that "Truffaut wrote later, 'while he was making *À bout de souffle*, Godard didn't have enough money in his pocket to buy a Metro ticket'" (Marie, 201).

Released in March 1960, the film was a hit with both the public and the critics, and Godard's career as a feature filmmaker was finally and definitively launched.

À bout de souffle is a remarkable feature film debut in a number of respects. It is audacious and assured, insouciant and knowing, calculated and spontaneous. The editorial structure of jump cuts within scenes has been much remarked upon; in assembling the film, Godard simply edited out those sections of a scene that were boring to him, and spliced together the remaining sections of the scene without the use of dissolves, wipes, or other traditional transitional devices. As late as 1994, this bold, jagged visual style was being remarked upon by Andrew Sarris, who interviewed Godard in New York, while the director was on a press junket to publicize the opening of *JLG/JLG*. *À bout de souffle* was, by this time, thirty-five years old, yet Sarris admitted to Godard that: "I've always wondered how you hit upon the electrifying jump cuts in *Breathless*. Was it instinct?"

Godard replied:

> Yes, partly. But the fact is that, unless you are very good, most first movies are too long, and you lose your rhythm and your audience over two or three hours. In fact, the first cut of *Breathless* was two and a half hours and the producer said, "You have to cut out one hour." We decided to do it mathematically. We cut three seconds here, three here, three here, and later I found out I wasn't the first director to do that. The same process was described in the memoir of Robert Parrish, who was an editor on Robert Rossen's *All the King's Men* [1949]—he was the third or fourth editor, actually, because his predecessors weren't capable of making the cuts. Parrish told Rossen: "Let's do something different. We'll look at each shot and we'll keep only what we think has more energy. If it's at the end of the shot, we'll throw out the beginning. If it's at the beginning, we'll throw out the end." They did exactly what I did later, without knowing what they had done. Only, I said, "Let's keep only what I like."

Of the film's "rough-hewn," near-documentary look, Godard noted we "couldn't afford to work in a studio, so our movies were not something we had planned in advance. In my case, it was my natural way of doing things. I mean, more or less I am always saying, 'Give me more. Let's do what has not been done'" (Sarris 1994, 89).

The plot of the film is slight; in the hands of a less gifted director, *À bout de souffle* might well have been another routine *policier*, a plodding chase film without distinction or excitement. Godard's film, however, takes a simple gangster story and uses it as the jumping-off point for a series of telling and incisive observations on life, the cinema, relationships between men and women, and the authority of the state. In *À bout de souffle*, Jean-Paul Belmondo plays a small-time hood named Michel Poiccard (who also uses the alias Laszlo Kovacs, in homage to the great cinematographer of the same name) who arbitrarily kills a policeman and is on the run from the law. Poiccard takes up with a young expatriate American woman, Patricia Franchini (Jean Seberg). Patricia sells the *New York Herald Tribune* in the streets of Paris to eke out a meager existence. The film chronicles Michel's attempts to flee the police, cash a check for getaway money, steal some cars, and sleep with Patricia, most of these activities being documented in a modified "newsreel" style by Raoul Coutard's handheld camera. In the end, Patricia arbitrarily betrays Michel to the authorities. Michel is shot down in the street while making one last attempt to escape. His life, and his death, are both seen as essentially random acts, devoid of meaning and/or consequence; Michel lives only for the moment, and *À bout de souffle* is shot in an appropriately spontaneous style. Long blocks of the film have the feel of spontaneous improvisation, and although the overall narrative structure of the work seems conventional in comparison to later Godard films, for 1959, the film seemed to flout every rule of established cinematic syntax. Godard dedicated this, his first feature film, to the memory of Monogram Studios, the legendary producers of numerous "B" gangster films in the 1940s and 1950s in Hollywood. Both Godard and Truffaut had always been attracted to the modesty and speed of production inherent to the Monogram production process; both men had written critical reviews praising little-known Monogram films for *Cahiers* and *Arts* that went against the grain of the prevailing school of film criticism. Now, with *À bout de souffle,* Godard constructed a film in much the same manner as a classic Monogram thriller. It had a low budget, it used existing locations whenever possible, it was shot quickly, and it aspired only to be a successful "action" picture. Indeed, with this first film more than any of his subsequent efforts, Godard was aiming for a commercial success above all else—a success that would ensure his future as a commercial feature filmmaker.

Seen today, *À bout de souffle* seems primitive, classic, not at all the audacious ground-breaker it seemed to be in 1959. The jump cuts which were so radical then are now a staple of MTV; shooting on location to enhance the illusion of reality is a staple of contemporary cinema practice. The "studio look" is now used only on films that require an utterly *unrealistic* vision, such as *The Shadow* (1994), and audiences will no longer accept the hyperreal glossiness of 1950s Hollywood glamour as a zone of genuine human habitation. Godard's use of natural locales is indebted to Rossellinian neo-realism, it is true, but like the German Trümmerfilm (or "Rubble-film," literally a film shot in the ruins of Germany after World War II) of the same period, Rossellini shot in the wreckage of newly liberated Rome to create a cinema of despair and renewal. For Godard (and his contemporaries in the New Wave), Paris was simply a huge set waiting to be discovered, magnificent in its architecture, and relatively undocumented by a cinematic tradition that had been confined to the sound stage since the early films of Alice Guy at Gaumont.

And yet *À bout de souffle* is not a realistic film. Godard himself realized this when he stated "although I felt ashamed of it at one time, I do like *À bout de souffle* very much, but now I see it where it belongs—along with *Alice in Wonderland.* I thought it was *Scarface"* (Milne, 175). On the construction of the film itself, Godard has these thoughts:

> *À bout de souffle* began this way. I had written the first scene (Jean Seberg on the Champs Elysees), and for the rest I had a pile of notes for each scene. I said to myself, this is terrible. I stopped everything. Then I thought: in a single day, if one knows how to go about it, one should be able to complete a dozen takes. Only instead of planning ahead, I shall

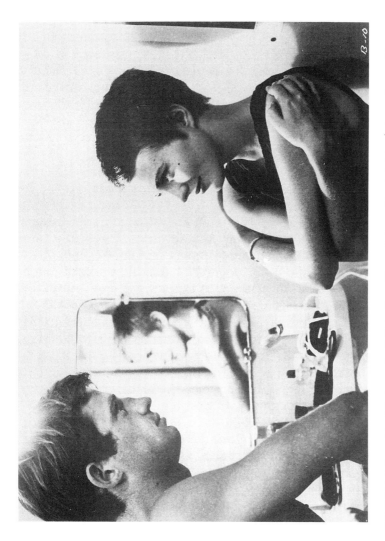

FIGURE 2. Jean-Paul Belmondo (Michel) and Jean Seberg (Patricia) in À bout de souffle (1959). Courtesy New Yorker Films.

invent at the last minute! . . . But [Jean-Paul] Belmondo [who played Michel] never invented his own dialogue. It was written. But the actors didn't learn it: the film was shot silent, and I cued the lines. . . . *À bout de souffle* was the sort of film where anything goes: that was what it was all about. . . . I also wanted to give the feeling that the techniques of filmmaking had just been discovered or experienced for the first time. The iris-in showed that one could return to the cinema's sources; the dissolve appeared, just once [in the transition to Mansard's junkyard], as though it had just been invented . . . if we used a handheld camera, it was simply for speed." (Milne, 172–73)

Nor was the crew of *À bout de souffle* sanguine about the film's technical execution. As Godard wrote during production of the film, "At the rushes, the entire crew, including the cameraman, thought the photography was revolting. Personally I like it. What's important is not that things should be filmed in any particular way, but simply that they should be filmed and be properly in focus. My main job is keeping the crew away from where we're shooting. . . . On Wednesday we shot a scene in full sunlight using Geva 36 film stock. They all think it stinks. My view is that it's fairly amazing" (Braunberger 1987, 183–84, as cited in Marie, 204–5). But Godard rushed ahead anyway, desirous of nothing more than getting the film shot at top speed despite any and all objections, pursuing an aesthetic that was all his own, pushing film "to the limits of its possibilities" (Braunberger 1987, 184, as cited in Marie, 205).

In *À bout de souffle*, Godard created a narrative cinema of simplicity and primitive charm, as befits the first film of a cinéaste, and a film which was an immediate commercial and critical success. Godard's colleague François Truffaut, as mentioned, had been barred from the 1958 Cannes festival because of the brutality of his cinema criticism; now Godard, Truffaut, and Alain Resnais all burst on the scene in 1959 with three major films, which in each case immediately established the reputations of their makers. The older French films were swept aside with a single brusque gesture; the Nouvelle Vague represented the generation of invention, vitality, speed, and improvisation. This new generation was also attractive to film financiers, for all of the early New Wave films were very cheaply made. Truffaut's *Les 400 coups* (*The 400 Blows*), his 1959 debut feature, cost a mere $50,000 to produce (Graham, 9), and was even shot in FranScope, the French equivalent of CinemaScope! Truffaut was still concerned that the film would never recoup its investment. But making films inexpensively during this period (before theatrical exploitation costs and the explosion of straight-to-tape features in the late 1980s made conventional distribution practices functionally obsolete) pretty much ensured that the film would turn a profit. In fact, the United States theatrical rights for *Les 400 coups* alone were sold for $70,000 (Graham, 9).

Thus, Godard and Truffaut proved Antonin Artaud correct when he stated, many years earlier, that "one of the main mistakes of producers, and especially French producers, is to think that a film must have been made at a high price to sell it at a high price" (1972, 69). The films of the New Wave prefigured the later films of such cinéastes as Ron Rice, whose feature film *The Flower Thief* (1960) cost less than $1,000, Andy Warhol, whose 3½-hour split-screen epic *The Chelsea Girls* (1966) cost less than $1,500 to shoot, and even Robert Rodriguez, whose debut feature *El Mariachi* (1993) completed principal photography for a mere $7,000. Significantly, Rodriguez has staked a claim for his individual vision in Hollywood (not an easy thing to do in 1997) by using the very same technique that Godard pioneered in *À bout de souffle.*

Rodriguez's first full-fledged Hollywood feature, the 1994 made-for-cable movie *Road Racers* (made for Showtime's *Rebel Highway* series), was shot in thirteen days for $1.3 million at at an average rate of forty-five setups (complete changes of camera and lighting) a day. On one particularly hectic day, Rodriguez knocked out seventy-eight setups for *Road Racers,* an unheard of figure for a Hollywood shoot. How did he do it? "I just ended up grabbing the camera, getting in a wheelchair, and shooting" (Clark, 77). At another point during the shoot, Rodriguez told the cameraman "to forget about the lighting" (Clark, 77). Yet the finished film was so visually audacious that it was considered the best of the series, was chosen to debut the series, and Rodriguez's outlaw methods helped to create *Road Racer's* raw, visceral impact. There's more than an echo of Godard's "full-speed ahead" method here. Rodriguez's use of the wheelchair for a dolly, the frenetic production pace, the use of a minimal crew, the short shooting schedule, and the use of shots done with improvised or minimal lighting—all of these production circumstances mimic *À bout de souffle*. In a medium where time is money, speed is freedom. Godard and his compatriots here demonstrated for an entire generation that you can make a film quickly and cheaply, without any artistic sacrifice; all it takes is genius.

Yet there is a crucial difference between Godard and Rodriguez's ambitions for their respective projects. Whereas Rodriguez simply sought to make a good action movie, Godard was using the mechanism of the action film as a vehicle for personal expression. With his long period as a *Cahiers* critic behind him, Godard seized upon the *policier* genre to create a document which ruptures not only the grammar and syntax of the classical cinema, but also the unspoken societal contract between spectacle and spectator implicit in the traditional narrative film. As Walter Benjamin notes,

> the technique of reproduction detaches the reproduced object from the domain of tradition . . . and in permitting the reproduction to meet the beholder or listener in his own particular situation, it reactivates the object reproduced. These two processes lead to a tremendous shattering of tradition which is the obverse of the contemporary crisis and the renewal of mankind. Both processes are intimately connected with the contemporary mass movements. Their most powerful agent is the film. Its social significance, particularly in its most positive form, is inconceivable without its destructive, cathartic aspect, that is, the liquidation of the traditional value of the cultural heritage. (223)

By creating an "Alice in Wonderland" gangster film, Godard called audience attention to the inherent reflexivity of his enterprise, and the manipulative and plastic nature of the cinema. *À bout de souffle* is everywhere a construct aware of its own constructedness. It is a film which follows the format of the tradi-

FIGURE 3. Natural lighting in *À bout de souffle*; Van Doude (the journalist) and Jean Seberg (Patricia). Courtesy New Yorker Films.

tional narrative only insofar as this adherence serves Godard's true critical project: the "reactivation" of the people and things he photographs within a glyphic framework of hyperreal jump-cuts, editorial elisions, sweeping tracking shots which call attention to their structural audaciousness, and characters whose entire existence lies in a series of gestures, motions, appearances, and escapes, all to disguise the essentially phantom nature of their ephemeral existence. We have no idea why Patricia betrays Michel to the police, nor do we need to know. By eschewing conventional causality in his scenario, and through the effective and inexpensive expedient of hundreds of jump-cuts to fragment *À bout de souffle's* minimalist narrative, Godard does indeed "shatter tradition," and points toward a renewal of the cinema based on the domain of the eye and nothing else. *À bout de souffle* still dazzles us because it remains a marker of rupture; the end of classicism, and the birth of "Bop" cinema on a commercial scale.

If *À bout de souffle* made a few modest bows to cinematic conventions, particularly to the gangster film, all such intellectual and generic debts would be erased with Godard's second feature, *Le Petit Soldat (The Little Soldier)*, shot in Geneva, Switzerland between April and May of 1960, begun only a month after the official opening of *À bout de souffle* in Paris on March 16, 1960. Godard was operating at top speed, inspired by events in the French/Algerian War. What particularly interested Godard was "torture, which had become the big question" (Milne, 177). This time, producer Georges de Beauregard willingly undertook the risk of backing the film, and Godard used Raoul Coutard again as his cameraman, signing on the gifted Agnès Guillemot as his editor-in-chief. Guillemot would become, over the next several years, one of Godard's most sensitive and intuitive artistic collaborators. The cast of *Le Petit Soldat* included Michel Subor as Bruno Forestier, Anna Karina as Veronica Dreyer, producer Georges de Beauregard as an activist leader, and Godard himself in a bit part. It was during the filming of *Le Petit Soldat* that Godard and Karina first became attracted to each other; Godard had cast her for the film simply because he liked her "look." By the time *Le Petit Soldat* was finished, Godard and Karina were solidly involved in a relationship that would have great artistic and personal consequences for both parties. Shortly after production of the film was finished, the couple were married on March 3, 1961, in Béquins, Switzerland (Mussman, 311).

But Godard's second feature was proving too controversial. As the director later said, "I wanted to show that the most terrible thing about torture is that people who practice it don't find it arguable at all. They all end up by justifying it" (Milne, 178). The completed film was immediately banned by the French censor, and not shown publicly in France until three years later, after a number of cuts had been made, on January 25, 1963. The film's first public showing in the Untied States didn't take place until two years after that, in September 1965 at the New York Film Festival. In no way can *Le Petit Soldat* be considered the same sort of runaway success that its immediate predecessor had been. In fact, one wonders what might have happened if Godard had made *Le Petit Soldat* before *À bout de souffle*. The entire history of French cinema might well have been a different affair altogether.

Le Petit Soldat tells the story of Bruno Forestier (Michel Subor), a reporter/photojournalist who is also a deserter from the French Army. He meets Veronica Dreyer (Anna Karina; the character name is no doubt an homage to Danish filmmaker Carl Th. Dreyer, whom Godard deeply admired), a member of FLN, the Algerian Liberation Front. Ordered by the Organization of the Secret Army (OAS), who helped him escape from military service, to murder a man named Arthur Palivoda, Bruno refuses. While the OAS pushes Bruno to commit the deed, Bruno is taken hostage by the FLN and tortured (in the film's most infamous sequence; see Roud 1970, 38–41, for more on this) in an attempt to gain information about the activities of the OAS. Bruno finally escapes, and declares his love for Veronica. The OAS agrees to provide Bruno and Veronica with fake passports that will take them to Brazil if Bruno carries out the execution of Palivoda, and Bruno complies. However, the OAS has reneged on their part of the deal; they have tortured and murdered Veronica for information on the FLN. Thus Bruno has simply been a pawn in a diabolic double-cross, an apolitical bystander swept away by politics.

Le Petit Soldat is thus a brutal and entirely unromantic film, a film of political activism, or the cinema of conscience. Everything about the film is flat and mundane, particularly the

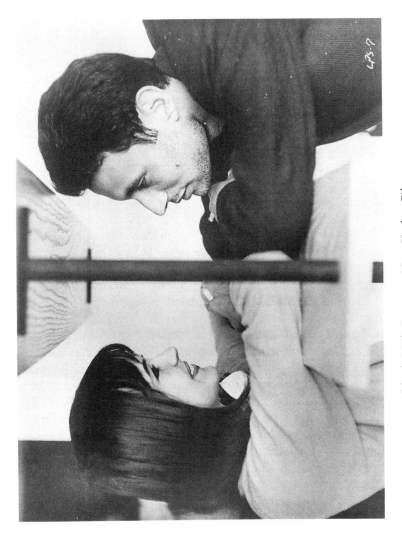

FIGURE 4. *Le petit soldat* (1960). Courtesy New Yorker Films.

torture sequence; Godard in *Le Petit Soldat* is making an utterly personal film which puts his audience effectively on trial. The graphic specificity of the torture sequences, as might be imagined, constituted one of the central controversies of *Le Petit Soldat*. As Richard Roud wrote, these scenes which probably contributed as much as anything to getting the film banned for three years, were an attempt not "to make the audience faint" but to make them think. The real horror was not so much in the actual torture as in the fact that the torturers did not find it particularly horrible—hence the frighteningly ordinary scenes in which the torture is interrupted by a girl delivering the weekly bundle of clean shirts. Or notice, too, the jar of hair-cream in the bathroom in which the torture takes place—another reminder of the banality of it all. . . . [P]eople accuse Godard of callousness, of unfeeling neutrality. And yet to be clear-sighted is not to be callous: understatement can often be more effective than pulling out all the stops; and perhaps the most frightening aspect of evil is its banality. (1970, 40).

As Bruno's face is wrapped in a towel, and he suffers repeated near-strangulation and/or asphyxiation, Godard's camera views the scene impassively, as if documenting an everyday occurrence—which is, of course, exactly what this process is for Bruno's torturers. The lighting and photography are flat, prefiguring Willy Kurant's drab black-and-white industrialized images in *Masculin Féminin*. The effect is that of Nazi concentration camp footage, the gaze that sees all, and yet nothing. It is not so much neutral, as clinical; not so much documentary, as utilitarian. Bruno is only an expendable commodity in the political/antihumanist landscape of *Le Petit Soldat*, and his figurative and literal death are preordained by external forces over which he has no control. As an indictment of the process of torture, and of French involvement in the war, the film is designed as a brutal and uncompromising piece, a confrontation rather than a seductive fantasy. Indeed, one can hardly imagine too more oppositional films than *À bout de souffle* and *Le Petit Soldat*. One belongs to the world of Spielberg and Tarantino; the other to Marcel Ophuls, Resnais's *Nuit et brouillard* (*Night and Fog*, 1956), and the diabolical depersonalization of the Other, as practiced by all nations during time of war. In its laconic montage, its fierce economy of shots, and the awful inexorability of its narrative, *Le Petit Soldat* is simultaneously an assured and nihilistic work signalling to his audience that Godard intended to be a great deal more than a cinematic mountebank. The complete lack of commercial success of *Le Petit Soldat* (even today the film is generally unavailable on video cassette) was no help to Godard's fledgling career, but he continued on at a relentless pace, unleashed at last after years of waiting. For his next project, however, Godard tried something that both he and his backers hoped would be slightly more commercial.

Moving quickly after *Le Petit Soldat*, Godard shot *Une Femme est une femme (A Woman is a Woman)* (1961) at Studio Saint-Maurice and on location in Paris from November 1960 to January 1961. In Techniscope and color, the film is a comedy/musical of sorts concerning Angéla (Anna Karina), who wants to have a child. Emile (Jean-Claude Brialy), her would-be fiancée, refuses to assist her unless they get married. Not to be dissuaded from her mission, Angéla asks Emile's friend Alfred Lubitsch (Jean-Paul Belmondo) to sleep with her. Godard wrote that "the subject of *Une Femme est une femme* . . . is a character who succeeds in resolving a certain situation, but I conceived the subject within the framework of a neo-realistic musical: an *absolute contradiction*, but that is precisely why I wanted to make the film" (Roud 1970, 7). In a number of ways, particularly in the use of 'scope and color, this film can be seen as a rehearsal for *Le Mépris (Contempt)*. *Une Femme est une femme* is generally considered lightweight Godard, even if the director did consciously (and intriguingly) work against most of the conventions of the movie musical. For one example, Godard insisted that his characters provide their own wardrobe for the film (as part of the "neo-realistic" approach); for another, the film seems barren and threadbare in its sets, as opposed to the lavishness one usually associates with films in the musical genre.

"To me, style is just the outside of content, and content the inside of style, like the outside of the human body—both go together, and can't be separated," Godard has said (Roud 1970, 13). If the narrative thread of *Une Femme est une femme* is exceedingly slight, the execution of the project can properly be seen as a comment on the inherent artifice of the musical, and as

FIGURE 5. Anna Karina (Angéla) and Jean-Paul Belmondo (Alfred Lubitsch) in *Une femme est une femme* (1961). Courtesy Jerry Ohlinger Archives.

an early exploration of the theme of prostitution (personal, social, political), which would preoccupy Godard for his entire career. As Roud notes, Angéla in *Une Femme est une femme* "sells her body; only as a strip-tease artist, to be sure, but the implications are clear, or at least they become so retrospectively" (1970, 30). While describing the film as "light-hearted," Roud has nevertheless hit upon an important truth buried in the froth of the film's flimsy scenario. The commodification of the human body (particularly the female body) becomes, in Godard's later works, the center of many of his key films, particularly *Le Week-end* (1967), *Deux ou Trois Choses que je sais d'elle* (1966), *Vivre sa vie* (1962), *Une Femme mariée* (1964), and *Le Mépris* (1963).

The body-display of Corinne Durand in *Le Week-end* is used to stop a truck to hitch a ride; the housewife protagonist of *Deux ou trois choses* turns to part-time prostitution to supplement her meager household allowance. Nana, in *Vivre sa vie*, is forced into prostitution as a means of survival, and in many ways, *Une Femme mariée* equates the marriage contract with a sort of metanarrative gift-exchange of one human body for/with another as a medium of commercial intercourse. Bardot's Camille in *Le Mépris* is desired by producer Prokosch as a trophy, a symbol of his "godlike" socioeconomic power, and his insatiable desire to acquire one object (human or otherwise) after another, without any heed of the consequences. Paul, Camille's husband, also becomes a prostitute, when he agrees to rewrite the Odyssey for producer Prokosch over the objections of Fritz Lang, playing himself, who serves as director of the film-within-a-film that forms the nucleus of *Le Mépris*.

Indeed, prostitution, no matter what form it takes, is an obsessive theme for Godard. In *King Lear* (1989), Godard's idiosyncratic version of the Shakespeare play, there is a moment when we see a copy of Virginia Woolf's *The Waves* washed up on the shore of a lake, the water swirling through the pages of the text as the sound of seagulls fills the soundtrack. And we can recall Woolf's admonition that "so long as you write what you wish to write, that is all that matters . . . but to sacrifice a hair of the head of your vision, a shade of its colour . . . is the most abject treachery" (110). In his choice of films as a director, Godard is uncompromising, and the vision that emerges from his works (either alone, or with Gorin or Miéville) is entirely original, and created without commercial compromise. One can understand how the theme of prostitution would attract Godard so powerfully; the history of cinema is cluttered with the dead dreams of ambitious yet unprincipled men and women who sacrificed their lives, their bodies, their integrity to achieve positions of power and prominence (like Prokosch), only to find success insipid, unless it is governed by a moral agency (such as Lang). Angéla's request that Alfred sleep with her in *Une femme est un femme*, so that she can have a child over the objections of her fiancé, Emile, is treated within the context of the film as a whimsicality, the sort of artificial complication that one might expect from a 1930s (pre-code) musical. But, at base, Godard's fascination with the mechanics of prostitution, and the economic, social and sexual consequences of this act, is absolutely serious, as is his next film, *Vivre sa vie* (1962), a work which seems closer to the nihilist nightmare world of *Le Petit Soldat* than the adolescent clowning of *À bout de souffle*.

Vivre sa vie, shot in February–March 1962 and released in the same year (known as *My Life to Live* in the United States and *It's My Life* in Britain) followed *Une Femme est une femme* almost immediately. Anna Karina stars in the film as Nana Kleinfrankenheim, a young woman who falls into prostitution to support herself. Shot in stark black and white, the film has a nearly documentary air, and was in fact inspired by Marcel Sacotte's study *Où en est la prostitution?* (Roud 1970, 175). The film is chopped up into a number of segments, including one coldly clinical section where Godard documents matter-of-factly the daily life of a Parisian prostitute with a dispassionate question-and-answer voiceover; there is also an exquisite sequence in which Nana goes to the movies to see Carl Th. Dreyer's *La Passion de Jeanne d'Arc* (1928), and weeps in empathy at the plight of Jeanne (Falconetti) condemned to die at the stake. Since *La Passion de Jeanne d'Arc* is a silent movie, this sequence is also silent, a structural conceit that works superbly.

Nana also meets and converses with the philosopher Brice Parain, in a metaphysical dialogue of considerable length and density; as mentioned before, these "dialogues" will become a hallmark of later Godard films. Nana is shot dead in the street in the final sequence of the film, as her pimp Raoul (Sady Rebbot) attempts to "sell" her to a gangster (Gerard Hoffman), creating a brutally abrupt conclusion for this brutally realistic film. Yet it seems almost as if this final sequence is simply "tacked on" to wrap the film up; Godard is interested in incident, not overall plot. Although the film's very premise objectifies the feminine corpus within the text of the film as a whole, Godard is aware of the level of scrutiny he subjects Nana to, and is uncomfortable with the idea of woman-as-victim, woman-as-object-to-be-saved, woman-as-prostitute, all of which are gender constructions of the feminine self as defined by patriarchal commerce.

In *Vivre sa vie*, a film that might be considered the first fully formed work of Godard's initial period as a filmmaker, the director gives Nana's character considerable depth and humanity, following her character more closely than any other in the film. Then, too, the men in *Vivre sa vie* are all thoroughly worthless and vile, with the exception of Parain; they view Nana as chattel, and Godard is clearly unsympathetic to this view. The entire film takes place in a Paris as drab and unromantic as one of Dickens' sweatshops; Truffaut, in his films, always took a more romantic view of prostitutes and their trade, but Godard here sees it clearly for the spectacle of human degradation that it truly represents. In the sequence in which Nana presents herself to Raoul as a potential employee of a professional house of prostitution, Godard's camera sweeps dispassionately back and forth behind her pimp, Raoul, as Nana and Raoul discuss the terms of her new trade while seated in a run-down café. Roud has dubbed this "the pendulum shot" and argues that it represents "a carefully worked out choreography for the camera" (1970, 89), but I would argue that although the shot presents the external structure of artifice, Godard's motivation for filming the scene in this manner might be his desire to identify the camera as the locus of the voyeur's gaze, peering over Raoul's shoulder to get a better view of this intimate conversation, merging the gaze of the cinema spectator with that of an overly inquisitive (and uninvited) onlooker.

Roud compares this shot to the back-and-forth camera movement during Paul and Camille's breakup in *Le Mépris*, but the two strategies do not seem to me to be equivalent. In *Le Mépris*, Paul and Camille are seen in profile, arguing meaninglessly over the dissolution of their marriage, as the camera dollies languidly from left to right, then right to left, emphasizing the emotional void between the estranged couple. The "pendulum" camera in *Vivre sa vie* is continuously angling for a more comprehensive, yet clandestine view of a private business transaction. In *Vivre sa vie*, as elsewhere, Godard clearly enjoys the luxury of a long take; the camera's somnolent gaze forces us to pay close attention, to absorb all that we can from a resistant image. In contrast to the hypermontage of *À bout de souffle*, Godard in *Vivre sa vie* is developing his strategy of real-time recording, forcing the spectator to create her/his own montage within the carefully composed frame that he presents.

In the world of *Vivre sa vie*, all is consumption, all is commerce. Women and men exist as commodities to be traded in exchange for goods or services, rather than independent agencies capable of controlling their respective fates. One can see in *Vivre sa vie* the beginnings of Godard's later interest in Marxist/Leninist discourse, in that he clearly views capitalism as the social structure responsible for this ceaseless human exploitation. What one desires in the world of *Vivre sa vie* is immaterial. Nana turns to prostitution because the society she lives in condones, and encourages, the objectification of the feminine. Although, as I have suggested, her death at the end of the film seems an arbitrary end to the narrative, it is also a logical one; prostitution equals the death of identity, the death of self. The dialogue between Brice Parain and Nana in *Vivre sa vie* suggests that Nana is dimly aware of the forces conspiring to destroy her, but is either unable or unwilling to escape the mechanism of prostitution. Although the film was made before the age of AIDS, and now (in retrospect) lacks the visceral punch of more recent examinations of prostitution such as Lizzie Borden's *Working Girls* (1986), *Vivre sa vie* remains a benchmark film in both Godard's career, and a compelling evocation of the plight of a woman forced into prostitution by economic exigency, into a life which can only end in violence. Shortly after the film was made, Godard stated that creating the film

> was both very simple and . . . it was as if I had to snatch the shots out of the night, as if they were at the bottom of a well and had to be brought to light. When I pulled out a

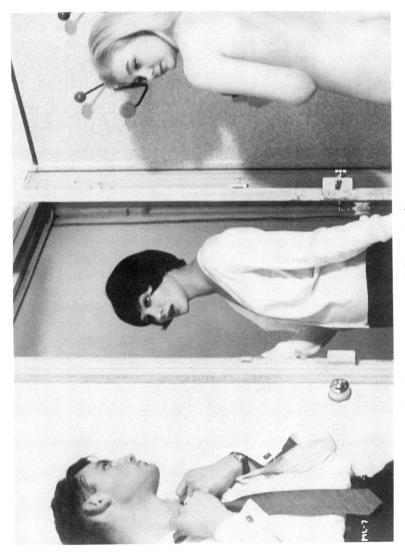

FIGURE 6. *Vivre sa vie* (1962). Courtesy Jerry Ohlinger Archives.

shot, I said to myself, 'Everything is there, no changes'; but there had to be no mistakes about what came out, and came out at the first try. . . . This way of getting shots meant there was no editing. All I had to do was put the shots end to end. What the crew saw at the rushes is more or less what the public sees. Moreover, I had shot the scenes in sequence. There was no mixing either. The film is a series of blocks. You just take them and set them side by side. The important thing is to choose the correct ones at first go. Ideally, I wanted to get what I needed right away, without retakes. If retakes were necessary, it was no good. The impromptu means chance. It is also definitive. What I wanted was to be definitive by chance. (Milne, 185)

One measure of Godard's success in this respect can be judged by the fact that *Vivre sa vie* won a special jury prize at the Venice Film Festival, and went on to a respectable "art house" release in the United States. The film thus consolidated Godard's reputation as one of the most prolific and politically engaged filmmakers of the New Wave, and increased audience anticipation for his next work.

But Godard's most ardent partisans were taken aback in 1963, when Godard released *Les Carabiniers* (*The Soldiers*), a serio-comic study of war shot on Kodak XX negative stock for a newsreel effect, intercut with existing stock footage of war newsreels. As part of Godard's design for the film, the "staged" sections of *Les Carabiniers* were duped several times over in the laboratory until all the greys and shadings were destroyed, and the "fictional" footage achieved the same visual verisimilitude as the old newsreels. Godard dedicated the film to the late Jean Vigo, one of the greatest French directors of the early sound era (best known for his boarding-school allegory *Zéro de conduite* (*Zero for Conduct*, made in 1933). When Godard's working methods were attacked by Parisian critics upon *Les Carabiniers'* initial release, Godard replied by reprinting the reviews that Vigo had been subjected to during his brief career, reviews which caused the commercial failure of both *Zéro de conduite* and Vigo's only feature-length film, *L'Atalante* (1934).

The plot of *Les Carabiniers* is deceptively simple. Two hapless everymen, Ulysse (Marino Masé) and Michel-Ange

(Albert Juross) are drafted to fight for their king. There follow a series of "battles" (culled from newsreel footage) in which Ulysse and Michel-Ange do not actually participate. The gap between the fictive and the real is demonstrably acknowledged by Godard's editorial structure, although his visuals have been matched to achieve photographic consistency as described earlier. As the two men stumble through their allegorical adventures, they send home postcards to their wives Venus (Geneviève Galéa) and Cléopâtre (Catherine Ribéro) that are striking in their banality; Godard later revealed that the hackneyed phrases used in the postcards from Ulysse and Michel-Ange were direct quotations from battlefield correspondence dating from the Napoleonic era to World War II (one of the postcards was originally written by Heinrich Himmler). Death in the film seems unscripted and spontaneous, as everyday an activity as making one's bed or drinking a cup of coffee. At the film's conclusion, the king's army loses the war. The two men who originally drafted Michel-Ange and Ulysse into the army are now on the other side; for their efforts, the two carabiniers are machine-gunned to death.

Fredric Jameson has argued that "the objects of the commodity world of capitalism . . . shed their independent 'being' and intrinsic qualities" when they are casually documented by vacationing tourists. "This is the meaning of the great scene in . . . Godard's *Les Carabiniers*, when the new world conquerors exhibit their spoils: unlike Alexander, 'Michel-Ange' and 'Ulysse' merely own *images* [my emphasis] of everything, and triumphantly display their postcards of the coliseum, the pyramids, Wall Street, Angkor Wat, like so many dirty pictures" (1990, 11). The Pyrrhic victory of Michel-Ange and Ulysse over the domain of the visible alone is further undermined by Godard's reflexive use of newsreel footage to depict the horrors of war. Thus the film emerges as a triumphantly fraudulent construct, a metaphorical conceit that brazenly revels in the artificiality of its syntactical structure. *Les Carabiniers* is an ugly film about a world bereft of beauty, in which meaningless conquests are followed by equally arbitrary betrayals. Michel-Ange and Ulysse are strikingly banal characters, empty vessels waiting to be filled with bourgeois ambition and guided by external, unquestionable governance.

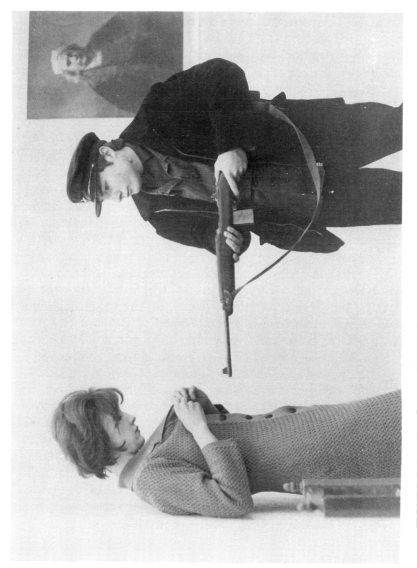

FIGURE 7. *Les Carabiniers* (1963). Courtesy New Yorker Films.

The banality of these two nonpersonages is matched by the degenerated, high-contrast imagery of the film, reducing the entire mechanism of war, and its existing documentation, to a series of visual and narratological clichés. "We will find in Godard formulas which express the problem," Deleuze has written; "if images have become clichés, 'just an image,' an autonomous mental image, an image *must* [Deleuze's emphasis] emerge from the set of clichés . . . with what politics and what consequences? What is an image which would not be a cliché?" (1986, 214). Perhaps such an image would be the abstraction of banality, the refinement of the everyday through reproduction and disintegration.

When Godard feeds the images of *Les Carabiniers* back into the laboratory for repeated reprinting, is he not turning the photographic process back upon itself? As Godard said at the time of the film's release, some of the shots in *Les Carabiniers*, "intrinsically too grey, were duped again sometimes two or three times, always to their highest contrast, to make them match the newsreel shots, which had themselves been duped more than usual" (Milne, 200). He further noted that the final prints for the film were made on high-contrast film, resulting in a further spatial flattening and abrasion of the film's images. To such critical comments as Michel Cournot's assertion that *Les Carabiniers* was "a badly made, badly lit, badly everything film" (Milne, 200), Godard replied, "I consider these lines as praise indeed" (Milne, 196). Only through the systematic corruption of the photographic process, the reification of the image through serial duplication, can one begin to create a fresh image out of the clichés offered to us by conventional, representational cinematography. By calling our attention to the structural processing of images by the filmic apparatus, and through the systematic visual reinterpretation of his chosen glyphic constructs, Godard creates an insular, self-referential visual wilderness of destruction and decay, in which the spectator is assaulted by an avalanche of hypermanipulated images and brutally cacophonous (and meticulously reconstructed) sounds. In *Les Carabiniers*, we see Godard moving even further away from his beginnings as a genre entertainer, toward his soon-to-be-adopted stance of visual essayist. In retrospect, it is not surprising that the film was both a commercial and critical failure at the time of its original release, but from our current perspective, the film seems both postmodern and postnarrativist, a construct that anticipates the later work of such filmmaker/theorists as Michael Snow, Trinh T. Minh-ha, Ernie Gehr, and the late Hollis Frampton.

By this point in his career, Godard was alternating films aimed at a wider audience with films paradoxically designed to alienate the conventional spectator. The semi-traditional narrative of *À bout de souffle* and the desultory stab at a musical in *Une Femme est une femme* was counterbalanced by the brutal intensity of *Le Petit Soldat* (which was released in Paris during the filming of *Les Carabiniers* after a three-year hiatus) and *Les Carabiniers*. Godard was using modest budgets and short shooting schedules to create his personal vision of the cinema, a cinema designed more to instruct than entertain. Predictably, the critics liked *À bout de souffle* and *Une Femme est une femme*; they disliked *Le Petit Soldat* and *Les Carabiniers*, both films that implicitly or explicitly criticized the government of Charles de Gaulle.

Godard was no longer the predictable purveyor of cinema entertainment, if he ever *had* been; already François Truffaut's films were becoming more conventional and somewhat softer and elegiac in tone, while Godard's films were ever more polemical in tone and content. With these first four features, Godard was making his own contribution to the history of the cinema. Now he sought to pay homage to its past, to the directors whose works he admired, to the Hollywood studio system, to the world of the big-budget movie, and the international co-production, in a film that celebrated both the star system and the *politique des auteurs*. This led to the creation of his first international co-production, the epic consideration of the history and practice of the cinema that constitutes the text of *Le Mépris*.

CHAPTER TWO

●

The Exhaustion of Narrative

Le Mépris (*Contempt*) was Godard's first lavishly budgeted feature film, produced at a cost of more than one million dollars (U.S.) for shooting alone. The film was shot in Rome, at the famed Cinecittà Studios, and Capri, "including Curzio Malaparte's villa" (Roud, 177). As with Godard's earlier efforts, the plot of *Le Mépris* is slight, but Godard worked directly from an existing narrative in creating his screenplay for the film: Alberto Moravia's novel *Il Disprezzo*. *Le Mépris* chronicles, in painful detail, the break-up of the marriage of Camille and Paul Javal, while Paul works on a "rewrite" of Homer's *Odyssey* for a crude American producer, Jeremy Prokosch. The production of the film-within-a-film, while a powerful element of the film's structure, seems almost peripheral to Godard's central interest in making *Le Mépris*; exactly how, and why (if such a thing is possible to comprehend), two people cease to love each other, due (in part) to a complete breakdown in communication.

Brigitte Bardot was cast as Camille Javal, and Michel Piccoli as Paul Javal, the screenwriter. Both Bardot and Piccoli were major French stars of the 1960s; Bardot's fame, of course, was worldwide. Jack Palance appeared as film producer Jeremy (Jeremiah) Prokosch, and Fritz Lang, the brilliant German-American director of *M* (1931), *Scarlet Street* (1945), and numerous other films, played himself, as the reluctant director of Prokosch's compromised version of *The Odyssey*. Georgia Moll played Francesca, Prokosch's bilingual assistant, and in a neatly handled self-reflexive touch, Godard appeared as Lang's assistant director for the film-within-a-film, a modern version of *The Odyssey* which Fritz Lang is directing for producer Prokosch. Three powerful real-life producers signed on to back the film: Carlo Ponti from Italy, Joseph E. Levine from America, and Georges de Beauregard from France. Each producer put up a portion of the budget in return for the rights to screen the completed film in their respective countries. Peter Lev points out, in his study *The Euro-American Cinema*, that although de Beauregard hoped that *Le Mépris* would be a wedding of the commercial and the artistic, everyone ultimately wanted something different out of the project, and clashes were perhaps inevitable (see Lev, 82–89 for a detailed discussion of the production history of *Le Mépris*, which I will draw upon here).

Brigitte Bardot, for her part, "wanted recognition as an actress, and she was excited to be working with Godard" (Lev, 84). Fritz Lang accepted because he admired Godard's work as a director, and agreed to act in the film, but to act *only*, and not interfere with Godard's creative process as a filmmaker. Lang, known for his authoritarian methods and unrelenting shooting schedules on his own projects, played himself as a very mellow, aging patriarch, creating his film-within-a-film of *The Odyssey* with quiet determination, despite producer Prokosch's continual interference. For Michel Piccoli, it was a chance to stretch his artistic wings with a celebrated director of the new generation; for Jack Palance, it seems to have been a chance to star in a big-budget feature film. Appropriately enough for the theme of *Le Mépris*, Godard and Palance didn't get along at all on the set of the film, and Godard reportedly shot scenes with an empty camera to placate Palance's desire to dominate the proceedings. Godard as an actor is barely visible in the film, as he darts about the set of Lang's *Odyssey* barking orders at the camera crew and shouting "ready, Mr. Lang." But he certainly looks the part of an assistant director; thin, ambitious, perpetually in motion. All of these disparate elements were combined in a film that would eventually be issued in three different versions (for Italy, France, and the United States).

FIGURE 8. Michel Piccoli, Fritz Lang, and Jack Palance (left to right) on the set of *Le Mépris* (1963). Courtesy Jerry Ohlinger Archives.

As Lev recounts, "*Contempt* was ultimately distributed in three different versions in the home territories of the three producers. It was 100 minutes long in France, 103 minutes long in the United States, 84 minutes long in Italy. The French and American (subtitled) versions of the film are almost identical; the opening scene requested by Joseph E. Levine is in both" (Lev, 88). What makes the United States version longer is the use of a series of "repeat montages," using footage from previous or forthcoming scenes in the film (along with other footage, seen only within these brief "montage" segments) which bracket key sections of *Le Mépris*. One montage "bracket" is used when Paul first arrives on the grounds of Prokosch's villa; another is used when he enters the villa itself. Delerue's mournful score is also chopped up during these brief segments, as if to remind the viewer that she/he is witnessing a visual and aural construct which has been edited together from existing photographic and sound materials.

In Italy, Carlo Ponti went several steps further in his mutilation of the film. As Lev states, Ponti "dubbed, shortened, and in other ways drastically changed the film. The dubbing destroyed the character of Francesca (she became an interpreter with nothing to interpret) and the film's theme of miscommunication" (Lev, 88). Ponti also chopped out most of the scenes of Lang's *Odyssey*, and dropped Delerue's score (one of the composer's finest efforts) and substituted "a jazzy score" (Lev, 88) by Piero Piccioni instead (Piccioni composed the music for another Levine/Ponti collaboration, Elio Petri's *The 10th Victim* [*La Decima Vittima*], produced in 1965).

Godard had to endure additional postproduction interference on the film, when producer Levine withheld *Le Mépris* from the 1963 Venice Film Festival until Godard bowed to his demands to add more nudity. "Godard found a way to [add additional nude scenes] without damaging his film. He shot, in France, an opening scene for the film with Camille nude on her stomach in bed, asking Paul which parts of her body he loves the most" (Lev, 87–88). Godard flips through a variety of colored filters as the scene progresses, turning the shot from red to blue, and running some of the sequence with natural lighting. Levine had complained that "you haven't got enough ass in it" (Lev, 88); Godard here complied "literally" to Levine's request.

Lev further notes that the "Italian critic Adriano Aprà wrote that the Italian copy of *Il Disprezzo* [the Italian release title of *Le Mépris*] . . . 'represents perhaps the most sensational case of betrayal of the original film in the history of film'" (Lev, 88). Nor does the interference with the film's original vision stop here. As Lev and many others have observed, video copies of the film destroy the original FranScope formatting in favor of television's use of standard Academy ratio (1.33 to 1), and *all* dubbed versions of the film (no matter what language it is dubbed into) destroy not only the character of Francesca, but also the monolingual arrogance of Palance's performance, as well as Piccoli's befuddled attempts to communicate with the producer in hopelessly broken English. Finally, the omni-lingual authority of director-within-the film Fritz Lang is deeply undercut by any such attempt to bring all the characters in *Le Mépris* into the domain of any one language. *Le Mépris* is, above all, a film that resists dubbing, resists "pan and scan" rephotographing of its CinemaScopic image for television, and requires the viewer to constantly focus on several levels of linguistic (and gestural) communication simultaneously.

In many ways, *Le Mépris* investigates the mechanics of feminine/masculine power relationships, and the ways in which these metanarrative exchanges of dominance inform either the rupture or the maintenance of marriage. What governs Godard's vision of relationships between the sexes is not so much misogyny as a fear of women, and of their supposedly instinctive understanding, and through this knowledge, control of sexual and emotional commerce. In *Le Mépris*, Godard presents Camille as the controlling force in a doomed relationship, and Paul as a confused, conflicted pawn in the game, unable to shape or influence the destiny which is about to engulf them both. Most of all, Paul lacks knowledge of self, an appreciation of his true motives for his actions. Although he is repellent, Prokosch is in control of his life because he readily assumes the mantle of dictator. Paul, unaware that in compromising his work he is also compromising his life, makes concession after concession for no appreciable gain.

Le Mépris is not only about miscommunication, as Lev suggests. It is also about compromise, the creation of art within the sphere of commercial enterprise, the struggle to hold on to one's individual vision in an industry dedicated to pleasing an anonymous public. Paul is blind in his work, in his relationship with Camille, and in his understanding of his own internal desires and motivations. Later in the film, Camille reminds Paul that when they first met, Paul was writing hack detective novels, and they were poor, but relatively content. But there is a purity in hack work that is not concomitant with rewriting Homer. Paul has dared to set his life against the will of the gods, and he lacks both the omniscience and moral resolution to win such a contest. Prokosch "likes the gods" because in his own small, self-created world, he can be one.

Above all, the hermetic and privileged world of *Le Mépris* is informed by the mechanics of prostitution, played out in a series of ephemeral film sets and rented villas. Everything is transient, all is illusion. Near the beginning of the film, producer Prokosch delivers a Lear-like tirade of despair to a bemused Paul; Prokosch has had to sell part of his studio and fire most of his staff to meet his current debts. "It's the end of cinema," his translator, Francesca, interjects theatrically, and though Paul immediately counters, "No, I think the cinema will last forever," one is tempted to agree with Francesca. The studio (Cinecittà) is deserted, abandoned. Left-over props abound. Decay is omnipresent. The studio system—the vertically integrated monolith that Godard celebrated (after a fashion) in his earlier writings—has decisively collapsed. Prokosch is a dinosaur who knows how the gods feel, because his existence, too, has been called into question.

Prokosch exists through the medium of personal prostitution, of himself and others; throughout *Le Mépris* he is depicted as being simultaneously ruthless, vain, childish, arrogant, stupid, greedy, self-deluding—he is, indeed, a veritable catalogue of negative character traits. Prokosch signs his checks on Francesca's back ("bend over" he commands), throws cans of rushes around the screening room, drives his sports car recklessly, never asks or cares about anyone else's beliefs or opinions, treats adultery as a mildly amusing hobby, holds intellectuals in contempt, and thinks that money can compromise anyone. He is, in short, the perfect producer, morally and spiritually bankrupt, desirous only of commercial success and material gain. If Lang's version of *The*

Odyssey is to be judged in any respect a success, it is because Lang alone holds out against Prokosch's relentless mercantilism, and finally finishes the film when Prokosch and Camille are killed in a car crash—artistic freedom at last. One can't help but wonder if Prokosch's violent death isn't something of a wish fulfillment for Godard, who continues to battle with his backers to the present day, resisting all outside attempts to vitiate his vision.

Lang is thus the moral center of *Le Mépris*, even if his victories are won at the cost of constant struggle; "to live is to suffer" he shrugs during one particularly unpleasant conference with his producer. Paul, who has just written a junk screenplay for cash, *Toto vs. Hercules*, nevertheless has a solid grounding in the classics (as an early conversation with Lang reveals). Yet Paul can be bought, made to compromise for cash. Prokosch uses his checkbook like a gun (as Lang notes, comparing Prokosch's tactics to those of the Nazis), demanding instant cash, "yes or no." At one point, Paul warns Prokosch that Lang will never compromise, even if Paul rewrites *The Odyssey*, reminding Prokosch that Lang fled the Nazis in 1933 rather than work for Goebbels and Hitler. But Prokosch is unmoved: "This is not 1933, this is 1963, and he will direct whatever is written." Although subsequent events will prove him wrong, Prokosch will never know it. The end of cinema is also Prokosch's death, a brutally apt conclusion for one who has spent his existence attempting to compromise the visions of others for personal gain.

It is this purity of evil which attracts Camille to Prokosch on the one hand, even as she is repulsed by Paul's willingness to prostitute himself. All the characters in the world of *Le Mépris* live in a world that is essentially negative, and yet they are attempting to create a work of beauty from the zone of deficit. As Foucault argued, "more than anything else, it is the *place* [emphasis mine] of prostitution that introduces a negative value" (1986, 19). The mercantilism of the commercial cinema is above all a locus of prostitution, where every person or idea remains a commodity for sale or display. Foucault continues, "it is not by analogy that slaves signify wealth; they are an integral part of it" (1986, 19). Prokosch's employees are in fact his slaves, and in his kingdom there is only one absolute—his will. Offenders are banished. There is no real life in *Le Mépris* ; all is artifice, a construct, a rehearsal for the disasters to come. Personal disasters (the break-up of Camille and Paul; Camille and Prokosch's death) and financial ruptures (the collapse of Prokosch's finances, the ultimate commercial mutilation of the filmic corpus of *Le Mépris* itself) are commingled in his film, in which Lang alone achieves victory through creative work despite all the forces arrayed against him. Prokosch is a portent of evil for both Godard and the cinema. The producer's ruthless negative ambition is fated to collapse back in upon itself, causing his own death, the death of his studio, the death of those whom he would dominate (particularly, in this last case, Camille). It has been observed that Paul, despite his acts of prostitution, is allowed to escape the trap of the cinema relatively unscathed, but this does not seem to me to be the case. He will bear to the end of his days the scars of his lost innocence, the death of one he loved, the spectacle of his own ruin through the medium of wretched self-compromise. It is implied, I would argue, that Lang will go on to direct other films; Paul, at the end of *Le Mépris*, is a drifting husk, bereft of direction.

Life in *Le Mépris* is conducted in deserted and abandoned studios, and in apartments and villas either rented (and furnished with rental furniture) or under construction (as is the case with Camille and Paul's mortgaged "luxury" flat). As Deleuze notes, "Godard's unfinished apartments permitted discordances and variations, like all the ways of passing through a door with a missing panel, which takes on an almost musical value" in *Le Mépris* (1986, 121), as Paul traverses and retraverses the space he shares with Camille, in search of a new connection with his estranged wife. As Prokosch's world collapses, so does the marriage of Camille and Paul, and Francesca is left by Prokosch's death to search for both a new job and a new life. *Le Mépris* presents a harrowing vision of the world as an arena of perpetual commerce, driven by ambition, greed, and the lust for the phantom immortality of the cinema.

Seen today, *Le Mépris* is still an exhausting film, a relentless examination of the politics of film production, the compromises one must make (and must *not* make) in order to realize one's dream, and the gap of communication between the self and others in both personal and professional relationships. The casting of

FIGURE 9. A rare production shot from *Le Mépris* (1963). Courtesy Jerry Ohlinger Archives.

Lang in the pivotal role as the philosopher/director of the film-within-a-film is a key factor here; it is also interesting to consider Lang's view of *Le Mépris*, and of Godard's work as a filmmaker in general. In his book *Fritz Lang in America*, Peter Bogdanovich recalls Lang's own views on the genesis and production of *Le Mépris*, in an interview Bogdanovich conducted with Lang in 1965.

> Godard asked Lang to play a director named Fritz Lang in his picture about a group of people filming an adaptation of *The Odyssey*; admiring the Frenchman's work, he agreed. Lang: "Godard improvised a lot. I remember when I read his first, very thick outline—I didn't know him well then—I was very amused by one thing: he wrote it in sequences and, let's say in sequence seven—after he had told what happened in terms of the whole story—he wrote, 'Now, dear producer, I couldn't tell you exactly how I will shoot this scene or what will happen in it. How can I know, now, how the furniture will be in the room, or how Brigitte Bardot will step into the bathtub? But, dear producer, after I have seen how Brigitte does this and this, I can tell you.' I was very amused: three or four times 'dear producer'—in four pages—and he never told him anything really. Much of the dialogue between us was improvised, but there is not one bit of it of which Godard didn't approve. After he convinced me I should play the part (which is quite different from the part in the book), I said to myself, 'I will not direct this picture—I will not give Godard any advice—I will contract as an actor. If he asks for advice, I will give it.' Sometimes he asked, mostly he did not. For example, I have a long talk with the husband [Piccoli], in which he speaks about the killing of Penelope's suitors in Odysseus' house and, because the husband is jealous, he defends the killing. Godard was not satisfied with his own ideas and he said, 'Fritz, do you have any idea how we can end this picture?' I had written something that I never used, so I said, 'How would it be if Lang says, "Murder—killing—is no solution."' And he loved it. That's how we worked—and it was really very pleasant. I think he is the greatest hope for motion pictures." (142)

Godard's working methods were, of course, rather different from Lang's. In his own work, Lang would control the gestures of the actors to the point of actually moving their hands in the precise manner he wished, which irritated such "natural" actors as Henry Fonda (with whom Lang worked in the film *The Return of Frank James* [1940]). During the shooting of *Scarlet Street* (1945), Lang spent an entire morning arranging a pile of dirty dishes in the sink of a Greenwich Village prostitute (Kitty, played by Joan Bennett), to get just the right image of filth and slothfulness required to convey Kitty's unsavory character to the audience. The finished shot is on screen for less than five seconds, but Lang felt justified in this strict attention to detail.

In *Le Mépris*, watching Godard at work, Lang "was astonished that Godard [did not show the final] car accident as action—as [Lang] himself had done, for instance in *Beyond a Reasonable Doubt* [1956]—but only *result* [original emphasis], that is, [Godard] simply shows the dead bodies in the car, revealed in flashes cut into the reading of Bardot's farewell letter" (Eisner, 403). Lotte Eisner goes on to state that, in her view, "the essential difference between [Lang] and the Godard [of 1963 is] that Godard improvises while [Lang] prepares everything in advance" (403). In many ways, as we have seen, Godard works against audience expectations, showing us not that which we wish or expect to see, but only those actions and results that he deems necessary to create the world as he sees it. What could be more appropriate for Godard than to show us a car crash *without* showing us a car crash? One of the most attractive and compelling qualities of Godard's work is precisely this strain of resistance to audience expectation, a desire on the part of the director to elevate the normally passive audience to the level of co-creators within the context of his films. Godard makes his audiences work, and demands their full attention and participation at all times.

The shooting of the film was lengthy, and the production went slightly overbudget, coming in at 500 million francs for the final negative cost (Aumont, 228). The excessive postproduction tinkering by the film's *troika* of producers also did nothing to help matters. Lacking a definitive version of the final work, *Le Mépris* at first failed to find a paying audience. The initial com-

mercial failure of *Le Mépris* except in France (Lev, 89) notwith-
standing, the film has become an accepted classic of the international cinema, and is widely distributed on video cassette, and
presented in the original FranScope format in revival houses
throughout the world. From a financial viewpoint, *Le Mépris*
may not have been an immediate success. As a turning point in
Godard's career, the film demonstrated a new depth and tragic
maturity not present in the director's earlier efforts.

Godard's next feature film, *Bande à part* (*Band of Outsiders*), was shot on location in Paris from February through
March of 1964 (Roud 1970, 178). The film has been accurately
described as a rather slight comedy/drama, and although it is
widely available on video cassette, the reputation of *Bande à part*
has not improved with age. As James Monaco notes:

> After one short film (*Montparnasse et Levallois*, for the
> compilation film *Paris Vu Par* . . . shot in December 1963),
> Godard turned in February and March of 1964 to shooting
> *Bande à part*, his seventh feature film in five years. It's a
> gangster film, but a simple one "about a girl and a gun" as
> Pauline Kael has said. For the first time Godard seems to
> be repeating himself or perhaps summarizing the film world
> he had been constructing for the past five years. Anna Karina
> plays the lead role in the triangle along with Sami Frey and
> Claude Brasseur. *Bande* is famous for the trio dancing the
> Madison in a cafe, and for their decision to "do" the Louvre,
> "beating the American record of nine minutes and forty-
> five seconds by two seconds!" (1988, 395)

Bande à part was widely screened at film festivals around the
world, including The London Film Festival in November 1964,
and the New York Film Festival in September 1964 (Roud 1970,
178), but the general consensus was and remains that *Bande à
part* is not one of the director's major works.

This film was followed by *Une Femme mariée* (1964, known
as *A Married Woman* in Great Britain and *The Married Woman*
in the United States. Shot very quickly between June and July of
1964, less than three full months after the end of principal photography on *Bande à part*, the film starred Macha Méril as Char-

FIGURE 10. Jean-Luc Godard and Anna Karina in the early 1960s.
Courtesy New Yorker Films.

lotte Giraud, and Bernard Noël as her lover, Robert, while Philippe Leroy played the role of Pierre, her husband (Roud 1970, 1979). Monaco notes that the film,

> Subtitled "Fragments of a film shot in 1964," it is a passionate essay about women, men, and the culture of sex. *"La" Femme mariée* was not passed by the French censors until four minutes had been cut and the title had been changed to *Une Femme mariée*, lest the unsuspecting viewer make the generalization from the definite article that Godard very much intended.
>
> Charlotte (Macha Méril) is a concept rather than a human being. She's been formed and molded by the media that surround her—film, magazines, literature, records, ads, billboards, TV, radio. Charlotte is shaped by Triumph Brassiere ads' "looming bosoms on billboards," Céline and Racine, Jean Cocteau, and *Elle* magazine. The film is punctuated by seven monologues on such subjects as "Memory, the Present, Childhood, and Intelligence." For the first time Godard allows himself the full freedom to pun. (1988, 395)

Milne is quite taken with the film; even in 1988, he still feels that *Une Femme mariée* "is one of [Godard's] best" (1988, 395), but I have to admit that I don't share his current enthusiasm for the work. Although the film is "dead on" in its examination of the objectificational forces that continually threaten to shape and even engulf our lives, *Une Femme mariée* seems to me so enamored by the surfaces of the advertisements it excoriates that it, too, is ultimately seduced by them. Macha Méril's conventional iconography of plastic perfection is every bit as much on display here as are the various external forces seeking to control her. One of the most interesting features of *Une Femme mariée* is the fact that it depicts an inversion of the usual patriarchal romantic triangle, that of two women and one man, something that has been attempted only intermittently in the cinema (as in Chantal Akerman's *Night and Day* [1991]). But the promising vignettes presented in *Une Femme mariée* never coalesce into a coherent whole (something that does not happen, for example, in *Le Mépris*), and both *Une Femme mariée* and *Bande à part*

FIGURE 11. Macha Méril in *Une Femme mariée* (1964). Courtesy Jerry Ohlinger Archives.

remain, for this viewer, interesting footnotes to Godard's career.

As 1964 came to a close, Godard had created eight features, five short films, and four "sketches," or segments, of longer feature-film "omnibus" projects. The "sketches," which have not been discussed thus far, will briefly be examined here. *La Paresse* (*Sloth*), a segment of the film *Les Sept Péchés capitaux* (*The Seven Capital Sins*), was shot in September 1961 in Paris. Photographed by Henri Decaë in Dyaliscope (yet another anamorphic process), the short film segment featured Eddie Constantine, an American-born fixture of French gangster films (playing himself) and the young Nicole Mirel (as "the Starlet"). The plot of the film is extremely thin: a young starlet throws herself at Constantine in the hope of getting into the movies, but Constantine is too lazy to bother with her. Other segments of the film were directed by Claude Chabrol, Edouard Molinaro, Jacques Demy, Roger Vadim, Phillipe de Broca, and Sylvain Dhomme. The sketch is intermittently amusing, but as with so many segments in multiple-story films, *La Paresse* is merely a brief fragment of a film that doesn't really come off.

The same cannot be said of *Le Nouveau Monde* (*The New World*), a twenty-minute segment of *RoGoPaG*, a 1962 release. Godard's section of the film was shot in Paris in November of 1962 (Roud 1970, 190) and stars Alexandra Stewart and Jean-Marc Bory in a futuristic science-fiction sketch that is both disturbing and off-beat. Critic Jean Collet writes this account of *Le Nouveau Monde*'s narrative: "He had slept a long time, then he went out. The world seemed strange to him and Alexandra, whom he loved, seemed stranger still. The newspapers announce a recent atomic super explosion above Paris. He tried to reach an understanding with Alexandra, who has made him jealous, but she seems alien, impermeable to all human sentiment or moral sensibility. He discovers how very much the world has changed. He decides to write down this discovery" (Collet 1970, 188). The other directors involved in the project were Roberto Rossellini, Pier Paolo Pasolini, and Ugo Gregoretti. Royal S. Brown writes that "*RoGoPaG* was banned shortly after its release and later re-released, with cuts in the Pasolini [segment], under the title of *Laviamoci il cervello*" (Brown, 176). This brief film is one of Godard's most evocative and personal efforts and his first film in the science-fiction genre, a genre he would explore more fully in his 1965 feature *Alphaville*.

Le Grand Escroc (*The Great Swindler*, a section of *Les Plus Belles Escroqueries du monde*) was filmed on location in Marrakesh, Morocco during January 1963, featuring Jean Seberg (Patricia Leacock), Charles Denner (the swindler), and Laszlo Szabo (police inspector) (Roud 1970, 191). Cut from the completed film before initial exhibition, *Le Grand Escroc* was first shown as a separate short film at the London Film Festival on November 24, 1967, nearly four years after the film's production. The other directors involved in the film were Roman Polanski, Ugo Gregoretti, Claude Chabrol, and Hiromishi Horikawa. Jean Collet offers this synopsis of *Le Grand Escroc*: "Patricia, an American TV reporter working in Morocco, meets a counterfeiter, whom she interviews. He makes counterfeit money for charitable purposes" (Collet 1970, 190). Godard himself provided the narrator's voice for this brief project, which was directed from his original script, photographed by the omnipresent Raoul Coutard, and edited by Agnès Guillemot. Why Godard's episode was cut from the finished film before release remains something of a mystery. Finally, *Montparnasse-Levallois*, a segment of *Paris vu par*, shot in December 1963 in Paris, represented something of a departure for Godard, in that it was shot originally in 16mm by veteran documentary cameraman Albert Maysles on Ektachrome reversal film, and later blown up to 35mm for theatrical. This brief bit of whimsy features Johanna Shimkus (Monika), Philippe Hiquilly (Ivan), and Serge Davri (Roger). Collet's synopsis of the plot is simple: "Monika sends simultaneous messages to Ivan and Roger. She mistakenly believes she has switched the envelopes around, and attempts to explain to one and then the other [how the supposed mix-up has occurred]" (Collet 1970, 192). As Collet notes, this story has previously been told by Jean-Paul Belmondo (as Alfred Lubitsch) in Godard's *Une Femme est une femme* (1961). Of all of Godard's episodic "sketches," this is perhaps the slightest. The other directors contributing to the film were Claude Chabrol, Jean Douchet, Jean-Daniel Pollet, Eric Rohmer, and Jean Rouch.

This frenzied burst of activity reflects a number of things, most notably Godard's impatience to make a mark of his own on cinema history after a long period of critical apprenticeship. The brief "sketch" films anticipate, in a sense, Godard's later work with the Dziga Vertov collective, and his willingness to work on collaborative projects. Nor was Godard about to slow down. In the next year alone (1965), Godard would direct two feature films; in 1966 he would even direct two feature films almost simultaneously, starting shooting on the second project during the final days of the shoot for the first film (the two films are *Made in U.S.A.* and *Deux ou Trois Choses que je sais d'elle.*) While all this work was eventually bound to take its toll, for the moment, at least, Godard moved from one project to the next with supreme confidence, adhering to his low-budget, highly improvisational style, creating works of dazzling brilliance and originality seemingly out of thin air. His next project would be one of his most unconventional, and would become a central work in Godard's development as an auteur. Working again with Eddie Constantine, whom he had first used in the short film *La Paresse*, Godard would next create a science-fiction detective thriller comedy with the unlikely title of *Alphaville: une étrange aventure de Lemmy Caution)*, a film which would combine several disparate genres into a new "hot-wired" hybrid.

Shot in the winter of 1965 in the streets of Paris (specifically during January and February of that year, as some of the worst weather in decades plagued the French capital), *Alphaville* is a science-fiction/detective thriller/romance comedy, with heavy political overtones. The film stars Eddie Constantine as Lemmy Caution, a private eye/secret agent already known through a string of low-budget genre films to the French public. Godard and Constantine had gotten along well during the shooting of *La Paresse;* now Godard proposed a feature film to the actor, who immediately accepted. While Constantine had long been a favorite of the public, the actor was becoming something of a tiresome figure for critics and producers alike, who despaired of ever getting a really first-rate film from a man of undeniable screen presence. In a review of Constantine's 1957 film *Le Grand Bluff,* François Truffaut summarized the problem with the actor's existing body of work: "[*Le Grand Bluff*] is neither more or less bad than all those [films] that Constantine has performed in. The producers used to surround him with second-rate elements and people used to say: And yet, it would be possible to make a good movie with Eddie Constantine. Today, he is very powerful, he is nearly his own producer, percentage on grosses and everything that goes with it, he chooses the script, the director, the musician, the main actors. Everything remains second-rate and people think: Eddie Constantine will never make a good film. . . . In other words, Constantine's stock is falling and that's his fault" (Dixon 1993, 113–14).

In short, Constantine's career as an actor by 1965 was beginning to seriously falter, and he hoped that working with Godard would restore some luster to his battered screen image, as indeed it did. Godard summed up the reason for his admiration of Constantine in a brief comment during the making of *La Paresse*: "Constantine [is] a solid block, a block of intelligence and precision, but a block just the same." Godard observed at the same time that Constantine was "a famous actor who was well known as a personality" (Roud 1970, 158). By capitalizing on the pre-sold character of Lemmy Caution, while repackaging Caution's iconic presence in a parodic science-fiction film, Godard shrewdly gave *Alphaville* a good deal of "pre-sold" marquee value, enabling him to secure financing with ease. Constantine would work with Godard only one more time after *Alphaville* (in *Allemagne année 90 neuf zéro* [*Germany Year 90 Nine Zero*], shot in 1991 but not released commercially in the United States until January 1995), again playing the character of Lemmy Caution. Shortly before his death, Constantine gave one of his greatest performances in Lars von Trier's *Zentropa* (1992) as a corrupt American military man (Colonel Harris) assigned to duty in post–World War II Germany. Constantine died in 1993.

Other members of the cast included Anna Karina as Natacha von Braun, Akim Tamiroff in a brief guest appearance as the aging, shabby secret agent Henri Dickson, and Howard Vernon as Professor Leonard Nosfératu (an obvious homage to F. W. Murnau's 1922 version of the Dracula myth, *Nosferatu*), aka Professor von Braun, Lemmy's nemesis in the film. But the real star (and the real threat) in *Alphaville* is Alpha 60, the gigantic computer that controls not only the physical existence of the capital city of Alphaville, but the lives of all of its inhabitants as well. Alpha 60's philosophical dialogue dominates the narrative of the

FIGURE 12. Eddie Constantine (Lemmy Caution) and Jean-Luc Godard in a publicity still from *Alphaville* (1965). Courtesy Budget Films.

film, erasing all other presences within the work, save for that of Lemmy, and to some degree, Natacha and her father, von Braun. Everyone else behaves like an automaton, which is precisely the condition they have been reduced to. In the world of Alpha 60, there is no room for individuality, conscience, or a personal exis- tence of any sort. Sex is commodified; so are both masculine and feminine bodies. The world of *Alphaville* offers "nothing for something," a void in exchange for one's soul. Lemmy Caution arrives in his Ford Galaxie across the vast reaches of interstellar space with a simple mission: find von Braun, kill him, and destroy Alpha 60. Only then can human independence be restored to the citizens of Alphaville.

The world of Alphaville is one of eternal night, and nearly all of the interior and exterior shots were photographed with existing light on Ilford HPS high-speed black and white film. In many ways, *Alphaville* is one of the most audacious black and white fiction films ever photographed. Often, what light there is will come from street lights, or Lemmy's cigarette lighter, or his Instamatic Flash Camera, or a simple two-cell flashlight. Dur- ing filming, Coutard often objected to pushing the film to these extremes, and would sometimes tell Godard before a shot that nothing would show up on the screen at all. Godard would shoot the scene anyway, with the aperture open all the way, and then "push" the film in the developing bath if necessary. The results are remarkable, and entirely suited to the totalitarian bleakness of Alphaville. Indeed, it is not too much to say that there has never been a film quite as radical as *Alphaville* in its use of existing, profoundly unnatural lighting as an informing visual strategy of the production's overall tactile physicality.

Numerous parallels between the novels *1984* and *Brave New World* and the world of *Alphaville* have been drawn in the decades since the film's first release, and there can be no doubt that Godard owes a considerable debt to the dystopic visions of Orwell and Huxley, not to mention H. G. Wells (in *Things to Come* [1935]) and other dispiriting futurists. But *Alphaville* was and remains an original creation, a world of grubby, quotidian despair fashioned out of the world of nighttime metropolitan Paris with practically no sets or props. Part of the authenticity of despair that pervades the world of Alphaville is this use of then-contemporary settings to depict the rundown shabbiness of the future. Like the broken-down spaceship run by the disgruntled crew in Ridley Scott's *Alien* (1979), the physical reality of Alphaville is that of a crumbling, ill-maintained behemoth, intent on self-perpetuation even as the exostructure of the city collapses on all fronts.

Vending machines dispense useless tokens emblazoned with a perfunctory "merci" in exchange for a franc; women are objectified both as "seductresses" in the hotels where Lemmy stays, and displayed in plexiglass showcases for visual/virtual consumption. People shake their head "no" when they mean "yes," and vice versa; the dictionary (constantly revised) has become the Bible. The authority of the police is unquestioned; citizens are routinely arrested merely for questioning Alpha 60's arbitrary dictates, having committed no crime other than that of expressing their free will. A man who cried when his wife died is summarily machine-gunned to death in a ritualistic execution held in an underground swimming pool. Sex is seen only as prostitution; every person (male or female) is for sale. *Alphaville* is a compelling vision of a heterodystopia; the protagonists of the film are either heterosexual or asexual (married to their jobs; that is, married to the giant computer Alpha 60), and gays, lesbians, bisexuals, or women/men of color are notably absent. Nor does this last aspect of the film seem to be solely a function of intentional design. Moving in a world of white, middle-class patriarchal privilege, Godard echoes the values of the society he partakes of. The later Dziga Vertov work is still remarkably circumspect in the screen space and/or time it affords Third World protagonists (or incidental characters), but in *Alphaville*, these questions of racial, social and/or political marginalization do not even seem to exist.

Yet what is most engaging in *Alphaville* is the sardonic distancing between author and audience, the acknowledgement at all times that we are witnesses to a highly stylized and deliberately artificial construct. Godard is growing distrustful of fictions, even parodies of fictions and/or genres, and longs to make the shift to the freedom of the cine-essayist. In discussing Kendall Walton's study *Mimesis as Make-Believe: On the Foundations of the Representational Arts*, Robert Newsom summarizes Wal-

FIGURE 13. Akim Tamiroff (Henri Dickson) and Eddie Constantine (Lemmy Caution) in *Alphaville* (1965). Courtesy Budget Films.

ton's central argument, a paradigmatic objection to narrative that certainly disturbed Godard during this period of his work as a reflexively fictional feature filmmaker.

> But the most interesting, strong, and controversial part of Walton's theory has always belonged to its core and remains there today. It is that, precisely because fictions are props in games of make-believe, we can only have make-believe encounters with them. . . . Walton does not deny that fictions can provide us with models upon which to shape our own behavior, or that they allow us to express otherwise repressed unarticulated and dangerous emotions. . . . Walton's account remains firm in its insistence that our feelings about fictional beings and happenings are not themselves real. No real interactions between real and fictional worlds are possible, including even the apparently quite limited emotional interaction of simply having feelings about fictions. (Newsom, 144)

As Walton notes, when we go to see a horror film, we are not truly horrified by the monster on the screen; rather, we wish to be, we have lulled ourselves into a state of acceptance, we conflate illusion with concrete substance. Fictive narratives may hold the power to transform our existence, but they exist within the realm of bourgeois spectacle, just as surely as Edison's films shot in the Black Maria differed from the "actualities" of the Lumières. Godard at this juncture in his career is growing impatient with the requirements of narrative, feels that it is exhausted, verging on cannibalistic bankruptcy. With the Dziga Vertov films, he does away with narrative altogether in a number of instances; the unsuccessful and artificial melding of narrative with cine-essayist diatribes in *Tout va bien* (1972) failed because it split the focus of the audience. Is *Tout va bien* a lecture, or an entertainment, a narrative fiction, or an index of then-current political engagement? Godard sees narrative collapsing under the weight of its own pretense, and he strips it down to the bare essentials in *Alphaville*, doing only those scenes essential to the advancement of the fragmentary scenario. It is the concept of unforgiving dystopia that engages Godard here most, and we will see in this film and the others that immediately follow it an abandoning of narrative in favor of an expanded interior, reciprocal dialogue between filmmaker and audience. Above all other considerations, *Alphaville* was created by Godard as an act of social conscience, and societal criticism.

Yet through the simple expedient of using existing locations of incomparable drabness, and shooting 90 percent of his scenes at night, Godard has made a futuristic nightmare world seem both real and tangible, on a miniscule budget. Seen from the vantage point of current cinema practice, *Alphaville* still seems fresh and immediate, as if a newsreel crew had photographed the film only a few days earlier. In its sincerity and simplicity, and its faith in the power of love, *Alphaville* is as transparently romantic as *Masculin Féminin* (1966), shot only eight months later (and also in Paris), is brutally cynical. The harsh lyricism of *Alphaville* ultimately derives from Godard's intense love for Anna Karina, who is seen throughout the film only to best advantage (of all the characters, it is she alone who is photographed with any attempt at glamorization, not that this is required), and Godard's faith in the power of the cinema to bring to life a moral fable in terms that the general public can understand. Indeed, nearly thirty years after its initial release, *Alphaville* remains one of Godard's most popular and often revived films of the 1960s, and one that certainly gained a wider audience than the film that immediately followed it, *Pierrot le fou* (1965).

With typical impatience, Godard began filming *Pierrot le fou* in Paris and the South of France in June 1965, completing filming in mid-July of the same year—another short schedule (Roud 1970, 180). This time, however, Godard attempted a nearly impossible feat; the creation of a modestly budgeted film shot in Eastman Color and Techniscope, starring Jean-Paul Belmondo and Anna Karina, with a cameo performance by film director Samuel Fuller as himself. The Techniscope process itself helped to keep costs down. Devised in the mid-1960s to cut down on raw stock costs, the Techniscope process photographed *two* anamorphic images for *each* frame of film, resulting in a 2 to 1 saving in raw stock cost and developing, and doubling the running time of a conventional 35mm film magazine from ten to twenty minutes. Still, *Pierrot le fou* had a large cast, and the extensive location work made the project that much more difficult.

The plot of *Pierrot le fou* is simple, and Jean Collet aptly summarizes it: "On the evening of July 14 [Bastille Day], Ferdinand [Belmondo] leaves his wife [Graziella Galvani] in the middle of a stupid and boring party [dominated by a bombastic Samuel Fuller, who pontificates to the crowd at large on the qualities of the ideal action film]. He meets Marianne Renoir [Karina], a young girl with whom he was in love five years earlier. Marianne is tied in with a sinister band of criminals. Ferdinand finds a dead man in [Marianne's] room. Ferdinand and Marianne travel across France without money, and go off to live a reprieve on a deserted island on the Mediterranean seacoast" (1970, 196). The one thing that Collet forgets to mention is that, struck by the meaninglessness of their flight, Belmondo paints himself bright blue, wraps several sticks of dynamite around his head, and blows himself up during the final moments of their seacoast idyll. "Shit, shit, I'm an idiot!" are Ferdinand's last words, an apt conclusion to a rather trancelike and formless film which is nevertheless stylistically accomplished. Perhaps the most interesting segment of *Pierrot le fou* is the long sequence on the road, as Ferdinand and Marianne's car "drives" through the night (barely suggested by a darkened studio cyclorama), while alternating red and green traffic lights sweep across the windshield in an unceasing series of phantasmal arcs, eerily prefiguring the "anti-naturalism" of Juliette Lewis and Woody Harrelson in Oliver Stone's *Natural Born Killers* (1994). Intercut with this, Godard offers us his usual panoply of neon signs flickering on and off (at one point the entire Techniscope screen is filled with a series of neon signs endlessly repeating "Las Vegas"), and the philosophical interludes we have come to expect from the director, as Ferdinand and Marianne ruminate on their uncertain future.

It is worth noting that this film, in particular, had a significant impact on a young person who would become a major force in French cinema in the 1980s and 1990s: Chantal Akerman. In a 1983 interview, Akerman commented that "I saw *Pierrot le fou* by chance. I got crazy about movies immediately and I decided to make movies the same night . . . I later went to a lot of movies trying to find the same *Pierrot le fou* . . . Each film I saw, I said, 'It's no good, it isn't *Pierrot le fou*'" (Indiana, 61). As always,

Godard's films forged a link between the past (as represented by Samuel Fuller) and the future (inspiring Akerman to go on to a major career as a filmmaker).

Yet the key aspect of *Pierrot le fou* in retrospect is its influence on the most spectacular, apocalyptic Godard film of the 1960s, the production of which was two years in the future at the time. *Le Week-end*, shot in September–October 1967, shares many of the preoccupations of *Pierrot*: flight across an endless landscape, faking roadside accidents to avert detection (foreshadowing the endless series of "nonstaged" road accidents that litter the landscape of *Week-end*), embracing the French countryside as a figurative and emotional locale. The compositions in *Pierrot* are flat and garish; but the overriding romance (between Ferdinand and Marianne) that forms much of the narrative structure of *Pierrot le fou* is completely absent from *Week-end*. In *Pierrot*, we see two lovers in flight; in *Week-end*, we are shown a married couple who desperately seek to kill each other on their way to claim an inheritance. There is one other aspect of *Pierrot* that intrigues in retrospect: Godard's love of painting, and his use of details from the works of the classical masters, begin to appear (intercut with advertisements) as part of the visual fabric of *Pierrot*. Antoine Duhamel's music for *Pierrot* recalls the tragic splendor of *Le Mépris*, but cannot match the earlier film's majestically assured sweep or scope.

In the wake of *Pierrot le fou*, Godard created one of his most compellingly bleak films of the 1960s, one which still holds up well today. Fascinated by pop music, and the concomitant merchandising of pop music stars, Godard contacted Chantal Goya, already a well-known *chanteuse* of "yé yé" music—a lushly orchestrated, bouncy, saccharine style of French pop music which ruled the airwaves in the mid-sixties. Godard proposed that Goya should appear as Madeleine in a film titled *Masculin Féminin*, working with Jean-Pierre Léaud (as Paul), Marlène Jobert (Elisabeth), and Michel Debord (Robert).

Goya essentially played herself, although in the film she is still establishing her career, climbing her way up the ladder to momentary stardom. Shot by Willy Kurant rather than Raoul Coutard, *Masculin Féminin* was rushed into production in November through December of 1965, and filmed almost entirely

FIGURE 14. Jean-Paul Belmondo (Ferdinand) and Anna Karina (Marianne) in *Pierrot le fou* (1965). Courtesy Jerry Ohlinger Archives.

on location in Paris. Nearly everything in the film is shot with synchronous sound, and Godard with this film deepened his love for long takes, utilizing complex dollies to hold audience interest. Ostensibly adapted from two stories by Guy de Maupassant, "La Femme de Paul" and "Le Signe," the film deals with the developing relationship between Paul and Madeleine, and the harsh throwaway world of the pop music business, which is seen by Godard as a brutally rapacious enterprise. Although Paul is a romantic of sorts, smitten with Madeleine's physical beauty (in a voice-over, Madeleine confides to the audience "maybe I'll screw him, if he isn't a drag"), Madeleine is interested only in the success of her first pop single, "First Tell Me Your Name." Elisabeth and Robert are subsidiary characters in the film; Robert is an impractical Marxist who wants to sleep with Elisabeth; Elisabeth, in turn, wants Paul all for herself.

The drab greyness of *Masculin Féminin* makes even the bleak, futuristic Paris of *Alphaville* seem glittering by comparison. Once again, Godard uses mostly natural light, and shoots much of the film at night (highlighting the depressing rush of the Parisian Christmas buying frenzy). Godard's camera assumes a near-documentary veracity in this film, particularly in a nearly ten-minute static take of "Miss Nineteen," framed in an office window, being relentlessly interviewed by Paul who by this point in the narrative works for the French Public Opinion Institute. The camerawork throughout the film is sparse and functional, and heavily "tripoded." There are only a few handheld shots in the film, mostly in Paul's office. The film abounds in petty cruelties and savage throwaway gags; during a murder in a Parisian café, Paul complains loudly that by leaving the café door open, he's caught in a draft. A man borrows some matches from Paul, not to light a cigarette, but rather to immolate himself (offscreen) to protest the war in Vietnam. Brief sections of the play *Dutchman* are hastily restaged on a subway train. Brigitte Bardot appears in a café, rehearsing dialogue. Paul interrupts one of Madeleine's recording sessions, as Madeleine sings in a breathy whisper a series of inane lyrics over a completely pre-recorded orchestral backdrop. In an arcade, a man menaces Paul with a knife before abruptly turning it on himself, plunging the knife fatally into his stomach. Paul engages a military officer in distracting conversation ("Killing lots of communists in Vietnam?" "Yes, yes." "That's great"), while Robert spray paints "PEACE IN VIETNAM" on the side of a limousine. The film ends with Paul, Madeleine, Robert, and Elisabeth moving into a new apartment, which is still under construction. Paul falls to his death offscreen when he backs up to take a snapshot of the group (perhaps suicide, perhaps accident, perhaps a coldly calculated murder by Madeleine, who is growing weary of him). In the film's final shot, Madeleine reveals that she is pregnant by Paul, and is thinking of inducing an abortion with a coat hanger.

In the entire world of *Masculin Féminin*, there is not an ounce of warmth or compassion. When the group goes to the movies, they are forced to view a sadistic porn film (shot in Sweden as part of a rather strange co-production deal with Svensk Filmindustri), but all Paul can think about is the fact that the film isn't being projected in its proper ratio. As Paul drifts from one meaningless job to the next, he grows to despise the people he comes into contact with every day, wondering if his questions don't in fact shape the public opinion they're supposed to reflect. Structured as a series of "15 precise acts," and interspersed with typically Godardian full-screen slogans ("Purity is not of this earth, but every ten years it shines and flashes"; "A mole has no consciousness, but it digs in a specific direction"; "This film could be called the children of Marx and Coca Cola—think of it what you like") accompanied by the random sounds of rifle fire, *Masculin Féminin* is a meditation on the seeming impossibility of relations between the sexes, and the complete commercialism of contemporary art and music. In view of Godard's own faltering relationship with Anna Karina (see MacCabe 1992, 18), Godard may well have been working out his own personal frustrations through the characters in the film, which seems more despairing and cynical than any of his other films up to that time. Karina herself is absent from the production, but Godard would feature her prominently in his next film, *Made in U.S.A.*, the last film that the couple would make together. It is also worth noting that *Masculin Féminin* is Godard's last film in black and white; the commercial necessity of color for subsequent sales to television had become, by 1966, an unavoidable reality.

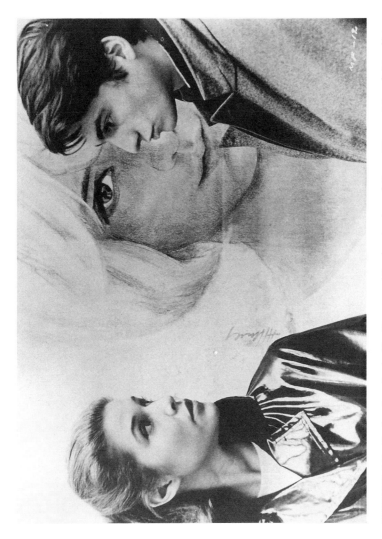

FIGURE 15. Catherine-Isabelle Dupont (Catherine) and Jean-Pierre Léaud (Paul) in *Masculin Féminin* (1966). Courtesy New Yorker Films.

Much of the notoriety of Godard's next two films, *Made in U.S.A.* and *Deux ou trois choses que je sais d'elle* (*Two or Three Things I Know about Her*) (both in 1966), derives from the fact that the two films were shot simultaneously, or nearly so, during the summer of 1966. The story has long been circulated that Godard shot *Deux ou trois choses* during the mornings and *Made in U.S.A.* after lunch, working with Raoul Coutard in Technicolor and Techniscope format on both films. However, it seems that this tale is apocryphal. Several production sources state that Godard began filming *Made in U.S.A.* in July 1966, and completed the shoot on August 11, 1966; shooting on *Deux ou trois choses* began on August 8th (Lesage 1979, 73). There is no question that Godard undertook the creation of two films back-to-back at the behest of his old producer, Georges de Beauregard (who produced *Made in U.S.A.*; François Truffaut, surprisingly enough, was a co-producer of *Deux ou trois choses*). The publicity value of this Herculean feat was, of course, played up in the press as much as possible, but *Made in U.S.A.* never achieved a substantial United States release because of rights problems associated with the source material, Richard Stark's suspense novel *The Jugger*. *Deux ou trois choses* also failed as a commercial enterprise in the United States, perhaps because of the usual and intellectual complexity of the film.

Godard was moving away from "plot" films more and more; *Masculin Féminin* was really a string of incidents strung together by an overall situation (the Parisian world of pop) rather than a fully-developed narrative. With *Made in U.S.A.*, Godard moved even further away from conventional filmmaking. Denied a theatrical release, *Made in U.S.A.* was screened at the Museum of Modern Art shortly after the film's initial release in an English-subtitled version, but even with such a sympathetic audience, the film was not well received. The stress of trying to compete with himself was beginning to show; furthermore, his relationship with Anna Karina was coming to an end. As James Monaco writes,

This, his last film with Karina, seems to be an almost forlorn attempt to capture her on film. The image of her face is on screen most of the time. The other characters are only vaguely realized. They all play minor supporting roles.

Godard explains it: "I tried to make a simple film, and, for the first time, to tell a story. But it's not in my nature. I don't know how to tell stories. I want to mix everything, to restore everything, to tell all at the same time. If I had to define myself, I'd say that I am a 'painter of letters' as others would say they are 'men of letters.'" (1988, 396)

Made in U.S.A. has only the barest suggestion of a plot. Karina appears as Paula Nelson, a reporter investigating the death of Richard Politzer, her lover. Paula arrives in Atlantic City, a "town somewhere in the French provinces. . . . Paula comes out of the affair having killed at least three men, and not really having discovered who murdered Richard" (Roud 1970, 105). The film is dedicated "to Nick [Ray] and Sam [Fuller]," and bears other traces of its affinity to the hard-boiled school of filmmaking. One of the characters is named Richard Widmark (Laszlo Szabo), another is called Donald Siegel (Jean-Pierre Léaud). Widmark's long career as a screen heavy needs no introduction; Siegel is most famous as the director of the 1956 version of *Invasion of the Body Snatchers.* Nor do the "in" jokes stop there; Godard also casts Jean-Claude Bouillon as "Inspector Aldrich" in homage to director Robert Aldrich, and Yves Alonso as "David Goodis," after the American mystery writer of the same name, whose novel *Down There* provided the source material for Truffaut's *Tirez sur le pianiste* (1960). Roud writes that in the summer of 1966, a revival of Howard Hawks's *The Big Sleep* (1946) was running in Paris, and Godard saw *Made in U.S.A.* as a kind of variation on the theme of that film, which is famous for its deliberately impenetrable series of mysteries which are only partially solved by the conclusion of the narrative (1970, 103). But despite a momentarily dazzling montage sequence (discussed at great length by Roud 1970, 106–14) of seventeen mysterious scenes, and a completely abstract non-narrative loosely based on "conspiracies, assassinations, torture and international connections between governmental figures, the press, and criminals" (Lesage 1979, 73), the image that stays in my mind the most is an extreme close-up of a cheap tape recorder playing back the last words of Rich and Politzer (as voiced by Godard himself), with the volume level

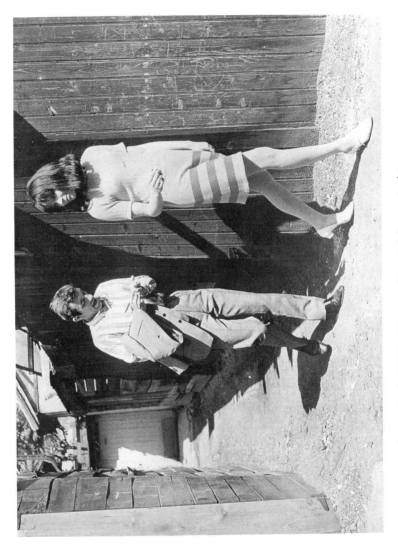

FIGURE 16. *Made in U.S.A.* (1966). Courtesy Jerry Ohlinger Archives.

turned up so high that it is almost impossible to decipher. In ret-rospect, *Made in U.S.A.* both reflects Godard's internal emotional crisis, and signals a new relationship with the audience. Up to this point, Godard had always made at least a token attempt at pleasing his audience, but here abandons all such ambitions alto-gether. *Made in U.S.A.* is a film that *attacks* the audience, daring them to make sense out of an inchoate jumble of words and images, scraps of music and political diatribes. It is perhaps for this reason that I respect *Made in U.S.A.* as much as I do; stripped of visual beauty, seeking to brutalize us with the stripped-down intensity of its primary-colored images, *Made in U.S.A.* prefigures not only the end of Godard's marriage to Karina, but the begin-ning of the end of Godard as a narrative filmmaker.

Deux ou Trois Choses was far more immediately popular; many viewers feel that this is perhaps the most usually and intel-lectually complex film of Godard's first period of work, and the claim is well justified. Shot in thirty days, from August 8 to September 8, 1966, and immaculately photographed by Raoul Coutard at the height of his customary brilliance, *Deux ou Trois Choses* is another Godardian study of prostitution, in which Juli-ette Janson (Marina Vlady), a young housewife in the suburbs of Paris, supplements her income through prostitution. Married to Robert (Roger Monsoret), Juliette is able to purchase a variety of household appliances and products with the extra money she earns as a prostitute, an activity her husband knows nothing about. The "her" of the title, incidentally, is not only Juliette, but also Paris, which has become a huge consumer metropolis ruled by the endless pursuit of material goods. In the beginning of the film, Godard announces that what we are about to witness is a fictive construct, as he first introduces (in voice-over) "Marina Vlady, an actress." A moment later, she is introduced again as "Juliette Janson . . . she lives here," in a huge high-rise apart-ment composed of an interminable series of identical flats. Throughout the film, which is structured within the confines of a typical day, Godard continually reminds us that we are watch-ing a film, telling us the time of day, what the weather is like, asking the viewer whether he should photograph this object or that. The two most famous sequences in the film are undoubt-edly the "cosmos in a coffee cup" scene, in which Godard allows cream to endlessly swirl in a cup of coffee while the director's voice delivers a desperate monologue on the soundtrack, and an extremely lengthy close-up of the end of a lit cigarette. Intercut throughout the film are a series of interviews about the difficulty of finding work for an older woman, shots of construction equipment at work building the new Paris, and still-life compositions of laundry detergents and other household products, neatly displayed in their pristine point-of-purchase packaging, silhouetted against a backdrop of summer grass.

Deux ou Trois Choses is a departure in other ways for Godard. The usual members of his "stock company" are absent. In their places are a group of actors who would begin to form the nucleus of the films of Godard's political years, particularly Juliet Berto, seen in a brief role. Producer/director Raoul Levy appears as "John Bogus;" the critic/historian Helen Scott appears playing a pinball machine. Many of the ideas in the film are in fact directly influenced by the writings of Francis Pouge (Lesage 1979, 78); much of the film is composed of shots of the various protagonists gazing off into the distance, lost in thought, either with or without a voice-over sound bridge. Structured into nine "chapters" (Roud 1970, 125), the film is a meditation, more peaceful and less grating than *Made in U.S.A.*, perhaps because Godard has made up his mind where he wants to go from here. Commercial filmmaking, it seems, even "genre-bending," has come to bore him intensely. Godard has become, with *Deux ou Trois Choses*, a philosopher filmmaker, considering the vicissitudes of human existence. In the "cosmic coffee cup" sequence, Godard ruminates on his past experience, considering his place as a sentient being within the universe. As the cream swirls on the coffee-cup, we hear Godard's voice-over telling us his innermost thoughts with naked simplicity, and hesitant artlessness.

Perhaps an object like this will make it possible to link up, to move from one subject to another, from living in society, to being together. But then, since social relationships are always ambiguous, since my thought is only a unit, since an immense moat separates the subjective certitude that I have for myself from the objective truth that I am for others, since I never stop finding myself guilty, even though I feel

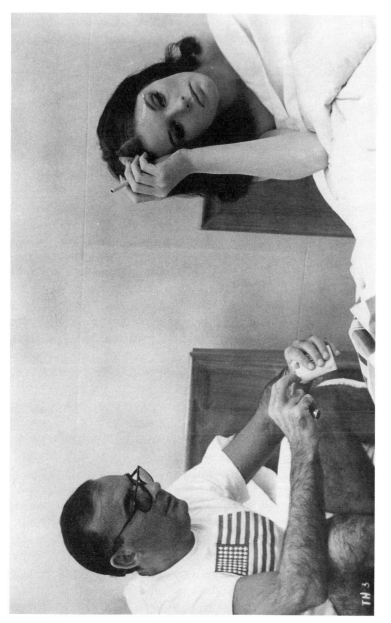

FIGURE 17. *Deux ou trois choses que je sais d'elle* (1966). Courtesy New Yorker Films.

innocent, since every event transforms my daily life, since I always seem to fail to communicate . . . since . . . since . . . since I can't tear myself away from the objectivity that crushes me, nor from the subjectivity that isolates me, since it isn't possible for me either to raise myself into Being, or to fall into Nothingness . . . , it's necessary that I listen, it's necessary that I look around me more than ever . . . the world . . . my fellow creatures . . . my brothers. (Monaco 1988, 366–67)

As Roud notes, *Deux ou Trois Choses* "succeeds on all levels" (1970, 125) because it has an overarching structure—one day in Juliette's life—which lends the film a certain grace and immediacy, akin to the near real-time structure employed in the films of Agnes Varda, Andy Warhol, or Shirley Clarke. There are scenes in *Deux ou trois choses*, as well, in which the characters turn directly to the camera and tells us their names, their occupations, their past failures and triumphs, their hopes for the future. The members of the proletariat—Godard's "brothers" (and sisters)—are the real protagonists of the film. An attendant in a beauty parlor tells us (with the camera recording her) that she didn't succeed as a typist, and so drifted into her present occupation. Functional dialogue is intermingled with introspection, and images that tell us of the dailiness of Juliette's life are intermingled with shots that convey the hidden and seemingly endless significance of a cigarette, a cup of coffee, an apartment building, a bulldozer, a gas station pump, a myriad of voices and images which are compressed into a mere 95 minutes of running time.

The resultant film is an essay of incomparable richness, a film which captures not only Godard's internal state in the summer of 1966, but also the external world of Paris during that same endless month of light and shadow. Marina Vlady brings to her performance a level of crisp, cool distanciation that Karina is seemingly incapable of. Although Juliette looks wistful and lost, staring off into the distance from the balcony of her high-rise apartment, another huge apartment block framed in the background behind her, the overall impression one gets is of control. Juliette may be a reactive agent, who deals with circumstances she does not create, but she copes with daily existence in an efficient if somewhat fatalistic fashion. For as Godard reminds us in the conclusion of *Deux ou Trois Choses*, what we have seen is simply one day in the life of Juliette and Robert. Tomorrow will be a day exactly like the one preceding it, full of errands, bills, compromises, and the false promise of consumer goods. Robert and Juliette return to their apartment, and Robert exclaims:

> "Well, here at last." Juliette replies: "Where?" ROBERT: "Home." JULIETTE: "And then what, what are we going to do?" ROBERT: "Sleep . . . what's got into you?" JULIETTE: "And then what?" ROBERT: "We'll get up." JULIETTE: "And then what?" ROBERT: "The same thing. We'll start all over again. We'll wake up, work, eat." JULIETTE: "And then what?" ROBERT: "I dunno . . . Die." JULIETTE: "And then what?" And as she pronounces those last words we get a flash of a petrol-pump, its dial immobile; then it begins to turn slowly, and then faster and faster. The figures whirl by in an obscene parody of life. (Roud 1970, 128)

This last shot offers a rather grim conclusion to a remarkable film, but it is clear by the end of *Deux ou Trois Choses* that there would be no turning back for Godard—his marriage, and his career as a creator of traditional cinematic narratives, were both over.

With *Deux ou Trois Choses* affording an early clue to a new direction for Godard, the director took time out to shoot a brief sketch "Anticipation, ou l'amour en l'an 2000" as part of the omnibus film *Le Plus Vieux Métier du monde, ou l'amour à travers les âges*, which was shot in Paris (using Orly Airport as one of the locations) during November 1966. In many ways, the plot of the brief segment, which runs approximately twenty minutes, is a throwback for Godard. "Anticipation" tells the story of John Demetrois (Jacques Charriér), an alien who lands from another world at Orly Airport. After a brief examination by the authorities, Demetrois is sent to the airport hotel to meet a prostitute, Marlène (Marilù Tolo). However, Marlène is simply a sex machine, incapable of dialogue during love-making. Demetrois objects and asks for a sentimental lover, and Natacha (Anna Karina) appears. In a nonstop torrent of words, Natacha and

Demetrois manage to communicate, and "invent the kiss" (Collet 1970, 199). The film starts out in various color tints, and only springs to life in full color during the final moments of the sketch: originally, as Lesage notes, "Some sequences were to be printed entirely in red, some in yellow, some in blue; each time the color of the sequence changed, the narrator would announce 'Coleur europeén,' 'Coleur soviétique,' or 'Coleur chinoise' . . . the first two attempts at lovemaking were to be printed in negative and the figure of the protagonist often blurred" (1979, 81). Not surprisingly for general release prints, the printing lab ignored these instructions, and printed the film in a "uniformly beige" tint (Lesage's words), with only the end of the short film in full color. The film was shown in proper color formatting at the Trieste Science Fiction Film Festival; and also during a run in a handful of "art houses" in Paris as part of a program dubbed Star Short Films. In addition to Karina's participation in the project, Jean-Pierre Léaud appears in a bit part as a bellboy. The overall effect of the film is slight, and Godard was intensely displeased that his color-printing instructions were not followed. When "*Anticipation*" was released in the monochromatic (except for the final scene) version as part of *Le Plus Vieux Métier du monde* for general release, Godard disowned the project. Other sequences in the film were directed by Franco Indovina, Philippe de Broca, Mauro Bologni, Claude Autant-Lara, and Michel Pfleghar. The film was released in a dubbed version only, and cut from 115 minutes to 97 minutes. The English release title for the feature was *The World's Oldest Profession, or Love through the Ages.*

Godard's next project after this brief diversion was *La Chinoise, ou plutôt à la Chinoise*, shot in 1.66:1 ratio by Raoul Coutard in striking Eastman Color, and edited by Agnès Guillemot. *La Chinoise*, perhaps one of Godard's simpler films, marked his first collaboration with Anne Wiazemsky, who would later marry Godard. Enthusiastically received by French and American critics upon its initial release, the film was nevertheless dismissed by several critics as a political fantasy, who apparently did not foresee the coming of the events of May 1968, which would shake the foundations of the French government. The plot of the film is really a pretext for a series of diatribes. *La Chinoise* chronicles the lives of five young "revolutionaries" who live in a bourgeois apartment in Paris during the summer of 1967. They are "a student, an actor, a country girl, a scientist, and a painter" (Collet 1970, 200), and they attempt throughout the summer to put into practical application the teachings of Marx and Lenin, as interpreted by Mao Tse Tung. The film is a small, intimate affair, with a cast of only seven, and was quickly shot in March of 1967 in Nanterre and Paris. The five students are Véronique (Wiazemsky), Guillaume (Jean-Pierre Léaud), Henri (Michel Sémeniako), Kirilov (Lex de Bruïjn), and Yvonne (Juliet Berto). The only other characters of consequence in the film are a mysterious "Comrade X" (Omar Diop) and the philosopher Francis Jeanson, playing himself.

Prophetic though the film may have been—as Monaco notes "it's about a Maoist cell at the Nanterre campus of the University of Paris, and it turned out to be an uncannily accurate forecast of things to come; less than a year later, the students at Nanterre were instrumental in beginning the university rebellion that led to the events of May 1968" (1988, 397)—it is also simplistic. It may not even be that prophetic: Godard met Jean-Pierre Gorin, his chief collaborator during his forthcoming Dziga Vertov period, in 1967, when Gorin was a member of the editorial board of *Cahiers Marxistes-Léninistes*, a radical left-wing journal (Lesage 1979, 6), and during this period he had extensive contact with radical student activists at Nanterre. *La Chinoise* may have been more of a rallying cry for an existing political faction, rather than a prognosticator of its future existence. Subtitled "a film in the making," *La Chinoise* features characters who are less fully realized creations than cardboard cutouts, which may have been precisely Godard's intention. Nevertheless, we never really feel that either these characters or their situations (and occupations) are real, and so the film becomes a tedious exercise in formalist propaganda. Godard's embrace of the teachings of Chairman Mao (as outlined in his Little Red Book) is alarmingly naive. Wiazemsky, who apparently was instructing Godard in the ways of political insurrection off-screen, harangues the other members of the group in the film, in an attempt to inculcate into the other members a sense of the historic importance of their shared mission. As Guillaume, Léaud carries off his part as an actor with flair and panache, but seems reflexively self-conscious of his work in the

FIGURE 18. *La Chinoise* (1967). Courtesy New Yorker Films.

film. Henri votes against violent action when the group, under Véronique's direction, decides to assassinate a member of the cultural/political elite as a positive act; for his efforts, he is excluded from the group. Subsequent interview sequences with Henri attempt to gain our trust by showing Coutard filming the interview as if to acknowledge directly the implicit staging of the entire narrative, but in retrospect, it seems both shallow and obvious, lacking the resonance of the same device at the beginning of *Le Mépris*.

Kirilov paints revolutionary posters; Yvonne does the housecleaning (and is supposed to be grateful to the other members of the group for rescuing her from a life of prostitution). Kirilov, convinced (rightly) of the futility of his acts, commits suicide. Véronique goes ahead with the assassination attempt, but kills the wrong person the first time (off-screen), and has to go back and kill another person (also off-screen) to accomplish her task. Brief skits of primitive political theater punctuate this skeletal narrative. A pop song praising "Mao, Mao" is heard on the soundtrack, promising all the answers to life's travails can be found in this little red book. Communist writer and theoretician Francis Jeanson argues with Véronique on a train about the proper way to conduct a revolution. As an organizing tool, *La Chinoise* is undeniably effective. The film makes revolution glamorous, a pop event. Indeed, the outbreak of Maoist passion at Nanterre can be seen as creating the film itself, rather than the film predicting the coming rebellion. The incendiary nature of the film was so pronounced that no conventional U.S. distributor would touch it. It was finally distributed in the U.S. by Leacock/Pennebaker, a small production/distribution company that specialized in low-budget documentaries such as *Don't Look Back* (1967), a film covering Bob Dylan's 1965 British tour, and *Monterey Pop* (1969).

The film opened in a "four wall" arrangement at the Kipps Bay Theater, and through astute "counter cultural" marketing by Leacock/Pennebaker, the film was Godard's biggest commercial hit in the United States since *Breathless*. Perhaps there is something to this phenomenon; both *La Chinoise* and *Breathless* are extremely linear films, easy to follow, easy to comprehend. The multilayered textual nuances of *Made in U.S.A.* and

Deux ou trois choses are nowhere apparent. *La Chinoise* is political filmmaking done with a very broad brush, on a highly stylized and eye-catching cinematic canvas, dominated by bright reds, blues, and yellows. In the most famous sequence of the film Véronique demonstrates to Guillaume that a person can indeed do two things at once, by playing some Schubert on a record player and simultaneously informing Guillaume that she doesn't love him any more. Her tirade against Guillaume is cruel and crushing ("I don't love your face, your eyes, your mouth, I don't love the color of your sweaters any more. You bore me more than you can imagine" [as cited in Roud 1970, 134]), and though she assures him later that she was simply demonstrating an abstract comment, Guillaume is understandably unnerved. Véronique, as confused and somewhat incompetent as she is (as evidenced by the botched assassination attempts later in the film), is clearly a force to be reckoned with, a very cool and calculating intellectual and physical presence. Godard seems to have come under Wiazemsky's spell quite completely during this period, which is understandable given the rupture in his marriage.

But in his fervent acceptance of Maoist doctrine without revision or reflection, Godard seems to be trying to prove to himself, and his public, that he hasn't lost touch with youth, or his ability to unsettle the conventions of the middle-class spectator. In 1994, Godard completely denied his association with Marxist/Leninist thought, in an interview with critic Andrew Sarris. Asked by Sarris, "What are your politics right now—that is, do you have any politics?," Godard responded: "Only what you see on the screen."

AS: "You were considered a Marxist activist at one time."

JLG: "Oh, no."

AS: "You were never a Marxist?"

JLG: "I never read Marx."

AS: "But you talked about Marx."

JLG: "Yes, but only as a provocation, mixing Mao and Coca-Cola and so forth." (Sarris 1994, 89)

In view of Godard's total immersion in the highly charged political events of the 1960s, this statement seems disingenuous in the extreme. Godard was, in fact, changing radically as a film-maker, becoming colder and less romantic. He was increasingly aligning himself with revolutionary youth movements in France, and in his work of the next few years he would almost entirely abandon the world of 35mm theatrical film production for the shadowland of 16mm political filmmaking, creating a highly problematic yet undeniably compelling body of personal and idiosyncratic work with the Dziga Vertov group (comprised, for the most part, of Godard and filmmaker Jean-Pierre Gorin). Films such as *Un Film comme les autres* (1968), known in the United States by a number of titles, the best of which is perhaps *A Film Like All the Others; British Sounds* (aka *See You at Mao*) (1969); and *Vent d'est* (*Wind from the East*) (1969) are primarily political tracts, advocating violent change and the radical overthrow of existing government. All were shot in 16mm; none were widely shown. Yet for those who saw them, their impact was undeniable. In many ways, these films were the result of Godard's work in *La Chinoise*. *La Chinoise* is a primer; the 16mm works are acts of direct political engagement.

However, for the moment, we see Godard basking in the glamorously controversial public reception of *La Chinoise*. During the filming of *La Chinoise*, Godard found time to contribute a brief but compelling sketch (perhaps his finest short film) to the collaborative feature, *Loin du Viêt-nam* (*Far from Vietnam*) (1967). Compiled by cine-essayist Chris Marker, the other contributors to the film included Claude Lelouch, Joris Ivens, Alain Resnais, William Klein, and Agnès Varda, though Roud notes that Varda's episode did not appear in the final film (1970, 184). Roud further mentions that it was rumored that Godard's first contribution to the project was also rejected by his fellow collaborators, for unspecified reasons (1970, 167), but in any event, Godard's final effort is simple and sparse, and altogether impassioned. During a screening of *Loin du Viêt-nam* at the New Arts Lab in Drury Lane during the summer of 1968, Godard's sequence was clearly the one that most impressed the audience.

As Lesage describes the visuals of Godard's segment, entitled *Caméra-Oeil* (*Camera Eye*, an obvious tribute to pioneering

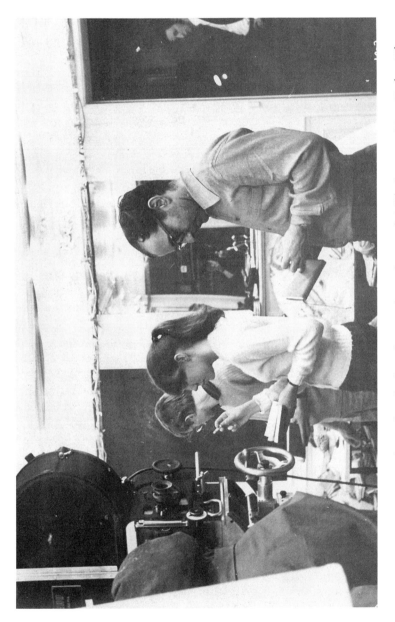

FIGURE 19. Anne Wiazemsky and Godard on the set of *La Chinoise* (1967). Courtesy New Yorker Films.

Soviet montagist/documentarist Dziga Vertov's Kino Eye),
"Godard peers through the viewfinder [of an enormous Mitchell
35mm camera, which almost totally blocks our view of the film-
maker] . . . and twiddles with the controls; the lights and the
camera itself are aimed directly at the audience. [There are
images of raw film stock being spooled on to a printer in a film
laboratory, as well as shots of arc lights flashing into the camera
lens] . . . intercut are some of the masks from the political theater
skits of *La Chinoise*, photos of [the corpse of political activist
Che Guevara], grainy newsreel images of military jets and bomb-
ings, scenes of striking French factory workers and demonstra-
tions" (1979, 85). On the soundtrack, Godard talks about his
desire to make a film about the Vietnam conflict, but because of
the requirements imposed upon him by the apparatus of commercial film production and distribution, he is unable to do so.
Godard tells the audience that from now on, he will include some
reference to Vietnam in every one of his films. He tells the audience that he wanted to go to Vietnam to make a movie, but got
turned down by the North Vietnamese government. "I was told
permission would not be granted because of my vague ideology. I
agreed that such a film by me might be dangerous" (as cited in
Lesage, 85).

Just how "dangerous" Godard was becoming is suggested
by this austere, structural film, in which Godard nakedly exposes
the inherent contradictions in making films (which cost money,
and are primarily consumer objects) about issues of conscience
which cannot be quantified. As a direct consequence of this insol-
uble paradox, Godard would make only one more major feature
film in the 1960s, which would sum up all the themes that had
been present in his work since becoming a feature filmmaker in
1959: *Le Week-end* (*Week-end*) (1968). After that, Godard would
navigate the increasingly rough political waters of the 16mm
phantom zone, and then return in the 1980s to 35mm feature
production.

As a footnote to this segment of his career, Godard made a
short film before tackling *Le Week-end*, a sketch entitled *L'Aller
et retour andate e ritorno des enfants prodigues dei figli prodighi*,
"filmed in 1967 on a roof garden in Paris" (Lesage 1979, 86), in a
project originally entitled *Vangelo 70*, then *La Contestation*

(*Amore e Rabbia/Love and Rage*). The other contributors to the film were Bernardo Bertolucci, Pier Paolo Pasolini, Carlo Lizzari, Marco Bellocchio, and Elda Tattoli. The 26-minute film was finished by Godard in 1967, as per schedule, but production difficulties involving the final choice of the title (at Bellocchio's insistence) pushed the final release up to 1969, when the completed film was screened at the Berlin Film Festival. The dialogue is in French and Italian, and traces the final break-up of a couple (he is Arab, she is Jewish) who have decided to go their separate ways to pursue their individual destinies. The visual look of this brief sketch is almost Straubian in its minimalism. There is only one set, and only two speaking parts, each of which is interpreted by two "witnesses" who facilitate the disintegration of the relationship. The resultant film is little more than a divertissement for Godard, who by this time had his mind on a project that would become perhaps his most hotly contested and widely influential work since his early days as a critic for *Cahiers*.

In August 1967, Godard and Wiazemsky were married. In September and October of 1967, Godard finally tackled the revolutionary narrative of *Le Week-end*, his last major 35mm production to reach commercial audiences for more than a decade (although he could not know this at the time). The resultant film would set Godard irrevocably on the path of a noncommercial, revolutionary cinema, and change the trajectory of his career as a *cinéaste* from that of an entertainer who wishes occasionally to instruct, to the stance of a teacher who brooks no interference when he lectures to his audience. Godard was moving away from cinema as commerce; as Walter Benjamin has argued, "by the absolute emphasis on its exhibition value[,] the work of art becomes a creation with entirely new functions" (227), and Godard was growing tired of a life of box-office subservience. *Le Week-end* can be seen as a farewell to the cinema as an object of commerce, and a foretaste of his entirely anti-commercial work with the Dziga Vertov collective. This period of his work would last for more than a decade, and create some of the most compellingly pure political anti-narratives in the history of the moving image.

CHAPTER THREE

———————————— ◉ ————————————

Jean-Pierre Gorin and the
Dziga Vertov Group

For Godard, *Le Week-end* is the beginning of the end, the jump-ing-off point into an entirely new form of cinema, a cinema that would embrace political action above all other considerations, and lead directly to this work with Jean-Pierre Gorin and the Dziga Vertov group. Godard in *Le Week-end* is often more inter-ested in language, spoken and/or written, than in visuals, and on occasion what we see on the screen is distinctly subsidiary to the various texts we hear on the soundtrack. Godard still plays with large intertitles to set off various episodes in the film, and his linguistic puns are present throughout, both visually and aurally. There is still a fragment of plot in the film: a husband (Roland) and wife (Corinne) plan to kill each other, yet form an uneasy alliance to cross the post-apocalyptic French countryside in the hopes of claiming an inheritance. This slight narrative is little more than a frame for a series of sight gags, street theatre, and stylistic flourishes which both celebrate and mock the death of the conventional image production system of the contempo-rary commercial cinema.

It is the unceasing replacement of one image with another, the tyranny of the visual, which most disturbs Godard in his films during this period. In contrast to the rapid cutting of *À bout de souffle,* and even the celebrated montage sequence in

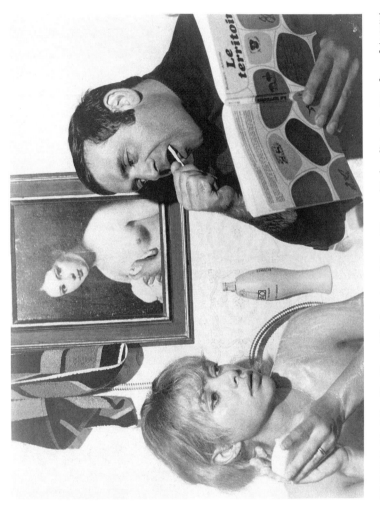

FIGURE 20. Mireille Darc (Corinne) and Jean Yanne (Roland) in *Le Week-end* (1967). Courtesy New Yorker Films.

Made in U.S.A., Godard now constructs his films in large blocks of images, held for long periods of time, requiring the audience to meditate on the visuals he creates. As Walter Benjamin notes, this is a possible solution to the imagistic ephemerality inherent in the cinema to graphic apparatus.

> The painting invites the spectator to contemplation; before it the spectator can abandon himself to his associations. Before the movie frame he cannot do so. No sooner has his eye grasped a scene than it is already changed. It cannot be arrested. Duhamel, who detests the film and knows nothing of its significance, though something of its structure, notes this circumstance as follows: "I can no longer think what I want to think. My thoughts have been replaced by moving images" [Duhamel, 52]. The spectator's process of association in view of these images is indeed interrupted by their constant, sudden change. (240)

When the image does not abruptly change—when, in fact, it lingers languorously on the screen for many minutes at a time, with only minor variations in framing and/or movement within the frame—we are forced to do that which we do when confronted with a painting in a museum or a gallery. We must *scrutinize* the image, deconstruct it, consider the margins and borders of the frame, and "contemplate" the mimetic structure of the iconic/representational strategies that informed the creation of this image. It is the birth of the cinema as a medium of spatial/temporal analysis.

Yet *Le Week-end's* most significant achievement is that it marks the definitive arrival of the artist as polemicist, using his camera as a scalpel and a weapon, as his soundtrack creates a defiantly oppositional mix of language, natural sound, and scraps of music. In Deleuze's words, Godard in his later works creates a series of dialectical "wanderings which have become analytic instruments of an analysis of the soul" (1986, 213). But for all of Godard's reliance on the variables of language, the most striking single sequence in *Le Week-end* is a nearly ten-minute traffic jam rendered entirely without dialogue in a single take (and a few intertitles), representing a triumph of the purely visual over

both narrative and linguistic syntactical structure. James Monaco
has written perhaps the best description of this landmark scene,
unique in the cinema. He describes the traffic jam as:

> a tour-de-force tracking shot that lasts almost a full reel as
> Godard slowly moves down a country road jammed with
> stalled cars. There's an ear-splitting symphony of horns to
> accompany the shot as we move with stately pace past men
> playing cards on the hood of their car, someone playing
> catch with a boy standing in a sun-roof, a crashed car lying
> upside-down, a crowd of children running around, a travel-
> ling circus, an empty bus, a horse and cart, some school
> children, more ball players, a car that is smashed into a tree,
> a huge red and yellow gas truck, a Fiat coupe, people playing
> chess, more card players, a man in oilskins in his yacht on a
> trailer hauling up sails, a driver urinating, and then finally
> the cause of the jam, a majestic multiple crash: a collage of
> color, crumpled steel, broken bodies, and blood. (1988, 397)

Coming as it does in the first thirty minutes of the film,
this magnificently choreographed sequence dominates our expectations for the rest of the film, but Godard willfully undercuts our
implicit spectatorial wish for a series of arresting and apocalyptic
tableaux. Most of *Le Week-end* is comprised of a series of functional, almost drab visuals backed up with intensely complicated
dialogue tracks, and the traffic jam sequence is the most memorable imagistic construct in the entire film. The rest is political
theater. An accident between a tractor driver and a young woman
with her boyfriend in a sports car serves as the backdrop for a
consideration of class privilege; bucolic picnics are interrupted by
groups of "guerrilla" hippies who massacre the guests and make
off with their food and clothing. An angel appears and offers
Corinne and Roland anything they desire, but is repelled by the
banality of their requests and abruptly departs, cursing their stu-
pidity. Corinne and Roland hitch a ride with a travelling pianist,
and must endure a piano recital in a farmyard before they can
continue their journey. The landscape of the French countryside,
in full summer bloom, is littered with car wrecks and dead bodies, but no one seems to care.

When Corinne's mother refuses to share her inheritance with the couple, they kill her with a huge kitchen knife, and then burn the body by the side of the road after stuffing the corpse into a particularly spectacular roadside wreck, involving a bright yellow airplane and a red Fiat. Often, Godard interrupts his scenes with intertitles ("A FILM FOUND ON THE SCRAPHEAP," "A FILM LOST IN THE COSMOS"), or shots of the odometer clicking away the miles on their useless voyage. At other times, Godard will conclude a scene with a staged grouping of all the protagonists standing against a wall, staring directly at the camera, in keeping with "post-modernism's rejection of all depth notions of virtuality for the shine of simulacral effects" (Polan 1989, 27). The end of the film seems designed to exhaust the spectator, involving as it does a series of "revolutionary" monologues and/or voice-overs by members of the guerrilla band, ritual animal and human sacrifices, and indecipherable radio communiqués. Several contemporary critics, in fact, complained that the film went on too long, particularly during the garbage truck monologues near the end of *Le Week-end*, in which an African and an Arab activist "speak for each other," while the camera stares clinically at their impassive nonspeaking faces (all of their dialogue is delivered as a nonsynchronous voice-over track). But I would submit that Godard is more interested in the political diatribes, and the stripping away of sound from image that accompanies their presentation within the film, than he is in the huge traffic jam near the start of the film.

Proof of this assertion can be found in the structural organization of the films directly following *Le Week-end*: *Le Gai Savoir* (long dialogues in a television studio) shot in December 1967/January 1968; Godard's cinetracts of May 1968 (a series of black-and-white silent three-minute political organizing films); *Un Film comme les autres* (a 1968 film in which the dialogue completely overshadows images of people sitting in a grassy field, listening to the asynchronous voices we hear on the soundtrack); and *One Plus One* (a series of lengthy takes of the Rolling Stones rehearsing their song "Sympathy for the Devil" in a recording studio, intercut with random political skits, shot in June and August 1968).

In each of these films, Godard is less interested in the external construction of his images than in the ideas that these images

94

FIGURE 21. The scene in the forest in *Le Week-end* (1967). Courtesy New Yorker Films.

present to his audience. Yet, at the same time, Godard cares less and less in these films about pleasing anyone other than himself and his fellow activists, and the monologues toward the end of *Le Week-end* point directly to this abrogation of the traditional role of the film director. When *Le Gai Savoir* was presented at the Berlin Film Festival, for example, Lesage notes that "the critical reaction was 'disastrous'" (1988, 90); during the film's screening at the New York Film Festival on September 27, 1969, the audience members disrupted the film repeatedly during its projection, eventually walking out *en masse*. A near-riot accompanied the screening of *Un Film comme les autres* on December 29, 1968, at Philharmonic Hall, Lincoln Center in New York. Of an audience of nearly a thousand people, less than 100 lasted through the second reel of the movie, which used a simultaneous French/English soundtrack that is well-nigh indecipherable. Furthermore, Godard included a note in the filmcan for the projectionist to "flip a coin" (Roud 1970, 147) to determine which reel of the two-reel film should be shown to the audience first. As Roud also notes, "legend has it that Godard was not there during much of the shooting" (1970, 147) of *Un Film commes les autres*, a further abdication of the director's usual role in the making of a film. The only possible concession to conventional audience expectation in *One Plus One* (a film which was later altered by the producer, Iain Quarrier, and retitled *Sympathy for the Devil*) is the inclusion of the Rolling Stones in the film. But the footage of the Stones working in the studio is quotidian and disinterested in the extreme, and the political theater surrounding this footage is hastily-staged and structured without visual conviction. This, then, is the new cinematic territory Godard was looking for when he completed *Le Week-end*, the near-complete erasure of his identity as a celebrity director, and the reinvention of both his professional and personal life as a political activist who happens to use film as his chosen medium. In the words of Walter Benjamin, "mechanical reproduction of art changes the reaction of the masses toward art . . . the conventional is uncritically enjoyed, and the truly new is criticized with aversion" (236). Godard certainly knew that his new, clearly radical films would infuriate bourgeois audiences, intent on being "entertained." Godard here signals that he is on to something altogether new, a film that does not even need an audience, a film existing primarily as a personal statement, as an abrogation of narrative, and the traditional filmmaker/viewer social/economic contract.

Viewed in this light, the monologues of the African and Arab truckers alluded to above form a crucial element of the text of *Le Week-end*. The two men compare contemporary colonialism to Nazism, and insist that Third World countries cannot, and must not, depend on the nonexistent "good will" of the exploitative superpowers to break free of their centuries of occupation and slavery. In contrast to the rest of *Le Week-end*, the two speeches we have just heard contain not a hint of reflexive self-mockery or cinematic stylishness. Visually, they are flat and seemingly without spectatorial interest in the usual sense of that phrase, but placed along side the political vaudeville that comprises the rest of *Le Week-end*'s narrative structure, these monologues are by welcome contrast compelling and real. Yet in these speeches, "The link to the workers' struggle is located in the desire to blow up power at any point of its application. This site is apparently based on a simple valorization of *any* destructive of *any* power" (Spivak, 272). This is the central problem with Godard's revolutionary strategy in *Le Week-end*; its dominant force lies in the infantilism of randomly destructive violence.

In the world of *Le Week-end*, all interest is self-interest, and moral responsibility is nonexistent. Roland can't be bothered to intervene on Corinne's behalf even when she is being raped in the ditch by a passing tramp. Perched atop a garbage truck symbolizing the wreck of civilization, half-listening to the two workers with obvious boredom, Corinne and Roland are the ideally complementary couple. The film begins with each planning to kill the other; by this point in *Le Week-end*, the last vestiges of pretense have been swept away. The audacity of these three shots, in which the Arab, the African, and the bourgeois couple stare directly into the lens of the camera, is stunning in its nonchalant assurance. Godard has grown both bored and suspicious of the elements of staging traditionally required by narrative cinema. Viewed today, much of the agitprop humor of *Le Week-end* is both forced and artificial, staged to satisfy the twin demands of entertainment value and international marketability. The traffic-jam sequence is a visual tour-de-force, without doubt, but the

Vietnam-era humor has dated badly. Yet the direct address of the Arab and the African speaking for each other remains vital, distressing, and prophetic.

In this sequence, Godard has not permitted "the cinema [to] exhaust itself in the model of an open totality of movement . . . because the cinematographic image ceases to be a movement—image in order to become a time—image" (Deleuze 1989b, 18). We must confront these two men, and the bored faces of Corinne and Roland, for many minutes at a time, the better to focus our attention not only on the words the men speak for each other, but also the phenomenon of the "time-image," a practice contrary to the dominant discourse of Hollywood cinema to graphic practice. If we are bored, then we have become one with the bourgeois couple, caring nothing for the plight of the marginalized citizens of the Third World. The sequence is an indictment of the audience, a clear signal of the collapse of narrative, and a criticism of the image production process and the concomitant cost involved in feature film production. A further indication of Godard's increasing distrust with conventional film narrative can also be seen in the sequence in the forest, as Corinne and Roland set fire to Tom Thumb and Emily Brontë, because "they're just fictional characters." Characterization is action in *Le Week-end* (actions of greed and malice) or else it is rendered in the form of a diatribe, an onslaught of discourse from which we are powerless to escape (short of leaving the theater).

Seen from the vantage point of recent feminist criticism, many aspects of *Le Week-end* seem both sexist and naive, although others have argued paradoxically that the film's vision is profoundly feminist, in depicting the woman's body as a commodity. Women are little more than props within the world of the FLSO, and have little or no say in the day-to-day activities of the group. However, all of the characters in the film are thoroughly selfish and corrupt (indeed, this is precisely the point of the work), so that any criticism of Corinne's actions alone within the film would be absurd; Roland is every bit as morally and spiritually bankrupt. All of the women and men in *Le Week-end* are participants in a world bereft of moral valence or emotional sensibility. Survival is all that matters. The bitterness and cynicism of *Le Week-end* are still resonant today, as is the cold and calcu-

98

FIGURE 22. Mireille Darc (Corinne) held at gunpoint in *Le Week-end* (1967). Courtesy New Yorker Films.

lating symmetry of Godard's camerawork within the film. In the few years between 1959 and 1967, Godard's view of both cinema and the world had been radically altered. His new marriage to Wiazemsky would open the door on his career as a cinematic activist, but the tenderness and emotional warmth of his earlier work have been erased. The Godard of *Le Week-end* seems embittered, remote, and somewhat stoic. He has become a philosopher with a camera, no longer driven exclusively by a love for the cinema. For the new Godard, direct political intervention is the most important question of cinema practice. Sadly, this was Godard's last collaboration with his long-time cinematographer Raoul Coutard. Asked in 1970 whether Coutard could work on Godard's new films, the director replied "I think not, because he is a reactionary mind and he can't [work with us]. We have nothing to say to each other" (Goodwin and Marcus, 29). Godard was clearly making a clean break with his classical cinematic past. Indeed, *Le Week-end's* last intertitle states flatly "fin de cinéma"; for Godard, the conventional narrative film was indeed over.

With the production of *Le Week-end* concluded, Godard began filming *Le Gai Savoir* (*Joyful Wisdom/The Gay Science*) in December 1967, less than two months after the completion of filming on *Le Week-end* (which wrapped in October 1967). Photographed entirely in the television studios of O.R.T.F., the French National Television and Radio Service, the film starred Jean-Pierre Léaud as Émile Rousseau, and Juliet Berto as Patricia Lumumba. The film was a watershed event for Godard, in that it was the first time he utterly abolished plot in one of his feature films. Instead, Godard used the film's 91-minute running time to consider the relationship between sound and image, the sign and the signified, "false images" and "false sounds," and those words/images/sounds that society conveniently suppresses in order to consolidate the power of the state, along with numerous other related issues. The philosophical dialogue is intense and densely structured, with considerable debts to Nietzche, Rousseau, Mao, Marx, and the writings of a number of pioneering Third World theorists. O.R.T.F. took one look at the finished film, which was shot in the relatively luxurious format of 35mm color, and refused to show it on television. Further, the French censor refused to issue a certificate for the film's general release, thus denying the film either a theatrical or television screening. Later, O.R.T.F. sold the rights to the film back to Godard (Lesage 1979, 90).

As one theorist aptly put it, "Many artists escape the restrictions of the media and do the work they want to do simply by calling it something other than what it is" (McDonald, 21). This certainly applies to Godard's work in *Le Gai Savoir*; it superficially masquerades as a feature film, while actually attacking the commodity/exchange system of the theatrical ciné-construct full force. It was also the beginning of Godard's long love/hate affair with the medium of television, which offers immediate distribution and audience assimilation without the bothersome technical details of a theatrical release (numerous prints of the film, advertising, distribution costs, and the like). Thus the film is structurally, conceptually, and thematically audacious, anticipating Godard's later work with Jean-Pierre Gorin and Anne-Marie Miéville. *Le Gai Savoir* also anticipates the collapse of the theatrical cinema apparatus, an event precipitated by the nascent rise of television, and a resultant drop in traditional cinema audiences. As Stuart Laing notes:

> Television's most dramatic effect on another medium was the collapse of the cinema. In 1955 cinema audiences stood at 1,082 million per year, still above prewar levels. By 1960 they had dropped to 600 million, fell to 326 million in 1965 and to under 20 million in 1970. There was a vicious circle of decrease in audience followed by closure of cinema followed by a further decline in the cinema-going habit; by 1970 the number of cinemas open was less than half those in 1959. (76)

Today the number of operational film theaters is exponentially less; even prestigious archival projection facilities such as the National Film Theatre of the British Film Institute are increasingly forced to run "blockbuster" films to lure videocassette-sated audiences out of their houses and into the cinema theatre. Only the attraction of the CinemaScope, digital sound super-spectacle can be relied upon to produce a satisfactory turnout; the black and white masterpieces of the thirties, forties, fifties and sixties have evaporated into the mists of memory, to be recycled in bits and pieces in commercials and videos. Godard sees this "fragmentation" of cinema's past rapidly approaching in *Le Gai Savoir*, and he celebrates the death of the old and the birth of the new with equal fervor.

The fact that *Le Gai Savoir* was so assiduously suppressed by the French government gives one some indication of the power of the work. Liberated from all narrative requirements, Godard in *Le Gai Savoir* emerges as a pure cinematic essayist, immediately at the top of his form, reinventing both the cinema and himself. The discussion of the manner in which society represses sexuality, and routinely distorts the meaning of texts/sound/images, particularly those that emanate from or treat Third World concerns, is both profound and richly detailed. Godard in this film is asking his audience to see the world with new eyes, to question all established modes of representation, to overthrow conventional iconic structures in favor of a process of continual and unceasing revision. He is attempting to train his audience to rethink the conventional ways of seeing people and things, as employed by the dominant cinema, which results in the enslavement and disempowerment of the average cinema/television viewer. *Le Gai Savoir* concludes with bursts of wild audience applause on the soundtrack, as if Godard wished to ensure the film's favorable reception, but the completed work was too rigorous and austere for most audiences. Even at the New York Film Festival, where the audience was primed to expect a rather challenging work from the press handout, the audience reaction was one of general hostility and bewilderment. *Le Gai Savoir* did not present Godard as the trickster, the punning entertainer the audience had come to expect, the director who might inject a bit of political rhetoric into an entertainment film, but then (even in *Le Week-end*) attempt to win his audience back with a crowd-pleasing spectacle or an "in" joke. *Le Gai Savoir* signalled the beginning of Godardian cinema as all-out political warfare, and it was only the beginning of a torrent of new films.

What Godard was after, and what he has been trying to do with his new series of *Histoire(s)* as well, is to redefine and reinvent the cinema, and above all to free it from the canonical orthodoxy which has been imposed upon the mechanism of the

FIGURE 23. Jean-Luc Godard in the early 1970s. Courtesy New Yorker Films.

recorded sound/image through exterior critical apparati. As Dana Polan notes, "Classical film theory is one of those imposing structures, a massive and weighty ontologising that we look back on with whimsical suspicion, understanding that the movement of history works to undo all ontologies" (1989, 23), a process Godard hoped to accelerate with *Le Gai Savoir* and his other, postclassical works. Polan continues: "filmic experimentation [serves] as a challenge not only to prior films but also to *a priori* theories" (1989, 23). This is precisely the challenge that Godard offered to cinema's past, practical and/or theoretical. Yet such work seems destined to be unpopular, even if only because it seeks to delimit the identification of the spectator-within-the-film, to establish new ground rules for interpretation and appreciation, to call into question all that has been known or done before in the cinema. Thus the critical/audience hostility Godard's new films experienced could not have been unexpected; indeed, the daring of his execution in the new films practically anticipated it.

After a tour of several American universities in February 1968 (Collet 1970, 202), Godard's next project was the creation of a series of *Ciné-tracts*, some shot at the University of Paris campus in Nanterre, some in Paris during the May–June 1968 political uprising of workers and students. Shot in black-and-white 16mm, each *Ciné-tracts* lasted 2 minutes and 50 seconds, the length of 100 feet of 16mm film at 24 FPS, and was edited entirely in the camera. Today, as in the events of Tiananmen Square in China, these films would no doubt be videotapes; in 1968, home video was in its absolute infancy, and the format was not practicable. Alain Resnais, Chris Marker and others also made *Ciné-tracts* during this period, and none of the *Ciné-tracts* were signed. The films were screened in France "in student assemblies, factories on strike and political action committees in May [and June] 1968" (Lesage 1979, 93), and in England at the New Arts Lab and elsewhere. Each *Ciné-tract* cost fifty francs to produce, and sold (in copies) for the same amount. Projected on portable 16mm machines at countless student meetings, they were an effective political organizing tool, particularly in view of their length. Godard, along with Jean-Pierre Léaud and others of his circle, were extremely active in the events of May, and the director's work on the *Ciné-tracts* reflects his increasing radicalization.

Godard was one of a number of directors (including Truffaut, Claude Berri, and Claude Lelouch) who staged a public disruption of the Cannes Film Festival, which culminated in a complete termination of that year's competition. When André Malraux tried unsuccessfully to fire Henri Langlois as director of the Cinémathèque Française in February 1968, Godard took to the barricades, physically battling with the French police on at least one occasion. He photographed the riots in the Latin Quarter of Paris during May 1968 for the *Ciné-tracts*, and marched on May 29, 1968 with a group of workers in a French labor union demonstration (Collet 1970, 202). On May 30, 1968, Godard left for London to shoot his next feature, *One Plus One.*

As recounted by Lesage, Godard shot the Rolling Stones footage (in 35mm color, using a British crew for the first time in his career) for three days in June, yielding two and a half hours of film (1979, 96). Around July 20, 1968, Godard went back and shot the rest of the film, a series of rather clumsy political skits set in a junkyard in a forest (the "Eve Democracy" skits, featuring Anne Wiazemsky as Eve), and in a pornographic book store. In between the first and second trips to England, Godard shot (or had shot for him) the footage that would become *Un Film comme les autres,* in which "some workers in the Renault auto factory engage in dispute with revolutionary students in a wasteland at the foot of the H.L.M. in Flins" (Collet 1970, 203). The Flins material is intercut with footage from Godard's *Ciné-tracts. Un Film comme les autres* opened in New York on December 29, 1968, provoking a near riot among the spectators. What upset viewers the most was probably the indecipherable French/English sound mix, which mingles the two dialogue tracks into one indecipherable wall of sound. The Flins images, in which we never see any of the faces of the protagonists of the film, also are designed to provoke an audience, rather than entertain. Calling the film "boring" (Roud 1970, 147) rather misses the point of the exercise. Searching for images of conventional visual "beauty" in *Un Film comme les autres* is a useless quest; this is a film which seeks to assault and enrage the normally passive spectator, something the film certainly did in its American premiere performance.

It is concomitantly significant that Mark Woodcock's *Two American Audiences: Godard on Godard,* a thirty-minute documentary that preceded *Un Film comme les autres* on the program, was well received; it's a very conventional film. In *Two American Audiences*, Godard talks about his work with *La Chinoise*, a film which was by the time of the screening nearly two years old, and a film made before the May riots in France. Woodcock's *mise-en-scène* is that of the traditional documentary, and the viewer is neither moved nor upset by the interview; it simply exists. With *Un Film comme les autres*, Godard has moved far beyond the territory he explored in *La Chinoise*, offering his audience an image/sound construct of considerable simplicity and (on the soundtrack) complexity. *Un Film comme les autres*, in a slightly more refined and less radical form, would prove to be the model for Godard's political work in cinema for the next several years. The Lincoln Center audience was obviously unwilling and/or unable to make the transition with the director to a more radical form of politically engaged cinema. As Godard said around this time, the cinema image in bourgeois filmmaking "has to be destroyed . . . this is one of the first things Dziga Vertov said . . . that we must liberate the sight of the . . . masses" (Goodwin and Marcus, 34–35). Yet even Godard could not escape his own fame, and his history, as a creator/disseminator of images. As Fredric Jameson argued, the

> films of Godard in hindsight seem susceptible to a kind of retroactive canonization-reification in which ostentatious marks of improvisation or editing interventions are frozen over after the fact (and by the sheer familiarity of numerous rescreenings) into the timeless features of the "masterwork." (1990, 188)

Renegade films though they were, Godard's most radical visual expressions would eventually be destined to fall into place in a sort of inverted filmic canon, along with the films of Jean-Isidore Isou, Andy Warhol, and other radical experimentalists. The Dziga Vertov group wanted, above all other considerations, to create a revolutionary cinema of illustration. But before one could create a "revolutionary" film text, a new film language had to be discovered. Sergei Eisenstein, in "Notes for a Film of *Capital*" wrote on October 13, 1927 that

> The most important tasks in a cultural revolution are not only *dialectical demonstrations but instruction in the dialectical method* [Eisenstein's emphasis], as well.
>
> Given the available data on cinema, such tasks are not yet permissible. Cinema does not possess those means of expression, since there has been, until now, no demand for tasks of that sort; only now do they begin to be defined. (138)

This was the task that faced Godard and Gorin in their work with the Dziga Vertov collective. It was a challenge that (perhaps predictably) ultimately overwhelmed the members of the collective, but at the very least, it represented a radical break from bourgeois cinematic tradition. Godard and his associates were exploring relatively new territory here, with only Eisenstein and Vertov as models, and they attacked their shared task with enthusiasm and defiance.

In the meantime, producer Iain Quarrier, who appeared in *One Plus One* as the proprietor of the pornographic bookshop where one of the film's political skits takes place, was fighting with Godard over the editing of *One Plus One*. Godard wanted the film to end with the song "Sympathy for the Devil" still uncompleted; on the soundtrack, Godard tells the viewer that he's "fed up and wants to go home" (Lesage 1979, 99). Godard added to the controversy when he punched producer Quarrier in the face during the London premier of *One Plus One*, which Quarrier had retitled *Sympathy for the Devil*, and slightly re-edited. In Quarrier's version of the film, we hear the Rolling Stones' final version of "Sympathy for the Devil" on the soundtrack with a full studio mix, thus lending the film some semblance of conventional narrative closure. This, of course, was precisely what Godard was working against. Although the film got regular commercial distribution in France, England, and the United States, probably because of the marquee value of the Rolling Stones participation in the project, in either version, *One Plus One/Sympathy for the Devil* is one of Godard's weaker efforts, memorable chiefly for the line "so what you're saying is, the only way to be an intellectual revolutionary, is to give up being an intellectual" (asked of Eve Democracy by a particularly persistent interviewer). Of all Godard's films, *One Plus One* seems the most perfunctory and dashed off, possessed of "the low-budget look of amateur actors, staged tableaux, and vaudeville-type numbers, essentially static and simply strung together—all of which must initially stun the viewer in search of vanguard of 'experimental' novelties" (Jameson 1990, 64), a charge that Jameson levels against the later work of the German experimental cinéaste Hans Jurgen Syberberg, but one which seems very appropriate here.

Roud recounts numerous incidents that disrupted the shooting of the film: the May riots themselves, Brian Jones's (the Stones' rhythm guitarist) arrest for illegal possession of drugs, the unrelated arrest of actor Terence Stamp (who was to appear in the film), and even a fire in the recording studio (1970, 151). But Roud, who also has problems with *One Plus One*, overstates the case when he claims that "Godard is uniquely unfitted to make the kind of film he thinks he *ought* to be making" (151). Roud bemoans the loss of Godard's "lyricism," but it is obvious that Godard abandoned any claims to conventional standards of visual beauty with the conclusion of *Le Week-end*. What is wrong with *One Plus One* is a timidity of execution, a thinness of material, and Quarrier's interference with the finished product (even today, it is the producer's version which predominantly circulates). As Godard later said of the film, "the whole thing was a mistake" (Goodwin and Marcus, 28). The presence of the Stones is mere window dressing for a hastily conceived and executed project designed to cash in on Godard's new "revolutionary" image, which not incidentally presents Anne Wiazemsky to the public with great insistence as Godard's new icon of feminine cinematic presence. The material is boring, didactic, and commercially compromised. It remains one of Godard's most public, and perhaps understandably his least intellectually satisfying, political films.

But what is most disturbing about *One Plus One* is that Godard seems to be, for the first time, repeating himself out of sheer exhaustion, as if his initial structural/ideological grid had collapsed beneath the weight of his past works. Perhaps this was inevitable:

[T]he avant-garde artist above all claims originality as his right—his birthright, so to speak. With his own self as the

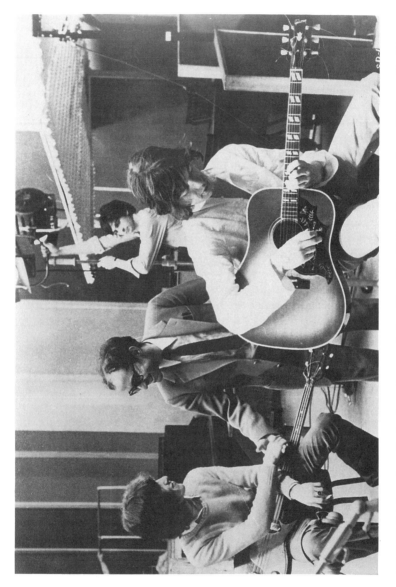

FIGURE 24. Jean-Luc Godard on the set of *One Plus One* (1968). Courtesy Jerry Ohlinger Archives.

origin of his work, that production will have the same uniqueness as he; the condition of his own singularity will guarantee the originality of what he makes. Having given himself this warrant, he goes on, in the example we are looking at, to enact his originality in the creation of grid. . . .

Structurally, logically, axiomatically, the grid *can only be repeated*. And, with an act of repetition or replication as the "original" occasion of its usage within the experience of a given artist, the extended life of the grid in the unfolding progression of his work will be one of still more repetition. (Krauss, 160)

Godard's *One Plus One* adds nothing new to the director's vision of the world; it is rather the initial manifestation of "the extended life of the grid" being allowed to supersede the textual/contextual concerns of the film itself.

It was also the last time that Godard would have the luxury of shooting in 35mm for quite a while, but this was something the director was absolutely ready to relinquish. With the low cost and portability of 16mm equipment, and the comparatively low cost of 16mm film stock itself (particularly in the 1960s,) came freedom—freedom from the interference of producers, freedom from the enormous costs of commercial filmmaking, freedom from the spectatorial demands of conventional cinema audiences. Godard was anxious to get on with this new phase of his career, and he turned to Richard Leacock and D. A. Pennebaker to help him puts his plans into motion.

In November 1968, Godard came to New York to consult with Leacock/Pennebaker, who had served as his American distributors for *La Chinoise*, about a new project to be titled *One American Movie (One A.M.)*, a typically Godardian pun. With Pennebaker and Leacock running the camera (as they had for *Don't Look Back* and *Monterey Pop*), Godard embarked on a film that featured the chic American radicals of the late sixties, including Rip Torn, Tom Hayden, Eldridge Cleaver, and the Jefferson Airplane. Godard began the project with high hopes, but soon clashed with his collaborators and abandoned the project. Speaking of the aborted film in March 1970, during an attempt to salvage the film at the Leacock/Pennebaker studios in New York,

Gorin observed (somewhat redundantly), "it's a dead corpse." Two things bothered Godard and Gorin in particular; first, that there was (in Godard's own words) "no context. We thought we could give it a context [now, by editing] but we can't, anymore, because it was originally made without context. We can't give it a context now because it's abstract and it means nothing" (Goodwin and Marcus, 10). The second problem concerned Pennebaker's handheld camerawork, which was very much in vogue at the time, but now seems distracting and self-conscious. As Godard said, "For the moment we prefer to work with steady shots, just to reduce things to more simplicity. It's not a law, but we think it's much better. Because even in a steady shot you have to think about where the camera is placed and how the shot is framed but at least you have limited questions raised, not unlimited ones" (Goodwin and Marcus, 29). Asked what would eventually happen to the film, Godard replied "We don't know . . . leave it unfinished. Or Pennebaker will do his own version without our finishing it, which means nothing to us" (Goodman and Marcus, 11). And Leacock and Pennebaker did in fact finish the film after a fashion, releasing it as *One P.M.* (or *One Parallel Movie*) in 1971.

By December of 1968, Godard was working in Quebec at a "private Canadian television station [where] he experiment[ed] with a new kind of 'free' television—listening to the voices of machine operators, technicians, labor union people, and students." However, "the project arouse[d] violent protests, and Godard return[ed] to France" (Collet 1970, 203). In early 1969, Godard was experimenting with primitive half-inch reel to reel videotape (the Sony Portapack), making black-and-white video "magazines" (Collet 1970, 203) around Paris. In February 1969, Godard began production of one of his most successful political films, *British Sounds* (aka *See You at Mao*), shot in 16mm for London Weekend Television (LWT). The film consisted of six long sequences. First is a ten-minute tracking shot of an MG assembly line at the British Motor Car Factory in Cowley, Oxford (Lesage 1979, 99). The soundtrack (actually two levels of noise, one synchronous and one added later) is an overwhelming din of heavy industrial sound. Second is a primitive stab at feminism, in which a nude woman walks around her flat, talks on the tele-

FIGURE 25. Rip Torn in Godard/Gorin/Pennebaker's *One American Movie (1 A.M.)*, shot in 1968, and subsequently re-edited and released by D. A. Pennebaker as *One Parallel Movie (1 P.M.)* in 1971. Courtesy Jerry Ohlinger Archives.

phone, and then directly faces the camera, which stares at her genital area for several hundred feet of film. On the soundtrack, a woman reads an early feminist text, describing the exploitation of women's bodies and images within bourgeois cinema and advertising.

In the third sequence, images of workers are intercut with a mock news broadcast, shown on a television monitor; in the fourth sequence, a group of workers discuss conditions in the workplace, with a few Godardian intertitles; in the fifth sequence, students at Essex University criticize pop music and construct posters advocating radical political change; in the sixth and final scene, "a hand covered with blood . . . moves slowly across mud and snow . . . to grasp a red flag (Lesage 1979, 101). In perhaps the film's most famous image, a fist punches through a Union Jack flag. Songs and political texts are heard on the soundtrack, and Godard cuts to the film's final title: "There's no end to the class struggle." LWT turned down the completed film for televising. There seems little doubt that the completed film was far too radical for LWT's liking, tame as it now seems. Two years later, on its own talk panel show entitled *Aquarius*, LWT analyzed and then disowned the film.

Of all of Godard's early political films, *British Sounds* is one of the most compact and precisely structured. The objectification of the feminine corpus in the film is still a disturbing issue, and a visual/political conundrum that Godard still struggles with to this day. You don't see any naked men marching about in the film, or any mention of the ways in which cinematic constructions of male sexuality constrain and commodify acceptable images of "masculinity" into a narrow range of rapidly exhausted stereotypes. Yet this is a common problem with much late 1960s/early 1970s "radical" work. To cite John Caughie:

> Perhaps even more seriously the language of cultural struggle comes out of a tradition of socialism which is aggressively masculine in its historical dependence on male industrial labour. It carries the weight of masculinism into the arena of popular culture . . . by defining the importance of popular culture, why it matters, in a historically masculine language of force, power and struggle. The concept of cul-

tural struggle was a strategic intervention to displace economism by asserting the effectiveness of struggles other than the struggle over the ownership of the means of production; but by polemically appropriating the language of class struggle it has placed culture within a discourse which makes it difficult to think other forms of engagement. Whatever the objects of the struggle, it is not easy to separate the history of the discourse from its assumption of a male subject. (162)

Godard and Gorin in *British Sounds* resolutely envision not only a "male subject" in their film, but also a male spectator. This primitive struggle to control the power of the significator will give way to greater self-knowledge of Godard and Miéville's *Soft and Hard*, but for the moment, Godard and Gorin's discourse is mined in phallocentricity. But the use of the long take within the film is a powerful focussing device, one which forces the viewer to directly confront, and meditate upon, the hierarchy of images produced by the dominant Hollywood cinema—or as Godard would have put it during this period of his career, "the bourgeois cinema." Yet *British Sounds* never reached its intended audience. Although designed to fit into a one-hour time slot, the film was effectively suppressed by the very entity that financed it, and then publicly dismissed by that same entity on national television sight unseen. The irony of this is immense, even if there is a reciprocal twist encoded within the history of *British Sounds'* production and nondistribution. Who remembers the panel show that LWT used to disassociate itself as a corporate entity from the film now, or even the names of the participants in that program? And yet the anonymous students and workers featured in *British Sounds*, and more importantly their ideas and concerns, have achieved a degree of immortality within the fifty-two minutes of the film's running time.

British Sounds also marks the dominant ascendence of the Dziga Vertov group as a productive entity within Godard's professional and personal life, although Godard's collaborator on the film was not Jean-Pierre Gorin, but rather Jean-Henri Roger. During 1969, Godard would work with a number of collaborators, including Paul Burron, Daniel Cohn-Bendit ("Danny the

Red"), Jean-Henri Roger, and Gorin. *British Sounds* was co-directed by Godard and Roger. *Pravda*, the next Dziga Vertov project, was co-directed by Godard, Roger, Burron, and Gorin. *Pravda's* genesis began during a trip to Czechoslovakia in March 1969, where Godard, Burron, and Roger surreptitiously filmed images in the streets of Prague, and also photographed additional material in 16mm directly off the television screen of his hotel room from Czech national television, but Godard put the footage aside for the moment and began production of another film, *Vent d'est*.

In May/June 1969, Godard went to Italy to film *Vent d'est*, described at the time as a "Marxist western," with a screenplay by Cohn-Bendit, Godard, Gorin, Gianni Barcelloni, and Sergio Bazzini. The project was rather ambitious, in that it featured several famous personages in the cast, including Italian actor Gian Maria Volonté, Vanessa Redgrave, film director Glauber Rocha (as himself), and former Andy Warhol impersonator Allen Midgette. The film also had fairly stable financial backing for a Godard film of this period, with Georges de Beauregard again involved on the financial end, along with the CCC Studios in Berlin, Godard and Karina's production company Anouchka, Berlin's Film Kunst, and Rome's Polifilm. Direction was officially credited to the Dziga Vertov group. Shot in 16mm by Mario Vulpiani, with a subsequent blow-up to 35mm, the film actually involved some studio shooting in an Italian "western street" set at Elios Studios, with interiors shot at De Paoli Studios, as well as additional exterior work at various locations (Lesage 1979, 103–4). Godard directed the film, but shooting was hindered by political and artistic differences between the various collaborators. At this point, Gorin arrived from Paris to assist in the production, and Godard and Gorin took over the project and brought the shooting to a conclusion. What emerged was something altogether different than what the producers probably had in mind, but in many ways, the most interesting part of the construction of both *Pravda* and *Vent d'Est* was happening behind the scenes.

Godard and Gorin were becoming increasingly close as artistic associates, and Jean-Henri Roger and the other members of the Dziga Vertov collective were dropping out. In an interview long

FIGURE 26. *Vent d'est* (1969). Courtesy Jerry Ohlinger Archives.

after the collapse of the Dziga Vertov group, Gorin observed that his priorities and outlook had changed a great deal since the late 1960s and early 1970s:

> The very idea of trying to think through the lenses of a guy who was thinking in the 30s seems to me, now, extraordinarily backward; what kind of madness tries to delay time and space and history? I'm hardly even a Marxist any more, so it opens my sights a little. (Walsh, 17)

But at the time, Gorin and Godard pursued their dream of a revolutionary cinema with nearly fanatical dedication. The two men became inseparable, working together as a political and creative entity through 1973. For all intents and purposes, the Dziga Vertov collective became simply Godard and Gorin, and the other members and associates of the group splintered off into their own projects. *Pravda* was post-produced by Godard; Gorin completed the editing on *Vent d'est*. The two men worked simultaneously, and at the conclusion of the editing, they found they had achieved a collective and creative synthesis of ideas, and that they were ideally complementary working companions (Lesage 1979, 7). Thus was founded the partnership that would shape Godard's political filmmaking, and his public pronouncements, for the next half-decade. Godard and Gorin sought to create a utilitarian cinema in their work with the Dziga Vertov collective, a cinema that was fresh, original, altogether new.

> The avant-garde artist has worn many guises over the first hundred years of his existence: revolutionary, dandy, anarchist, aesthete, technologist, mystic. He has also preached a variety of creeds. One thing only seems to hold fairly constant in the vanguardist discourse and that is the theme of originality. . . . More than a rejection or dissolution of the past, avant-garde originality is conceived as a literal origin, a beginning from ground zero, a birth. (Krauss, 157)

In Godard and Gorin's case, this "literal origin, a beginning from ground zero, a birth" was an essential part of their creative enterprise. With the Dziga Vertov group, and his later work with

Miéville as part of Sonimage, Godard hoped to create "a really significant work, the originality of which does not reside in numerous technical devices or external and superficial sequences of shape, but in a profound renewal of the plastic matter of images, a veritable liberation, by no means hazardous, but intricate and precise, of all the dark forces of the mind" (Artaud 1972b, 68). Paradoxically, during the 1969–70 period Godard was briefly involved in what would have been his first real Hollywood film, a filming of the Jules Feiffer play *Little Murders*. This idea never got beyond the stage of preliminary discussions, however, and actor Alan Arkin eventually directed the project in late 1970 for a 1971 release (Collet 1970, 204).

Based on the writings of Mao Tse Tung and Brecht, *Pravda* is certainly the more minimalist of the two films, and perhaps the more interesting because of it. Only two voices predominate on the soundtrack, that of Godard and an anonymous woman. The images—everything from Western commercial imagery to footage of Russian military presence in Czechoslovakia—conclude with an image of the Agfa logo (the film was shot on Agfa color film stock) and laboratory color test footage (Lesage 1979, 102–3). At fifty-eight minutes, the film seems designed for exhibition on television, but screenings were confined to workshops, collectives, and film societies. The real problem with *Pravda* is not an impoverishment of ideas, but rather the inadequacy of the distribution methods used to bring the film to the public. Although working to please himself alone, Godard still thought of his films as clarion calls to action, but increasingly, his audience was confined to fellow cinéastes and a narrow band of militants. The problem of widescale distribution is one Godard would continue to address with all of his 16mm political efforts, and remains an issue in Godard's work to the present day. A simple fact had to be faced: none of these films was making any money. Even worse, they were signal failures in their attempts to present revolutionary ideas to the public, because the public seldom got a chance to see the finished films.

Vent d'est is a barrage of political commentary, political theater, and the usual Godardian intertitles (of which my favorite is IT'S NOT A JUST IMAGE, IT'S JUST AN IMAGE), wrapped in a package of Marxist/Leninist self-criticism and self-reflexivity which seems more parody than polemic. The factions within the collective during shooting manifest themselves in *Vent d'est* in a sort of fatigued playfulness, as if the participants managed to shoot a series of scenes in a desultory manner over a fairly long period of time (nearly two months), but without any sort of cohesive vision that would have brought the film together. The organization of the images is all done in the editorial stage; the sequences as shot seem fragments, in itself not atypical of Godard, but fragments that lack both focus and conviction. The dialectic between female and male power relationships is perhaps the film's most interesting avenue of exploration, but *Vent d'est* needed greater discipline during the actual production of the film. Even with Gorin's eventual intervention, there's an air of careless insubstantiality to the film, which never coalesces into a wholly satisfying intellectual treatise.

Ultimately, it is the film's improvisational and appropriational stance which defeats the success of the enterprise. Jargonistic and vague, it uses political rhetoric in a hazy, unsubstantial fashion.

> Maoism [in French intellectual discourse] simply creates an aura of narrative specificity, which would be a harmless rhetorical banality were it not that the innocent appropriation of the proper name "Maoism" for the eccentric phenomenon of French intellectual "Maoism" and subsequent "New Philosophy" symptomatically renders "Asia" transparent. (Spivak, 272)

The same could easily be said of *La Chinoise*, particularly the "Mao, Mao" pop song sequence, but here the very real (and often harshly corrupt) ideology of Maoist Marxist/Leninism is reduced to the status of a privileged pastime.

Next was *Lotte in Italia* (*Luttes en Italie/Struggle in Italy*), a film never released in English, but one which Godard and Gorin, speaking during a 1970 lecture tour of the United States, seemed more pleased with than the previous Dziga Vertov efforts. As Gorin stated at the time of the film's production,

> *Struggle in Italy* is a film about the transformation of a girl who, in the beginning, says she is involved in the revolu-

tionary movement and is a Marxist. The film has three parts. During the first part of the film, while she speaks, you discover bit by bit that she isn't really as Marxist as she has said. In various aspects of her life there is a victory of the bourgeois ideology. What we try to explain in the second and third parts is how things have happened. So the whole film is made of reflections of the few images in the first part. (Goodwin and Marcus, 21–23)

In the same interview, Godard and Gorin mention they have no funding to create an English-language version of the film, but that they will press ahead and create a "dubbed" English version in Super 8mm magnetic sound. Godard then makes a rather accurate prediction on the future of cinema activism, demonstrating that for him, there is essentially no difference between film and video. Both are information storage and retrieval systems, and both are useful in getting one's message to the public.

We think the best way of projecting [*Luttes en Italie*] is to project it to a very small group, a family, things like that. Videotape is still very expensive—if not, we would have done it with videotape. I think in five or six years we'll be able to, especially when the video cassette is better developed. (Goodwin and Marcus, 24)

These comments foreshadow Godard's embrace of videotape in the late 1970s, and his willingness to mix the two mediums together within a single format, to blend images and sounds into a coherent yet plastic whole.

In February 1970, Godard and Gorin accepted an offer from the militant Palestinian group Al Fatah to make a film about the political situation in Lebanon and Jordan, provisionally titled *Jusqu'à la victoire* (*Till Victory*). Godard and Gorin described the process of working with the Palestinian political group. Godard remembered:

. . . when we arrived, they asked us, "Where do you want to go? Do you want to shoot a training camp? An operation? A hospital? Where do you want to go?" I said, "Yes, we want to *see* a training camp, we want to *see* an operation, but for the moment we don't know if we are going to build our picture from them. To know, we have to discuss it with you." And it took us three weeks before we could start shooting. (Goodwin and Marcus, 45)

However, although Godard asserted at the time that "two-thirds" of the filming of the project had been completed, the project was never finished in its original form because "the Jordanians killed most of the film's participants in Amman in September 1970" (Lesage 1979, 8). Thus the film went on the shelf, until, long after the collapse of the Dziga Vertov group, it would be re-edited by Anne-Marie Miéville and Godard through 1974, and retitled *Ici et ailleurs* (*Here and Elsewhere*). It was released theatrically in its final form in 1976, and on video in 1993. The film will thus be discussed in the next chapter in its final version, as a project that affords an interesting bridge between the Godard of the Dziga Vertov collective, and the Godard who would collaborate on his later films with Anne-Marie Miéville. It was also about this time that Godard's marriage with Anne Wiazemsky disintegrated, and the couple were soon divorced.

Vladimir and Rosa was the next Dziga Vertov project, a co-production between Grove Press in the United States and Munich Tele-Pool in Berlin. Directed by Godard and Gorin, the film also stars the two directors as Vladimir Lenin (Godard) and Karl Rosa [Luxemburg] (Gorin). At 106 minutes, this was one of the lengthier Dziga Vertov films, but as with the other political films, it was not well received. Writing in *Cinéaste*, Joan Mellen stated that the film

offers us, once again, Godard mistaking the political tract for political art. Godard reveals singular contempt for his audience whom he believes he can politicize through the browbeating of a steady drone of pseudo-Marxist cliché. He further insults us by asserting that this film is of no importance to him, that he made it only to finance another, one on the Palestinian revolution.

"Vladimir" is Godard himself, appearing in his own film and "modestly" choosing to call himself after Lenin.

His counterpart is his associate in the Dziga Vertov film collective, Jean-Pierre Gorin, who plays "Rosa" Luxemburg. In one scene the two discuss revolutionary art on a tennis court, seemingly oblivious to the game going on about them, heroically pursuing revolutionary aims in the midst of bourgeois indifference. (39)

But the technical aspects of the cinema were undergoing a radical shift, as the two filmmakers had predicted during the production of *Luttes en Italie*. Sixteen millimeter film was becoming an obsolete format (one that would be entirely eclipsed by video in the mid-1980s, not much more than a decade later), and Godard and Gorin had to face the unpleasant fact that their films were not being widely distributed, were not financially profitable, and were not attracting sizable audiences. Even in the early 1970s, primitive Sony black-and-white Portapack reel-to-reel machines were coming into use, either as tools to create works of purely formal/structural content, or else as aids in cultural anthropology. Critic and filmmaker Laura Mulvey commented recently on this fundamental shift in image recording/reproduction:

> I don't think that [the] 16 millimeter filmmaking world really had a future. I mean in a sense the medium still exists and people still go on working with it. I am actually working on a film at the moment which was shot on 16 mil, just to contradict everything I've said, but it's being edited on video. (Suárez and Manglis, 8)

Thus, for Godard and Gorin, there seemed to be only two options: either work in video and distribute to "home theatres" (as they had hoped to do with *Luttes en Italie*), or co-opt the traditional 35mm narrative cinema, and use the theatrical feature film medium as a mass-distributed, mass-consumed tool of political disruption.

Thus Godard and Gorin still hoped for a major breakthrough in their quest for a politically committed cinema. They wanted to make a big budget, 35mm color revolutionary film, using major stars to assure international distribution on a wide commercial scale. This project became *Tout va bien,* photographed in 1.66:1 (widescreen) ratio in 35mm Eastman Color by Armand Marco in Paris from December 1971 to January 1972. To make the project commercially viable, Godard and Gorin recruited Yves Montand and Jane Fonda for the title roles. The film was budgeted at slightly over a million dollars, and shot both on location, and on a stylized studio set of a factory that recalls the "cutaway" hotel seen in Jerry Lewis's 1960 comedy, *The Bell Boy.* Montand had wanted to work with Godard for quite some time; the actor and singer was no stranger to political activism. His appearance in Costa-Gavras's political thriller *Z* (1969) had been an international critical and commercial success. Jane Fonda apparently required more persuasion, although she, too, was then at the height of her activities as a political activist, earning for herself the unwelcome nickname "Hanoi Jane" for her advocacy of North Vietnamese forces during the war in Vietnam. At the time, though separated from director Roger Vadim, Fonda was staying with Vadim, visiting their daughter, Vanessa. As Vadim recounts it,

> Jane arrived in France to discuss a film with Jean-Luc Godard. . . . Having learned that Jane had serious doubts about the screenplay—she didn't agree with the political content—Jean-Luc lost no time in sending his associate, Jean-Pierre Gorin, to meet her. Two hours after Jane's arrival in Megève, Gorin was in the living room of the house I had rented for the summer, submerging her in political/artistic explanations of the profundity and historic significance of [*Tout va bien*]. . . . He harassed her for three hours. Jane was so exhausted she hardly had the strength to reply. (Vadim 313–14)

Before the film could get underway, however, tragedy struck. In June 1971, Godard was seriously injured in a motorcycle accident, along with his editor, Christine Marsollier, in which Godard was a passenger (Locke and Warren, 127). The incident marked the beginning of the end for the Dziga Vertov collective. Godard was in and out of hospitals for more than two and a half years following the accident, nursed back to health by Anne-Marie Miéville.

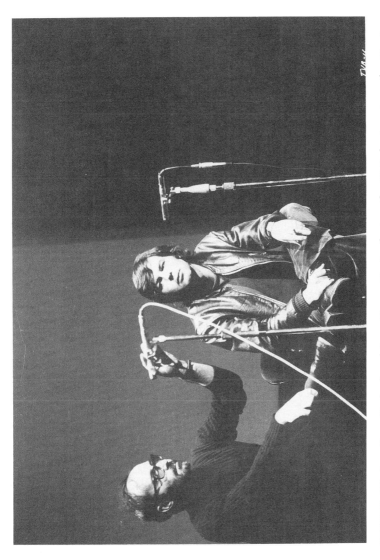

FIGURE 27. Jean-Luc Godard and Jean-Pierre Gorin during the U.S. lecture tour for *Tout va bien* (1972). Photograph by Norma McLain Stoop; courtesy New Yorker Films.

Miéville, a still photographer who worked in this capacity of the set of *Tout va bien*, refused to idolize Godard, and the two began a relationship that would eventually alter the way that Godard looked at both cinema and his personal relationships with others. By December 1971, everything was in place for *Tout va bien*, and although he was still recovering from the motorcycle accident, Godard had no choice but to go ahead with the project.

Tout va bien is not first-rate Godard, or even first-rate Dziga Vertov collective work. The best sequences occur in the beginning of the film, as Godard hurriedly signs a batch of checks to finance the production of the film in extreme close-up; there are also some striking lateral tracking shots on the factory set, the outline of which is highlighted with neon for added structural impact, a telling homage to the work of Jerry Lewis. There is also a seemingly endless tracking shot in an enormous supermarket that reminds one of the traffic-jam sequence in *Le Weekend*, and Montand turns in a creditable performance as a director of commercials who is sick of what he does for a living. Jane Fonda, who hosts a radio show entitled "Survey of France Today" within the film for the fictional American Broadcasting System, keeps the entire project at a distance, and fails to connect with either the material or her two directors.

But perhaps the most telling problem with *Tout va bien* is the central failure, or shortcoming, of the work of the Dziga Vertov group. Godard and Gorin insisted on dominating their audience, instructing them in a totalitarian manner that left no room for free will. As Habermas puts it,

> Socialism too ought never to have been conceived of as the concrete whole of a determinate, future form of life—this was the greatest *philosophical* error of this tradition. I've always said that "socialism" is useful only if it serves as the idea of the epitome of the necessary conditions for emancipated forms of life, about which the participants *themselves* would have to reach understanding. (1994, 113)

But Godard and Gorin never allow the "participants *themselves . . .* to reach understanding" of the imagistic process they criticize, and so *Tout va bien* seems sealed off from common human experience, too intent on shaping individual vision to allow for it. To again cite Habermas, "The 'emancipated society' is an ideal construction that invites misunderstanding. I'd rather speak of the idea of the undisabled subject" (1994, 112).

Jane Fonda's reluctance to become fully involved with the production might explain the creation of the ferocious companion piece to *Tout va bien*, *Lettre à Jane* (*Letter to Jane*), which deconstructs a photograph of Jane Fonda visiting Hanoi in a thoroughly brilliant but cruel examination of the iconics of Hollywood stardom. Intercut with shots from *Klute*, *The Grapes of Wrath*, *The Magnificent Ambersons*, and publicity stills from *Tout va bien*, the photo of Fonda (taken by photographer Joseph Kraft, and subsequently published in *L'Express* [Lesage 1979, 120]) is seen either in its original format, or cropped to show various details of the image. Though the film is undeniably vicious, and now all but impossible to see, it remains one of the most vigorous of the Dziga Vertov films, precisely because it is so minimal and simplistic in its structure, even more so than *British Sounds*. The soundtrack of *Lettre à Jane* is simply Godard and Gorin talking about the still photograph, with no music, just pure visual and political analysis of a manufactured image. It's brilliant, if difficult, filmmaking.

But yet again, significant commercial success had eluded the Dziga Vertov collective. *Tout va bien* opened for an extremely brief commercial run in Paris, and was a commercial and critical flop. Although Godard appeared in a Belgian documentary in 1972 (directed by Jean-Pierre Berckmans) titled *La Longue Marche de Jean-Luc Godard* and briefly toyed with a project for video entitled *Moi, je* in 1973 which never materialized, the political period of Godard's prolific career was drawing to a close. It would not be until 1975 that Godard would make another film. That film, *Numéro deux*, would mark the return of Godard to the world of commercial cinema, introduce his audience to an entirely new set of values and priorities in his work, and pave the way for the later, profoundly melancholic and introspective works produced by Godard in the late 1980s and early 1990s, among them *Je vous salue, Marie* (1985).

As for Jean-Pierre Gorin, his work with Godard was essentially over. In a remarkably candid interview first published in

126

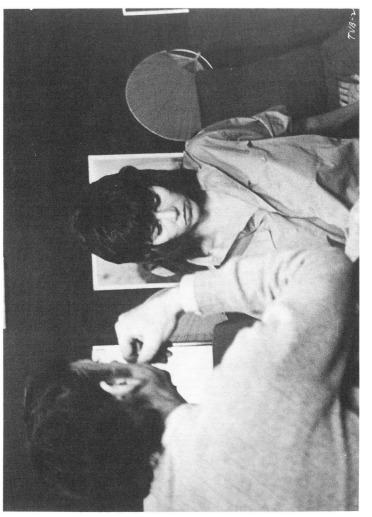

FIGURE 28. Yves Montand (Jacques) and Jane Fonda (Susan) in *Tout va bien* (1972). Courtesy New Yorker Films.

Take One magazine in January 1976, Gorin discussed why he was no longer involved in the work of the Dziga Vertov collective.

> With Jean-Luc and me, it was a love story; we really were deeply in love with each other, with no shame, no guilt; it was a very deep involved sexual thing; we played on our fears and neuroses, it was something which went far beyond movies, and that's why it was effective. What happened is that we really worked together for five years, thirteen hours a day, which is absolutely enormous. You don't get together saying, "Look, ah, we're going to do that masterpiece together," but rather, you get into a process which is absolutely, totally, out of control. But when you work in those conditions there comes a point where you're strangling yourself, you just want to breathe and take some air. So Jean-Luc is more and more into very theoretical, rhetorical film, and working in video. (Walsh, 123)

In the late 1970s, Gorin directed and produced the film *Poto and Cabengo*, "a feature-length documentary film about twin sisters who had supposedly developed their own language" (Walsh 116). By 1981 Gorin was teaching at the University of California at San Diego. Gorin continues to work in film and video to this day, but his work with Godard and the Dziga Vertov collective remains, arguably, the high point of his career.

CHAPTER FOUR

$\bullet$

Anne-Marie Miéville and the Sonimage Workshop

Following the break-up with Gorin, Godard went to Grenoble with Anne-Marie Miéville, who would become his partner in all his new works. Several years of convalescence lay ahead. During the period 1973–75, Godard husbanded his strength, endured several operations, and prepared for new work in video/film. Miéville was already conversant with video equipment, as was Godard, to a degree, and before their departure for Grenoble, Miéville and Godard had established a small studio in Paris which they dubbed the "Sonimage" workshop ("sound plus image"). Gorin was initially involved in this enterprise, but soon decided that his interests were moving in other directions. Gorin moved to California, and Godard and Miéville, established in Grenoble, began their life and work together.

Working as a team which still functions to this day, Miéville and Godard began to create a torrential series of films and videotapes, some signed by Godard, others by Miéville, and some officially credited to both Miéville and Godard. Yet most texts persist in examining Godard/Miéville's post-Vertov work as being created solely by Godard, with Miéville functioning in some subsidiary role as a facilitator or glorified assistant director/production manager. It seems to me that nothing could be further from the truth. When *Sauve qui peut (la vie)* was released in 1980, and interviewers attributed the film solely to Godard, he responded that "she [Anne-Marie Miéville] is at least 50% of this film" (Pajaczkowska, 241).

Miéville's best-known film is perhaps *Le Livre de Marie* (1984), a short film which was "packaged" with *Je vous salue, Marie* (1984) upon that film's initial release; thus, *Le livre de Marie*, a compelling story of the break-up of a family unit as seen through the eyes of a young girl, reached a relatively wide audience. The notoriety of *Je vous salue, Marie* also ensured effective international distribution of Miéville's film, but for the most part, Miéville has kept a relatively low profile in her life and work. This much is known about Ms. Miéville: she was born in Lausanne, Switzerland on November 11, 1945. Moving to Paris in 1960, she began a career as a singer, and cut two records. When her career in Paris stalled, Miéville returned to Lausanne and collaborated on two films with François Reusser. In 1972, she first worked with Godard professionally as a still photographer on *Tout va bien*. Following the move to Grenoble and the establishment of the Sonimage studio, Miéville and Godard began their collaborative work in earnest (Gianvito, 125).

Since then, Miéville's collaboration with Godard has been extensive. Miéville completed final editing on *Ici et ailleurs* with Godard in 1974; served as co-scenarist on *Numéro deux* and *Comment ça va?* in 1975 (Miéville also acted in *Comment ça va?*); co-directed with Godard *Six fois deux (Sur et sous la communication)*, a remarkably ambitious series of videotaped television programs; wrote, produced and directed her own short film *Papa comme Maman* in 1978, in addition to co-directing another series of videotapes for television with Godard, *France/tour/détour/deux/enfants* (also 1978); co-wrote, co-edited, and served as stills photographer on *Sauve qui peut (la vie)*, in addition to serving as co-writer and stills photographer for *L'Amour des femmes* (both in 1980); did still photography for *Passion* (1981); collaborated as co-director on *Scénario du film Passion* in 1982; wrote the screenplay for *Prénom: Carmen* in 1983, in addition to writing and directing her own film *How Can I Love a Man (When I know he don't want me)* during that same year; wrote, produced and directed *Le Livre du Marie* in 1984; co-wrote the screenplay for *Détective* in 1985, in addition to co-directing *Soft and Hard* with Godard, also in 1985; wrote, produced, and directed her film *Faire la fête* in 1987; wrote, produced, and directed the film *Mon cher sujet* in 1988; co-directed *Le Rapport Darty* with Godard in 1989; served as art director on Godard's *Nouvelle Vague* in 1990, in addition to co-directing the episode *L'Enfance de l'art* for the omnibus film *How Are the Kids?* (1990) with Godard; in 1991 wrote, produced, and directed her own film *Mars et Venus*, as well as co-directing an episode in the political activist film *Contre l'oubli* (Lest We Forget); and in 1993 wrote, produced and directed her own film, *Lou n'a pas dit non* (Gianvito, 125).

This is a considerable amount of creative activity in the realms of video and film production for one who has stated flatly "I hate cinema" (to critic Colin MacCabe in October 1980, as cited in Pajaczkowska, 241), but I think what Miéville refers to here is the canonical aspect of cinema, as well as the pernicious hold that cinema so readily obtains over individual consciousness. It is important to cite Miéville's extensive credits here, both in collaboration with Godard and on her own projects, to underscore the essentiality of creative collaboration in Godard's working methods. Godard's earliest short films (and critical enterprises) were created in concert with François Truffaut, although these two strong personalities parted company early on. Next, Anna Karina took center stage in Godard's life and work, appearing in a string of his films as a latter-day Marlene Dietrich to Godard's revisionist von Sternberg. (Parenthetically, it is worth noting that after her break with Godard in 1967, Karina sought to direct her own film, finally realizing this goal with the production of *Vivre ensemble* [1973], a feature film that she wrote, directed, and starred in. In 1978, Karina married French director Daniel-Georges Duval.)

Following the break with Karina, Godard sought refuge in the Marxist environs of the nascent student political movement of France just before the events of May 1968, and in a relationship with Anne Wiazemsky. At this point, Jean-Pierre Gorin entered Godard's life, and the Dziga Vertov collective was born. With the collapse of this creative enterprise, Godard immediately segued into his work with Anne-Marie Miéville as part of the Sonimage workshop. But also significantly, and unlike Godard's other collaborators, Miéville keeps up a furious pace of individual and co-production without concomitantly seeking the spotlight of publicity, leaving most of the interviews and other public relations work to Godard. I would argue that precisely because of this focus on privacy, this rejection of the "cult of personality," Miéville is in many ways the most effective creative partner of Godard's long and prolific career. Yet, as Whitney Chadwick and Isabelle de Courtviron note in their study *Significant Others: Creativity and Intimate Partnership*, "given our culture's emphasis on solitary creation, one is always constructed as significant, and the partner as Other" (10), signifying that one partner in the creative enterprise will almost inevitably be valued (or commodified) at the expenses of the other. Miéville's apparent self-effacement might seem to superficially play into this inequitable arrangement, yet despite persistent and archaic canonical and cultural prejudices, and our tradition of valuing individual achievement over collaborative work, in the case of Miéville and Godard (and Gorin and Godard) during their period of work, we have a true case of mutual interdependence and co-creation, in which both partners to the enterprise are equally important to the production of the finished work. It may be more *convenient* to credit Godard as the principal creative factor in any of his films or video productions from 1973, but it is the artificial convenience of canonical taxonomy. As with the films of Danielle Huillet and Jean-Marie Straub, or Joy Batchelor and John Halas, to cite one of many earlier examples, Anne-Marie Miéville and Jean-Luc Godard since roughly 1973 have functioned as a co-equal team in the creation of their videos and films, each being indispensable to the other.

The first project that Godard and Miéville pursued was a leftover from the Dziga Vertov days; the still unused footage shot in Jordan for *Jusqu'à la victoire*. As Godard regained his strength, he and Miéville began to look over the raw material from the shoot, attempting to criticize the material and structure a new film from the harvest of images. The resultant film is fifty minutes long, and confronts the emotional, physical, and historical distance between the original footage, shot in 1970, and the ways in which Godard and Miéville now manipulate these images to address issues of genocide, social injustice, theatrical presentation, and the endless contradictions and internal complications involved in creating any sound/image construct, fictive or documentary. *Ici et ailleurs* acknowledges that although the 1970 footage in the film is "real," the editorial decisions involved in constructing the final film are equally "real," and they shape, distort, reconstruct, and otherwise transform the flickering images of the dead Palestinians into a work which is a meditation on the creation of history, and the images that record (and transmute) that history into the fabric of our lives. On the soundtrack, Miéville offers telling criticisms of Godard's use of actors and editorial strategies within the film. Although *Ici et ailleurs* uses, for the most part, recycled imagery, and is a work which speaks to Godard's filmic past rather than his future, it marked the beginning of his new period of work, in which the filmmaker questioned not only his "bourgeois" films, but also the works of his Dziga Vertov period.

Ici et ailleurs was followed by *Numéro deux* (1975), ostensibly a remake of his first feature film, *À bout de souffle*. The film was shot on video by William Lubtchansky, and was produced for approximately the same cost as *À bout de souffle*, and then transferred to 35mm for exhibition. Directed by Godard from a screenplay by Godard and Miéville, the film marked a return to at least one old professional relationship for the director. Among the film's producers was Georges de Beauregard, who had also funded the shooting of Godard's first feature in 1959. Germaine Greer provided some narrative text used in the film; Miéville wrote the dialogue which constitutes the woman's text in the film. Sandrine Battistella appeared as the wife, Pierre Dufy as the husband, and the film was shot at the Sonimage studios in Grenoble in 1975. Despite Godard's claim that *Numéro deux* is a remake of *À bout de souffle*, however, the two films have little in common. Rather, *Numéro deux* is an examination of sexual and domestic politics within the domestic sphere, intercut with computer generated intertitles and the usual Godardian puns, creating an interplay between word and image. "Is this a film about sex or politics? Why always ask is it that or is it this? Perhaps it is about both at the same time," the film asks. Banks of television monitors display a variety of familiar images of political activity, clips from pornographic films and Kung Fu action movies, recalling the Godard of the Dziga Vertov period. The young girl in the family talks about her sexuality, and asks questions about her period, and what she will feel like when she grows up. The film has a preoccupation with anal intercourse, and the relationship between the husband and wife is often seen as a power struggle: who initiates sex, who decides what sort of sexual acts will be performed, who controls sexual activity, and the relationship between sex and politics in everyday life.

In may ways, *Numéro deux* carries forward many of the syntactical strategies of the Dziga Vertov films, but the major difference is that in this film Godard is criticizing and examining himself, and his life with Miéville, as Miéville criticizes Godard and the context of her relationship with him. Further, the film moves beyond the primordial examination of gender politics presented in the Dziga Vertov films by insisting on the domesticity of the participants. Rather than inhabiting a fantasy world where everyone is young, handsome, well-dressed, and involved in political theater and/or engagement, *Numéro deux* takes political struggle into the arena of the family and the bedroom, so that the resultant mix of sound and image is both intimate and disquieting. This is a view of Godard and Miéville struggling toward equality as artists and as human beings, as circumstances (political, social, sexual) conspire to alter and rupture their developing relationship.

As the wife says in the film, "What do you do when it's the state and the whole social system that's rape?" Mother, wife, sexual partner; these are all roles that delimit and circumscribe the individuality of the woman in both the public and private sphere. The presence of the grandfather (Alexandre Rignault) and grandmother (Rachel Stéfanopoli) only complicate matters further, as they carry forward their own lifetime accumulation of resentments and injustices into the relationship between the younger couple and their children. When *À bout de souffle* is, as Godard observed, "Alice in Wonderland," *Numéro deux* is a film about unceasing struggle, in which the personal is profoundly political, and all everyday acts (cooking, washing dishes, listening to music, having sex) constitute an endless series of negotiations, power exchanges, and compromises. *Numéro deux* is both difficult and disturbing to watch, but the film (distributed theatrically in 35mm format) was a substantial commercial success for the director, and signalled the beginning of a renaissance both personally and professionally for Godard.

Comment ça va, completed in 1975 and screened for the first time in the United States in 1976 (at the Pacific Film Archive) and 1977 (in a brief commercial run at the Bleecker Street Theatre) (Lesage 1979, 130), is a 78-minute political essay. Co-directed and co-scripted by Godard and Miéville, and shot by William Lubtchansky, the film "is about two workers in a newspaper plant who are attempting to make a video-film about [a] newspaper and its printing plant. But it is also a film about the mass media, about the transformation of information in the press, on the radio, on TV, in a film like this one" (Lesage 1979, 130). Richard Roud described the film as "a rather hectoring essay on the problems of running a Communist newspaper . . . a disappointment after *Ici et ailleurs* and *Numéro deux*" (as cited in Monaco 1988, 399). This project was followed by the creation of two sets of television programs: *Six fois deux/Sur et sous la communication*, shot in video and broadcast on six successive Sundays from July 25, 1977 to August 29, 1977 on F.R. 3 (the third channel on French television), co-directed and co-scripted by Miéville and Godard, each program running 100 minutes in length (Lesage 1979, 132–33); and *France/tour/détour/deux/enfants*, twelve 26-minute video programs scripted and directed jointly by Godard and Miéville, produced and screened for the French television network Antenne 2 by Sonimage (Grenoble), Godard, and Miéville's production company (Bellour and Bandy, 234). Godard had flirted with video before, but in reaching out to these major television networks, he acknowledged both the practicality of television distribution (one tape copy reaches millions of viewers) and the changing face of film/video formatting.

Six fois deux/Sur et sous la communications, *France/tour/détour/deux/enfants*, as well as the later video works *Scénario du film Passion* (1982), a video chronicling the creation of Godard's 1982 film *Passion*, and *Soft and Hard* (*A Soft Conversation between Two Friends on a Hard Subject*), made in 1986, are distributed in the United States through Electronic Art Intermix in New York City. All of these projects might more properly be considered video essays than fictional narrative projects, and they resemble the films of the Dziga Vertov period in their intense

136

FIGURE 29. *Six fois deux: Sur et sous la communication.* Part 2: *Leçons de choses* (1976). Courtesy Marita Sturken/Electronic Arts Intermix.

political commitment to questions of cinematic representation. But since this is the late 1970s, and the cost of film production has substantially risen, Godard chooses to work in video rather than film for primarily (it seems to me) economic reasons. The length of the projects alone would make production in even 16mm prohibitively expensive; *Six fois deux* runs 600 minutes alone. In view of Godard and Miéville's passion for the long take, video production seems the most reasonable option. The first series of tapes, *Six fois deux*, uses six interviews on the politics of labor and recreation interposed with illustrative video "essays" on the questions raised by Godard, Miéville, and the other participants in the project; *France/tour/détour/deux/enfants* focuses on two schoolchildren, and examines the ways in which their lives are structured by both television, and the family unit.

But there is a troubling aspect to *France/tour/détour/deux/ enfants*, a subtext in which Godard the schoolmaster/interrogator becomes an implacable bully, demanding comprehension and acquiescence from those who are incapable either of understanding his project, or even defending themselves against his verbal assault. In Godard's films the interview is the moment in which the fictional characters are tormented and put to the ultimate test: full-face, head and shoulders against a dazzling monochrome wall, they reply with hesitant assent or inarticulate half-phrases to the demand that they formulate their experiences, their truth, in words. The truth of the interview, however, lies not in what is said or betrayed, but in the silence, in the fragility of insufficiency of the stammered response, in the massive and overwhelming power of the visual image, and in the lack of neutrality of the badgering, off-screen interviewer. It is in *France/tour/détour/deux/enfants* (1978), that the tyrannical and manipulative power of this investigative position is most clearly exposed. There the still-Maoist interviewer questions school children whose interests, obviously, are radically different from his own. At one point he asks a little girl if she knows what revolution is (she does not). Jameson then speculates that there may be "something obscene" (1990, 65) in Godard's persistent interrogation of the young child, implying, to my way of thinking, that the girl is more victim than participant (or unwitting dupe) in the videotaped interviews which are featured prominently throughout *France/tour/détour/deux/enfants*. The interrogation of "Mademoiselle 19 ans" in *Masculin Féminin* was brutal enough; this apolitical infant has no hope of shielding herself from Godard's ideological attack.

The visual style of the videotapes is at once densely structured and anarchic. Godard uses superimposition of several images within one frame to blur and redefine the boundaries of the image, in addition to handwritten slogans scrawled over the television frame, thus "renaming" various commonplace activities and objects within the context of his discussion. As with the Dziga Vertov films, Godard works with Miéville as an equal partner, and seems far more interested in pleasing himself than in captivating an audience with any conventional tricks of film/video narrative. Uncompromising and resolutely difficult, these videotapes remind one of the epic structural films of Trinh T. Minh-ha and/or Hollis Frampton. The length of the piece is a function of a desire to create an epic work—a huge video/film canvas upon which the director meditates on the subtleties and nuances of a single image. More recently, as we shall see, Godard's cinema essays have become increasingly compact (with *Allemagne année 90 neuf zéro* and *JLG/JLG*), and tellingly, he has returned to 35mm film as his preferred format for these two-hour–length films, rather than videotape.

In 1978, Godard, ever fascinated by the concept of the self-empowerment of people through control over the images that shape their lives, embarked with Anne-Marie Miéville on an ambitious project to bring video technology to Mozambique. Working with Carlos Gambo, Godard and Miéville initiated an ambitious program of production and training, designed to put video technology into the hands of the ordinary citizens of Mozambique. According to Manthia Diawara, Godard and Miéville set to work on the production of five videotape projects, working with the Mozambique Ministry of Information, and also tried to set up a permanent facility for the maintenance of the video equipment and the training of new video technicians. But video was still, in 1978, a relatively bulky medium, and had not yet progressed to the ultralight camcorders we take for granted today. Because of this, Godard's experiment in bringing video production technology to Mozambique ultimately failed, but nevertheless, from the vantage point of contemporary video-equip-

FIGURE 30. *France/tour/détour/deux/enfants* (1977–78). Courtesy Marita Sturken/Electronic Arts Intermix.

ment capabilities, we can see that Godard was prescient, as usual in his desire to bring image production/reproduction/distribution to the general populace.

Godard returned home in 1979, and later admitted that it would have been better (given the then-current state of video technology) to shoot on Super 8mm film first and transfer the finished projects to videotape afterwards. This approach would now be obsolete, but at the time, this self-criticism was entirely on target. However, at the same time that Godard was working with Miéville to bring video to Mozambique, the cultural anthropologist and filmmaker Jean Rouch *was* working on a separate project to bring Super 8mm filmmaking to Mozambique. Rouch ran into several unexpected problems, not the least of which was Mozambique filmmaker Ruy Guerra's charge that Rouch's films were neo-colonialist, and, in their informal shooting and editing style, that they flaunted the basic structural principles of cinematic *mise-en-scène*. Rouch himself was working toward something like the early Dziga Vertov films in his original intent; he wanted to make "postcard" films of life as it was actually lived by the citizens of Mozambique. But Godard, Miéville, and Rouch failed to recognize sufficiently that empowering the common citizen of any country with the ability to create her/his own images from life carries with it an implicit threat to the established social structure of the ruling government forces.

Thus, the government could not allow the re-representation of the Other to succeed—and Godard and Miéville's project was undermined from the start. Indeed, the very act of making a film is inherently a radical rupture of the existing political discourse, because "the technique of reproduction detaches the reproduced object from the domain of tradition" (Benjamin, 223). Thus freed of "tradition" the object/or person reproduced can inhabit the domain of a new hypertaxonomy of images, and assist in the creation of an entirely new order of visual signifiers. The visual structures implicitly imposed by Godard and Miéville, working as they did in concert with the official government Ministry of Information of Mozambique, remained within the domain of the colonial, or mimicked the colonial, and thus, through the lens of a government-controlled enterprise, the citizens of Mozambique remained signifiers of the Other, the foreign, the person-as-subject. "The effect of mimicry on the authority of colonial discourse is profound and disturbing. For in 'normalizing' the colonial state or subject, the dream of post-Enlightenment civility alienates its own language of liberty and produces another knowledge of its norms" (Bhabha 1987, 318). This new "knowledge of its norms" constitutes a rule of the look in which the subaltern is continually the subject of neo-colonialist enterprise, seen only as the shadow figure of the cultural determinist. As Gayatri Chakravorty Spivak puts it, "In the face of the possibility that the intellectual is complicit in the persistent constitution of Other as the Self's shadow, a possibility of political practice for the intellectual would be to put the economic 'under erasure,' to see the economic factor as irreducible as it reinscribes the social text, even as it is erased, however imperfectly, when it claims to be the final determinant or the transcendental signified" (280). But is this possible, given the physical/social/political/economic exigencies imposed by the cinema/video apparatus? And is it not true that "Every gaze is like this, according to Lacan: it designates the person who is looking as that which is concealed, no longer viewer but viewed, one spot in a totally exteriorized space?" (Foss, 33).

If this is so, then we must accept Spivak's assertion that "the subaltern cannot speak" (308) until that which is not the subject becomes the dominant voice within a given discourse, a project which neither the imagistic colonialists of globally dominant Hollywood or the political colonialists of Western Europe will support. In fact, as Spivak notes, "Some of the most radical criticism coming out of the West today is the result of an interested desire to conserve the subject of the West, or the West as Subject" (271). In direct opposition to this "epistemic violence is the remotely orchestrated, far-flung, and heterogeneous project to constitute the colonial subject as Other" (Spivak, 280–81), a process celebrated and relentlessly pursued in such dominant films as *Congo* (1995), where the project of Othering is both brazen and blatant, to such seemingly "innocent" films as *The Indian in the Cupboard* (1995), which disguises its racism and colonialism in the cloak of juvenile fantasy. Godard, Miéville, and Rouch were on the right track with their experiment, but they were simply a bit too early in implementing their plans, and ignored (or hoped to supersede) the colonialist project inherent in the Mozambique government's desire to retain control over the production apparatus at all times. Today, cheap, convenient image production has become a nearly universal reality, thanks to the video camcorder; but without distribution on a global scale, the subaltern will continue to be silenced (Diawara, 97–103).

This ambitious project was followed by a short twenty-minute videotape anticipating the production of *Sauve qui peut (la vie)* (*Every Man for Himself*), entitled *Scénario de Sauve qui peut (la vie)*. When the film itself was released, also in 1979, it received generally favorable reviews. Shot in 35mm color from a script by Miéville and Godard, the film centers on three protagonists, Isabelle (Isabelle Huppert), Godard (Jacques Dutronc), and Denise (Nathalie Baye). The film is less a narrative than a series of incidents, as the three people's lives intersect at seemingly random intervals, without any artificial explanatory material. Dutronc's character, "Godard," works at a hotel taking care of the various guests. Denise (Nathalie Baye) is romantically involved with Godard, but seems unsatisfied with their relationship. This is not surprising, as "Godard" has managed to complicate his life with an estranged spouse and a daughter who has become sullen and cynical with the passage of time. When "Godard" meets Isabelle (Isabelle Huppert), a prostitute, he spends the night with her, in an episode reminiscent of *Vivre sa vie*, in that the film examines (albeit peripherally) the problems that prostitution presents to those who practice it.

But *Sauve qui peut (la vie)* moves beyond the territory of commodification/prostitution/objectification that Godard has mapped in the past. Working with Miéville, he creates an entirely new vision of the merchandising and mechanics of the sex trade, a film which explores the possibility of genuine communication between men and women, rather than the prostitute/pimp dialectic informing the narrative locus of *Vivre sa vie*.

> In *Sauve qui peut (la vie)* Godard and Miéville have explored this tendency to project sexuality on to "woman," and violence on to an external cause. If the film claims that a progressive and productive collaboration between men and women is "impossible," it nevertheless explores the effects

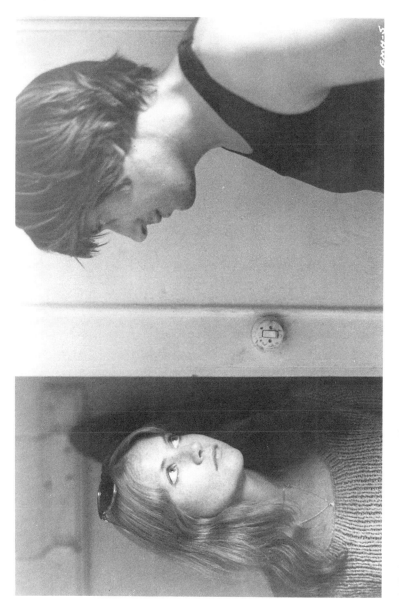

FIGURE 31. *Sauve qui peut (la vie)* (1979). Courtesy Jerry Ohlinger Archives.

of that impossibility on the masculine self, and represents these as a combination of despair and violent eroticism. . . . Although the film does represent the reality of subjectivity, alongside social reality and textual reality, the exploration of masculine subjectivity stops short of recognizing the Oedipus complex. Instead the film attacks the idea of a productive and meaningful relationship between men and women, which, in the unconscious, is an attack on the Oedipal parents. (Pajaczkowska, 253)

Two brief video projects, *Lettre à Freddy Buache* (1981) and *Changer d'image* (1982) were produced by Godard and Miéville before the creation of Godard's next major effort, *Passion* (1982). *Lettre à Freddy Buache* is a typically intransigent Godardian conceit: hired to make a film to celebrate the 500th anniversary of Lausanne, Godard declares that he can't create such a work, and then dedicates the resultant refusal to Robert Flaherty and Ernst Lubitsch. *Changer d'image* is a nine-minute section from the broadcast *Le Changement a plus d'un titre*, a brief film starring and directed by Godard. It was also during this period that Godard participated in the production of using Wenders's *Chamber 666*, a 45-minute meditation on the question, "Is the cinema a lost language, an art about to die?" Shot in a hotel room at the 1982 Cannes Film Festival, Godard, along with such other directors as Ana Carolina, Monte Hellman, Susan Seidelman, Paul Morrissey, Rainer Werner Fassbinder, Steven Spielberg, Michelangelo Antonioni, and Yilmaz Guney, appear before Wenders's camera to share their thoughts on the subject.

The responses vary widely, as might be expected, and Wenders cuts the resultant footage with ruthless authority. Spielberg, seeming both earnest and utterly unfazed by the question, describes his life as a commercial filmmaker without insight or undue self-examination. He makes commercial films, and personal films aren't a part of his life. Susan Seidelman gets cut off abruptly, as does Paul Morrissey, and Monte Hellman tells the camera that he doesn't watch movies that much anymore.

Of all the interviewees, Godard (who appears near the beginning of the film, shortly after a framing shot of a huge, apparently dead tree, which both begins and ends *Chambre 666* as a metaphoric visual bracket) is the most loquacious and deliberate, taking the question seriously, and offering some engagingly direct thoughts on the topic at hand. Godard refuses to be intimidated by the camera, pausing when he needs to frame a sentence, unhurried by the ineluctable flow of film through the camera gate, telling the audience (and the camera) that Wenders's film is "an inquest on the future of films." Not surprisingly, although he recognizes the numerous differences between the film and video image, as well as television and theatrical distribution and presentation, Godard embraces the future, and refuses to be imprisoned by the past. Significantly, he is also the only director interviewed (at least after Wenders' editorial intervention) who directly takes control of the camera itself, rising near the end of the twelve-minute reel of film, walking slowly toward the camera and gravely turning the machine off.

Chambre 666 deserves to be more widely seen for the insight it offers into Godard's work, and also for the view of Godard as a theoretician that the film affords. In his own films, despite his often paradoxical desire to distance his audiences from the spectacle he creates, Godard leavens even his most sincere imagistic constructs (such as *Je vous salue, Marie*) with little asides, jokes, quotations and self-referential framing devices. *Chambre 666* gives us Godard shorn of nearly any editorial interference; of all the directors in the film, he gets the most screen time, and his interview seems to have been subjected to no editing at all, recalling the insistent gaze of Andy Warhol's immobile camera in such films as *Vinyl* (1965) and *My Hustler* (1965). Taken as a group, *Lettre à Freddy Buache, Changer d'image* and Wenders's *Chambre 666* show us Godard as the contemplative master of the film and video image, and lead up to the creation of *Passion,* an altogether breathtakingly gorgeous catalogue of the difficulties and inherent transcendence afforded by the waking dream of the cinematographic process. As Fredric Jameson commented, "the filmic apparatus [is] now challenged to do battle not with its traditional rivals—the theatre or the photograph or video—but with the painted image itself, and with the *wall* (a challenge . . . accepted by Godard, in *Passion)"* (1990, 58).

Passion opens with a series of shots of the clouds overhead drifting idyllically past the camera, as Gabriel Fauré's *Requiem* plays on the soundtrack. As the film progresses, it chronicles the efforts of Jerzy (Jerzy Radziwilowicz) to create a feature film despite the absence of a coherent narrative script, a situation that mirrored the production of the film itself. Hanna Schygulla (as Hanna), famous for her work with the late Rainer Werner Fassbinder, was recruited by Godard to appear in *Passion*, but found it difficult to work with the director, who created the scenario on a day-to-day basis as the film was being shot. Godard stalwarts Isabelle Huppert (as Isabelle) and Michel Piccoli (as Michel) returned to work with the director, and lend considerable depth to the proceedings, creating resonant characters out of their iconic presences rather than predestined, scripted characterizations. What is most striking about *Passion* is the film's physical beauty, and the gorgeous *tableaux vivantes* created by the director Jerzy for the film-within-a-film that serves as the locus of the film's action. Scenes of Jerzy stalking about a café while he waits for inspiration mimic Godard's own difficulties with the film's production, as do a number of scenes in which the director Jerzy sets up shots for his film and then silently contemplates them, wondering if he should commit them to film or not.

Godard essentially reworks his commitment to film by restaging other forms of visual arts within the competing frame of *Passion*. While Deleuze argues for "the politics of the image," (1989a, 10), particularly as these images are staged by the performative bodies in *Passion*, Jameson responds that Godard seeks to confirm "the superiority of film itself as a medium over these disparate competitors" (1995, 159). In *Passion*, Godard simultaneously challenges and affirms the validity of film practice. This struggle revolves not only around the politics of the visual, but also around the theory and politics of image production itself. As Jameson (1995, 159) concludes:

> Godard's strategy is to pose the strongest objections to the medium—to foreground its most urgent problems and crises, beginning with that of financing itself, omnipresent in these late films and above all here [in *Passion*]—in order the more triumphantly to surmount them.

Passion tangentially addresses political issues, but seems more concerned with the process and problems of making a feature film than in Godard's past preoccupations with personal/domestic governing structures. This said, one remembers the film because of the beauty of Raoul Coutard's cinematography (of all of Godard's camerapersons, it seems to me that Coutard is undeniably the most accomplished), and because of the film's frank depiction of the agony (and "passion") that must inevitably go into any creative enterprise. The film was a modest theatrical success, and was accompanied by the production of a companion videotape, the previously mentioned *Scénario du film Passion* (1982). As described by Amy Taubin,

> *Scénario du film "Passion"* (1982), the video Godard made after completing the film *Passion*, opens with the image of a naked woman climbing onto a stage, which then slowly dissolves into an image of the director seated, his back to the camera, in front of an audio/video control board. He's also going to expose himself—expose the processes by which he shapes ideas into images and sounds, expose the means of production. . . . (Godard can't resist flashing a construction of sexual difference in which woman is body and man is culture.) (1992, 45).

The video is a fitting complement to a film intent upon the objectification of the female body for the sake of artistic signification, in which the patriarchal concept of "beauty" is obtained through personal compromise and the specification of gender.

Godard, however, was rapidly moving onto new projects, and in early 1983 he made a brief video entitled *Petites notes à propos du film "Je vous salue, Marie"* at roughly the same time that he created his next 35mm feature, *Prénom: Carmen* (1983), "a patchwork, a heterogeneous, encyclopaedic collocation of signs, of fragments whose assemblage constitutes a meditation on the image" (Powrie, 64). Ostensibly based on Bizet's *Carmen*, "*Prénom: Carmen* [in fact] inhabits an intertextual interstice . . . between Mérimée's short story *Carmen* and Preminger's film musical version (*Carmen Jones*, 1954); in between a literary text and musical texts" (Powrie, 64). This intermingling of variable and competing texts in *Prénom: Carmen* has the effect of creating a new narrative, evoking the memory of the numerous alterna-

FIGURE 32. Isabelle Huppert (Isabelle) and Jean-Luc Godard during the shooting of *Passion* (1981). Courtesy Jerry Ohlinger Archives.

149

FIGURE 33. A scene from *Passion* (1981). Courtesy Jerry Ohlinger Archives.

FIGURE 34. *Scénario du film Passion* (1982). Courtesy Marita Sturken/Electronic Arts Intermix.

tive versions available. Thus, these intertexts "have a double function. They conjure up a distant, indeed absent, narrative, so that *Prénom: Carmen* comes into being only as a palimpsestic gesture which structures the original Carmen narrative as loss" (Powrie, 65). In addition to Prosper Mérimée's short story, Preminger's *Carmen Jones* and Bizet's musical version, there are citations from Beethoven's notebooks, Giraudoux's *Électre*, Harry Langdon and Rodin's sculptures, woven into the text of *Prénom; Carmen*, as Powrie notes (63–67). The film's narrative centers on Carmen X (Maruschka Detmers), a radical terrorist who robs a bank and then falls in love with Joseph Bonaffe (Jacques Bonaffé), a policeman who tries to arrest her in a rather half-hearted manner. Godard himself appears in the film as "Uncle Jean," an irascible and crotchety film director detained in a mental institution who falls in with the plans of Carmen X's terrorists in a typically ineffectual fashion. All of this is intercut with footage of the Quator Prat chamber ensemble endlessly rehearsing fragments of various Beethoven quartets, a process that, in the tradition of *One Plus One*, they never entirely complete. As Phil Powrie notes,

> The choice of a Beethoven score rather than Bizet is significant, as Godard himself pointed out. . . . It is by no means fortuitous that this might remind us of Godard's wish to create a spectacle along with its analysis. *Prénom: Carmen* is an attempt to score the image, in the literal sense of scratching the surface of the image, so as to destroy its value as a commodity exchanged with the spectator, and, in the figurative sense, orchestrating what remains, its trace, the desire of/for an image. (65)

The film is structured in Godard's typically jagged fashion, and features the same sort of brutal slapstick humor that underscored the structure of *Week-end*. Violence in *Prénom: Carmen* is, on the whole, treated as a joke, and the film features several signature sequences of black comedy in which a cleaning lady mops up the floor of the bank after a robbery without disturbing the numerous corpses resting at her feet, and a group of impassive bystanders ignore a massacre that takes place right under their

FIGURE 35. Jean-Luc Godard in *Prénom: Carmen* (1983). Courtesy New Yorker Films.

noses (these sequences remind one of *Masculin Féminin* and *La Chinoise*, the films in which the physical consequences of direct revolutionary political action are treated as a series of grim jests). Indeed, "The film's constant self-referentiality coupled with self-destruction as a realist artefact suggests the denial of (sexual) difference" (Powrie, 71). Significantly, however, it is not the political or sexual which is foregrounded in *Prénom: Carmen*, but rather the difficulty of creating a politically correct or "truthful" series of images to illustrate a philosophical tract. "The truth is that for Godard Truth in film is impossible because of the way images lie. At the beginning of the film, Oncle Jean types out the following phrase: 'mal vu, mal dit.' The film exists in the in-between of 'mal vu, mal dit,' in between sound and image, in between Godard and Oncle Jean, in between humour and tragedy, in between thriller and myth" (Powrie, 67). It is Godard who is the center of our attention in this film, as a sort of anti-celebrity, behaving badly on purpose to shock and annoy his audience. Shot in the most unflattering fashion possible, the gruff, cigar-chomping "Uncle Jean" resembles no one so much as Samuel Fuller, the director of American "B" action films who popped up as himself in Godard's *Pierrot le fou*. Then, in the mid-1960s, Godard revered the figures of cinema's past; now Godard himself has become a part of cinema history, and so he seems content to present himself as a figure of functional memory, as were Fuller and Lang in his earlier works. *Prénom: Carmen* won first prize at the Venice Festival (The Golden Lion) in 1983, and was enthusiastically received both commercially and critically, but next came Godard's most controversial film in years: *Je vous salue, Marie* (1985), released in the United States and Britain as *Hail Mary*.

The film was invariably presented in conjunction with a brief film by Anne-Marie Miéville, entitled *Le livre de Marie* (1984). This twenty-five-minute short film was photographed by Jean-Bernard Ménoud, Caroline Champetier, Jacques Firman, and Yvan Niclass, and edited, scripted and directed by Miéville. The cast of Miéville's film was comprised of Rebecca Hampton (Marie), her mother (Aurore Clément), her father (Bruno Cremer), a traveller (Copi), and two young girls (played by Valentine Mercier and Cléa Rédalier). In several sad, clinically documented "blocks," Miéville's film depicts the break-up of a marriage, as

seen through the eyes of the couple's young daughter, Mary
(Marie). In a neatly sardonic touch, footage from Godard's *Le
Mépris (Contempt)* plays on a television set during one key
sequence of the film, offering a fictive counterpoint to the brutal,
banal reality of the final breakdown between Mary's mother and
father. Miéville uses additional music in her film from Chopin
and Mahler, but Delerue's original score for *Le Mépris* dominates
the film's soundtrack, and the matter-of-fact presentation of the
film's narrative seems coldly modern in contrast with the stylized
angst presented in the earlier film. Composed of a striking series
of sunsets, still lives and darkly lit interior shots that perfectly
convey the tragedy of the impending break-up of the couple's
relationship, Miéville's film is intensely structured and epigram-
matically intense, conveying in shorthand sequences a love in
terminal collapse. Miéville uses a synchronous sound in the film
to telling effect, and often presents the character's dialogue in
voiceover, rather than as the directly spoken word.

Miéville's short has seemingly nothing to do with Godard's
film directly, although one might persuasively argue that
Miéville's film is about the dissolution of a marriage due to a
breakdown in communication (Marie's mother and father are
seen constantly fighting), and *Je vous salue, Marie* concerns itself
with a marriage that nearly collapses. *Je vous salue, Marie* is, of
course, Godard's retelling of the story of the Virgin Mary. The
film was denounced by numerous church groups as blasphemous
and obscene, a charge that seems difficult to support when one
sees the film itself. It almost seemed that Godard, the hard-line
Marxist of the late 1960s and 1970s, was now in the mid-1980s
re-anchoring his faith in the divine. Production of *Je vous salue,
Marie* began on February 6, 1984.

Je vous salue, Marie is a film of simple visuals and complex
sounds; the structure of the narrative is remarkably easy to follow, and is presented in a surprisingly straightforward fashion.
There are the usual Godardian intertitles—the phrase AT THAT
TIME, for one example, is repeated throughout the film as an
image block on a number of occasions—but for the most part, *Je
vous salue, Marie* tells the story of Mary (Myriem Roussel), a
young woman who works in her father's gas station. Joseph, her
husband (Thierry Rode) is a taxi driver, who through the course of

FIGURE 36. Myriem Roussel (Mary) in *Je vous salue, Marie* (1984). Courtesy New Yorker Films.

the film is transformed from an indignant spouse, certain of his wife's infidelity, into Mary's platonic helpmate. In a slightly parodic, modern touch, the angel Gabriel (Philippe Lacoste) arrives in a jet plane to bring the glad tidings to Mary. What distinguishes *Je vous salue, Marie* from the rest of Godard's films during this period is the absolute seriousness of the project, and the intensity with which Godard presents his subject matter. Above all, *Je vous salue, Marie* is a film of nature, of the purity of things as they are, taken on faith, devoid of abstraction.

In her discussion of *Je vous value, Marie*, Laura Mulvey notes that "[t]he film manages to pay tribute to the spirit of the Christian myth and still derive from themes and motifs latent in Godard's past work, so that there are unexpected elements of continuity between this, and the older, more familiar Godard." Mulvey locates "the persistence of [Godard's] preoccupation with the woman's body and her sexuality in the story of the Annunciation" as one of these latent motifs. Further, Mulvey notes that "the film dwells on Joseph's almost unbearable sexual frustration" for much of its running time, and objectifies the feminine figure of Mary even as it celebrates her role within the film's narrative (1993, 39).

But intriguingly, Mulvey also cites the early influence of Catholic André Bazin, founder of *Cahiers du Cinéma*, as a possible informing agency in the creation of the work. Godard, at this stage of his career, is in direct confrontation with his own mortality; indeed, ever since his motorcycle accident, he has been in an extended state of recuperation/degeneration documented by his performances in *King Lear, Prénom: Carmen*, and other of his late films. By reaching toward the figure of Mary, Godard may simultaneously be recalling the world of his early apprenticeship in the cinema, when he wrote reviews as "Hans Lucas" for *Cahiers*, and lived for the world of film alone (1993, 43). Mulvey concludes that, for Godard,

> the female body is bound to remain an enigma and a threat. It is interesting that Godard, no longer able to approach historical, political reality, should attempt to construct the image of the Virgin Mary as a fetishized substitute. It is, however, characteristic of Godard's rigor and his honesty

that he reveals the impossibility of his own construction, just as he used to reveal the illusionistic nature of the cinema machine. (1993, 52)

The film's opening sequences show stones being thrown in the water, the ripples endlessly cascading out into infinity, mirroring the impact of Christ's teachings upon his followers. Sections of Bach's Toccata and Fugue in D Minor underscore a tense conversation between Joseph and Juliette (Juliette Binoche), exploring what women and men expect from a relationship. Juliette offers to marry Joseph, who is apparently undergoing a rocky period in his relationship with Mary, but Joseph tells Juliette that his relationship with Mary, who is at this point in the narrative Joseph's fiancée, is none of her business. Godard cuts to a women's basketball game. Mary sits on the sidelines, watching. In a brief voiceover, Mary speaks: "I wondered if some event would happen in my life." The coach sends Mary into the game; she pauses, basketball in hand, and seems about to shoot a penalty shot. Godard here presents both Mary and Joseph as ordinary people, with quotidian conflicts and ambitions. Yet in their internal suffering and torment (Joseph's frustration, Mary's gradually dawning comprehension after her initial resistance), and in the meticulously observed details of their "blue-collar" physical existence, both Mary and Joseph take on aspects of martyrdom.

> The exemplary Christian masochist also seeks to remake him or herself according to the model of the suffering Christ, the very picture of earthly divestiture and loss. Insofar as such an identification implies the complete and utter negation of all phallic values, Christian masochism has radically emasculating implications, and is in its purest forms intrinsically incompatible with the pretensions of masculinity. (Silverman 1992, 198)

Joseph must thus forego any sexual relationship with Mary as an act of faith, with the concomitant "radically emasculating implications this requires," in order to be part of the miracle of Christ's birth. Mary must place her faith in the Divine over her trust in the mechanism of traditional scientific inquiry. As a subsequent scene demonstrates, Godard himself now seems to question the concept of random indeterminacy in the creation of the earth, and with it, the smug nihilism of many of his earlier philosopher figures in *La Chinoise*, *Vivre sa vie*, *Made in U.S.A.*, and other of his films.

In a classroom, a young woman, Eva (Anne Gauthier) listens as a professor (Johan Leysen) holds forth on the creation of life on the earth, which, he asserts, happened entirely "by chance." But then the professor immediately questions himself. "What if it wasn't chance?" As the professor continues his lecture, it becomes clear that he believes in a divine structure to all events on earth, and has rejected the explanation of "pure chance" for the earth's origin. "The astonishing truth is that life was willed, desired, anticipated, organized, programmed by a determined intelligence." We might reasonably assume that this "determined intelligence" can be construed as a "divine intelligence." It's interesting to note that in a film such as *La Chinoise*, the professor's lecture would have most probably been a Marxian diatribe; in *Je vous salue, Marie*, Godard gives us the professor as catechist. This makes the furor of the religious right in this matter all the more unfathomable; in *Je vous salue, Marie*, Godard performs the astonishing feat of bringing religion into the classroom, something that fundamentalist Christians have been attempting to do in recent years with great insistence. Godard here has become their ally in this effort; it seems to me altogether remarkable that so few have noticed this.

The film shifts to the airport, where Gabriel (Philippe Lacoste) and his assistant, a young girl (Manon Anderson), arrive to bring the news of the Annunciation to Mary and Joseph. Godard indulges in a bit of humor here, involving a near confrontation between Gabriel and another patron of the airport, but intercuts this scene with a serenely devotional shot of Joseph feeding his dog inside his taxi, while simultaneously reading a book. Without warning, Gabriel and his assistant jump into the back seat of the taxi, hand Joseph an enormous amount of money, and order him to drive off. Driving through the rain, the group comes upon the gas station operated by Mary's father, and jump out of the taxi. Gabriel confronts Mary: "You're going to have a child." Mary responds, "I sleep with no one." Gabriel replies,

FIGURE 37. Myriem Roussel (Mary) in *Je vous salue, Marie* (1984). Courtesy New Yorker Films.

indicating Joseph, "It won't be his. Never!" Godard cuts to a tight close-up of Gabriel's assistant, who admonishes Mary, "Be pure, be rough. Follow thy way." The act of "making sex" is thus introduced in the beginning of the film, and as Charles Warren notes,

> Making love is inextricably tied up with the scientific pursuit of the film, in the present scene and throughout. And making love, living sexually at all, is an aspect to Mary that Mary is curious about, wants and shies off from, projects and creates. "God counts on ass," Mary says much later in the film, somewhat bitterly, though she is reconciled to giving her own. (20)

It's interesting to note here that the angel Gabriel, as conceived here by Godard, bears more than a passing resemblance to Joseph Balsamo, the illegitimate son of God and Dumas in *Le Week-end*. Brusque and commanding, Gabriel arrives to tell Mary, Joseph, and Mary's father of the coming miracle, but does so in a decidedly worldly fashion. The young girl who serves as his assistant is equally stern, but yet there is something simultaneously sacred and comic in their shared demeanor. Why should anyone understand their actions? Gabriel and the young girl come from another sphere, and follow divine law. The governances of the world are both immaterial and inconsequential to them. By placing the action in the humble precincts of a gas station, Godard draws a direct parallel with the manger in which Christ was born.

Mary accepts her situation with a modicum grace and candor, although Joseph (as in the Bible) is still confounded by the events which have rapidly overtaken them. "What is this?" asks Joseph. "Miracles don't exist. Kiss me." Mary responds, "There's no escape for us." We are then shown several shots in which Joseph attempts to force Mary to kiss him, but she resists his advances. These shots are intercut with scenes of nature: sunlight on the water, trees, the sky at twilight. The professor reappears, and continues his lecture, "That Voice deep in our consciences whispers, if we listen: You're born of something, somewhere else, in Heaven." Surely Godard's intent here could not be more direct, or more sublime.

As the film progresses, it becomes a meditation on the relationship between Mary and Joseph, and the growing certainty of Mary's faith in her role within the divine scheme of things. Mary goes to a skeptical gynecologist, who confirms that she is pregnant, yet still a virgin. Joseph does not believe this is possible: "It must be mine!" he cries. Mary, however, has come to "rejoice . . . in giving my body to Him who has become my master forever." By placing Mary at the center of the narrative, Godard seems to be stressing the primacy of the feminine in the story of the birth of Jesus. "Is Mary God? Is she so by virtue of loving a man?" (Warren 24). Or is she so by virtue of loving God more than any man; loving her nature (and the origins of her divine existence) more than the pleasure of any earthly embrace? Throughout the film, Mary's divine pregnancy is repeatedly linked to nature, and to daily acts such as taking a bath, or eating an apple while talking on the telephone. Joseph, becoming ever more frustrated, threatens to leave Mary, but as the film concludes, he promises, "I'll stay . . . I'll never touch you. I'll stay." Jesus (Malachi Jara Kohan) is born, and states directly in the film's final minutes, "I am He who is . . . I must tend to my Father's affairs." The film's final shots depict Gabriel saluting Mary for her service to God. And on this note of reverence and mystery, the film quite properly ends.

Seeing the film, which is simultaneously hushed and reverent in its depiction of the nativity, one wonders what all the fuss was about. There are several sequences in the film in which a semi-nude Mary examines her swelling body with wonder, and perhaps some viewers were offended by this; it is also true that by retelling the story of the birth of Christ in modern-day dress, Godard runs the risk of being perceived as parodic (and he does occasionally indulge in bits of throwaway humor, as in a brief sequence where Gabriel and his young assistant shop for a sportscoat). But to me the most interesting aspect of the film is simply that Godard chose to do the project, and that he agreed to direct his next film, *Détective*, a straightforward commercial venture, precisely in order to direct *Je vous salue, Marie*. As with other of Godard's late films, the visual structure of *Je vous salue, Marie* is both highly stylized and simple. Scenes are presented in large blocks, manipulated through sound bridges and voiceovers, and bracketed with shots of the sun, the man, and carefully composed still life shots that elevate the mundane elements of domesticity into the realm of the celestial. The film is not so much the story of the Nativity as a variation of the theme of the Virgin Birth, as *King Lear* (1987) is a variation on Shakespeare's text. As Warren notes:

> This story's gestures toward God's story do not so much *explain*, or alternatively *confound*, this story as *develop* it. This film, in Eliot's phrase, "tends toward" being a recognizable modern story and also toward being the divine story, without allowing us to have it either way definitely. (24)

The crew Godard uses gets smaller with each of the late films, and *Je vous salue, Marie* looks both modest and unassuming in its physical presentation. Yet it is undeniable that the film remarks a return to a faith beyond Marxism-Leninism for Godard, and a reassessment of what it means to be human in the latter half of the twentieth century. Far from being a *retelling* of the Christ tale, I would argue that *Je vous salue, Marie* represents a *rebirth* of the vision of the divine. One might almost call the film a vision of the second coming of Christ, or a reaffirmation of the centrality of God in matters of daily existence. Considering the path that Godard has charted for himself in the years since he directed his first short film in 1954, it seems that in three decades Godard has worked through the personal and the political to come back to the divine. No one who has seen the film can doubt the fact that it is, at base, absolutely serious. In *Je vous salue, Marie*, Godard has moved beyond contemplation of the concerns and problems of the physical world to explore the mysteries of the divine.

Détective (1985), which directly followed *Je vous salue, Marie*, is another matter altogether. A commercial enterprise in every respect, it is redolent of Godard's early fascination with the American "B" gangster film. Sporting an all-star cast, including Johnny Hallyday (the French "Elvis Presley" of the 1950s), Jean-Pierre Léaud, Nathalie Baye, Claude Brasseur, and many others, the film is dedicated to John Cassavetes (famous for his own iconoclastic vision as an *auteur*, in addition to his work as an actor in conventional Hollywood cinema), Edgar Ulmer (creator of some of the most broodingly doomed films in Hollywood history, particularly the spectacularly impoverished thriller *Detour* [1946]), and Clint Eastwood, another actor/director known for his dark and violent vision of American society. *Détective*, however, is more playful than hard-boiled, and recalls the Godard of *À bout de souffle* without the handheld camerawork, and the gritty formalism of the black-and-white frame.

As with most late Godard films, the plot is so slight as to be nonexistent; in any event, the narrative of the film is clearly not one of Godard's chief concerns. As Dana Polan points out, the cinema at the end of the twentieth century constitutes "a period of return to strong narrativity" (1989, 27), with such films as *Forrest Gump, Apollo 13, Dumb and Dumber, Pocahontas,* and other Hollywood blockbusters dominating the box office, in direct contrast to Godard's work during this period. The Hollywood film of the late 1990s "intensely invest[s] in chronology, eschew[s] all flashback, [and offers] the visualization of temporality as reduced to mere and simple accounts" (Polan 1989, 27), as witness *Forrest Gump*'s simplistic narrational thread which binds together the strictly linear structure of the film itself. In *Détective* as in his other late films, even when he creates a "commercial project," Godard always works against the dominant grain. *Détective* pretends to concern itself with the activities of several rival groups of gangsters: in fact, it is a homage to the history of the crime film, the cinema itself, and yet another manifestation of Godard's insistence on the uselessness of narrative. In *Détective,* four different crime "families" interact in the rooms of the Hotel Concorde at Saint Lazare in Paris, and perhaps to facilitate ease of shooting, nearly all of the film takes place inside the hotel. Only the last sequence contains any exterior shots at all, and that exterior is the street in front of the hotel. Characterization is also slight; the actors present not realized portraits of imaginary personages, but rather inhabit a series of preordained roles, or situations. Émile Chenal (Claude Brasseur) and Françoise Chenal (Nathalie Baye) spend their time trying to force unethical fight promoter Jim Fox-Warner/Impresario (Johnny Hallyday) to repay an enormous debt he owes the Chenals; the "house dick" William Prospero (Laurent Terzieff) and his nephew Inspector

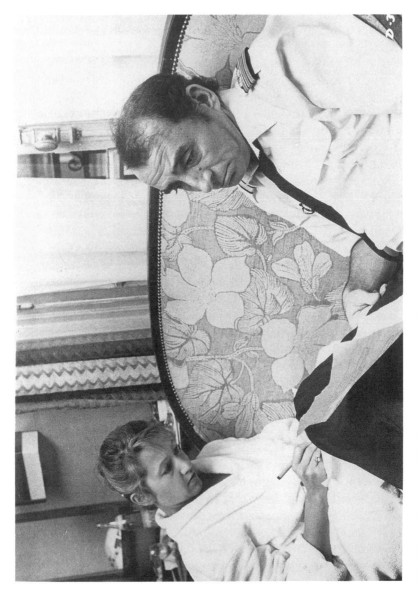

FIGURE 38. *Détective* (1985). Courtesy Jerry Ohlinger Archives.

Neveu (Jean-Pierre Léaud) dash about the hotel trying to solve the murder of a prince. Alain Cuny plays an old Mafioso who spends his time in the company of a bodyguard/accountant (Xavier Saint Macary) and a young girl (Julie Delpy). Jim Fox-Warner, down on his luck, dodges the Chenals while trying half-heartedly to train his new discovery, Tiger Jones (Stephane Ferrara), in a room of the hotel. The motivation for the swirling action in the film is never made particularly clear, but no matter; this is *Grand Hotel* meets *A Night at the Opera* and *The Big Sleep*, and the entire piece is played more as a comedy than anything else.

Bruno Nuytten's cinematography is as gorgeous as one might expect, framing Godard's protagonists at the edges of the frame with masterly insouciance, and the film is peppered with more than the usual quota of Godardian anecdotes, references to cinema's past, maxims, and "in" jokes. *Détective* not only invokes Ulmer, Cassavetes, and Eastwood, but also contains excerpts from director George Archainbaud's *The Last Squadron* (1932) starring Erich von Stroheim, Jean Marais in Cocteau's *La Belle et la bête* (1946), and literary references to Saint Exupéry's *Vol de nuit*, Gide's *École des femmes*, and Conrad's *Lord Jim*. There are also the pithy comments on the state of modern technological society ("Seeing is deceiving"), and Godard's ensemble cast seem to be having a fine time essaying their various caricatured roles, although as a whole *Détective* is, not surprisingly, rather claustrophobic. At the center of the film, however, behind the allusions and quotations, one senses that Godard's commitment to the material is far from total, and that he views *Détective* as a stylistic and cometic exercise lacking in serious resonance. As Godard noted of *Détective's* genesis in a recent interview with Gavin Smith, "*Détective* was well-lit, a good photographer. He lit the unknown actors well because they were not afraid if they were not seen. But as soon as the so-called stars like Nathalie Baye or Johnny Hallyday came, then he [used] artificial light and it was not good. He put light on them because they want to see the speakers [i.e., those actors delivering dialogue] on TV . . . there was a fight. But I couldn't avoid it because it was signed on the contract. It was a compromise. A movie is always a compromise" (Smith, 41).

A great deal of the fun in *Détective* can be found in the exaggerated portrayals afforded by Godard's performers, in the painterly cinematography of Nuytten, and in the controlled frenzy of the film's picaresque narrative structure. As the cast members of *Détective* hurtle or glide through the hallways of the vast hotel they seem doomed to inhabit, their various quests for love, money, or clues trail away into inconsequential and ineffectual gestures. There is more than a touch of Alain Resnais's *L'Année dernière à Marienbad* (1961) in *Détective*, and we sometimes feel as if the protagonists of Godard's films are fated to pursue their essentially meaningless ventures for eternity. For example, we never find out who murdered the prince, nor do we really expect to, although Alain Cuny's aging Mafia don is also referred to as the prince throughout the film. As with all late Godard films, the external structure of *Détective* is a device that facilitates the creation of a philosophical essay. Any homage to the genre of the mystery or thriller in *Détective* resides in an appreciation and/or consideration of the requirements and expectations of the classical Hollywood mystery film.

Godard followed *Detective* with one of his least seen, and simultaneously most bitterly hilarious films, *Grandeur et décadence d'un petit commerce de cinéma* (1986), released in the United States as *The Grandeur and Decadence of a Small-Time Filmmaker*. An absurdly brutal and minimalist examination of the desperate search for financial backing by two small-time filmmakers (Jean-Pierre Léaud and Jean-Pierre Mocky), *Grandeur et décadence* is knowingly self-referential, sad, and appropriately enough, a film shot on a miniscule budget in 16mm. Nominally based on a novel by James Hadley Chase, with script and direction by Godard, the film was photographed by Caroline Champetier and Serge Le François. The film is a made-for-television movie (a format that Godard would increasingly embrace in the 1980s and 1990s), with a running time of ninety minutes. It received only a few desultory screenings, most notably at the Montreal Film Festival in 1986, before being shelved. This is a shame, because *Grandeur et décadence* is a quintessentially Godardian examination of the process of filmmaking, at once vicious and joyous, compromised and unfettered. To me, the film seems to be one of Godard's key works of his later period.

Léaud and Mocky are two harried, endlessly pressured commercial filmmakers who desperately scheme to put together the funding for a low-budget French/German co-production made-for-television feature film. This dubious enterprise consumes their every waking moment, as they audition a number of actors for the film in hastily concocted "cattle calls," count their spare change to pay for coffees in the local café, and fruitlessly attempt to scheme their way into the rarified world of theatrical motion pictures, all the while facing the nightmarish probability of imminent financial collapse from the quarters of their absurdly tiny office. Holding forth in the local café with a mixture of absurd posturing and reflexive self-loathing, the faltering film producer and his manic director partner present us with a compelling vision of the filmmaker as huckster and con man, willing to go to any lengths to get even the most utterly banal and corrupt scenario filmed. More hustlers than filmmakers, Léaud and Mocky sustain themselves with visions of cinema's past, as they repeatedly audition a young actress (Marie Valera), discuss the glories of classical cinema, art, and music, and dream fruitlessly of the day that they will finally make a comeback. These pathetic shells of humanity have long since relinquished any connection with life outside the commercial film industry; Léaud, in particular, is frenzied beyond all reason in his quest for money and fleeting glory. Filmmaking in *Grandeur et décadence* is seen as being centered on money, connections, deadlines, seductions, under-the-table payoffs, and endless compromise.

The pathetic, Sisyphian cycle of commercial production is perhaps most tellingly foregrounded in a brief appearance within the film by Godard, as he meets with the producer for a futile discussion on the problems of finding backing for a film, and the growing United States/Hollywood stranglehold on the film production, distribution, and exhibition. Godard ultimately leaves the producer to his shabby fate, withholding any assistance he might have afforded him. The producer and one of his lackeys are subsequently murdered in a somewhat battered Mercedes Benz that the producer has somehow managed to hold on to while all else collapsed around him, but the endless grind of low-budget filmmaking goes on without him. Godard's production company on *Grandeur et décadence* is aptly named Hamster Productions. One immediately remembers the image of a pathetic, directionless hamster tirelessly running in place on a stationary wheel in a small, smelly cage. The hamster will never get anywhere; his existence is an unceasing quest for an unreachable goal. *Grandeur et décadence* is, as is *Je vous salue, Marie*, an unrelenting, serious work, and a bitter and knowing indictment of an industry which sacrifices dreams and ambition for the endless proliferation of mass-consumption hackwork. Concomitantly, some find fault with Godard for making television commercials and "industrial" videos; after all, isn't he the quintessence of a free spirit within the ordinarily ultracommercial world of the dominant cinema? As I see it, however, Godard's art compromises no one (except perhaps the consumer, who is always at a disadvantage in the production and dissemination of any advertisement), and allows him the relative freedom to create a cheerfully vicious commentary (in *Grandeur et décadence*) on the very system that seeks to exploit him. In this metanarrative exchange, Godard creates a commercial and uses the proceeds to finance two resolutely noncommercial works, which, given the realities of film finance, seems an altogether satisfactory arrangement.

This savage comedy was followed by *Soft and Hard (A Soft Conversation between Two Friends on a Hard Subject)*, a 48-minute videotape co-directed by Godard and Miéville as a co-production between JLG Films and Britain's Channel 4 television network. The tape is structured in two parts, and is most accurately described as an exercise in self-criticism, or, if you will, self-abasement. In the first section of the tape, Godard and Miéville putter about their home, both occupied by various daily tasks. Godard fools around with a tennis racket and conducts some business on the telephone, while Miéville labors on an editing table with some film and later attends to the laundry. Part two of the tape is an extended discussion by Godard and Miéville on their recent work, and the impact of television on their projects, but what surfaces is a thinly veiled contest between the two over domestic issues of power, control, and social obligation. Miéville confronts Godard with a series of precise observations, but Godard manages to deflect most of her criticisms in the same fashion that he handles a zealous interviewer for a cinema

FIGURE 39. *Soft and Hard* (1985). Courtesy Marita Sturken/Electronic Arts Intermix.

journal. One thinks of John Ford deliberately provoking his would-be interrogators with a series of noncommittal comebacks to equally sincere queries, refusing to let himself be seen while simultaneously ensuring his dominance within the sphere of inquiry. When Miéville finds fault with the romantic interludes in his recent films, Godard lets the criticism pass; in return, Godard subtly patronizes Miéville, and, as Kathleen Rowe notes, "keeps turning the conversation back to himself. . . . 'So what really bothers you?' [Godard asks.] 'I'm sure that if I could understand that, I would be able to measure up to television" (Rowe, 59), making a feeble joke of the situation. Miéville persists, telling him that "You never doubt that what you have to say is interesting . . . at times I feel that any originality in me is very fragile. For you, there's only film. For me it's more fragile" (Rowe, 59). As the title suggests, the conversation in this film is indeed "soft," and no direct confrontations are forthcoming from either Godard or Miéville. Indeed, the discussion finally ends on a note of spectacular inconclusiveness, as Godard wistfully asks Miéville, "Where has it all gone? All those projects? All those projects to be enlarged into subjects?" [and Miéville answers] "It's hard to say!" (Rowe, 59).

In 1986, Godard shot *J.L.G. Meets W.A.* (*Meetin' W.A.*), a 26-minute project featuring Woody Allen and Godard engaged in a discussion of cinema history and aesthetics. This extremely slight videotape nevertheless has a link to Godard's *King Lear* (1987), as it was sort of an introduction between the two filmmakers, and Allen would appear the next year as "Mr. Alien" in *Lear*. In early 1987, Godard also directed an episode for Don Boyd's omnibus film *Aria*, a twelve-minute visualization of Jean-Baptiste Lully's *Armide* ("Enfin, il-est en ma puissance"), sung by Rachel Yakar, Zeger Wandersteene, and Danièle Borst. The other directors involved in the project were Nicolas Roeg, Charles Sturridge, Julien Temple (best known as a director of rock videos for MTV), Robert Altman, Derek Jarman, Franc Roddam, Bruce Beresford, and Bill Bryden. Indeed, the completed film represents nothing so much as an extended string of classical music videos, with various celebrity directors engaged in the project to add marquee value to the finished work. Godard's section of the film is typically audacious; staging the action in a gymnasium, he

FIGURE 40. Jean-Luc Godard during the shooting of *Armide*, his segment of the omnibus film *Aria* (1987). Courtesy Jerry Ohlinger Archives.

juxtaposes an unsuccessful seduction (two nude women try to attract a group of men who are working out) while cleaning women (a recurring theme in late Godard; one thinks of the cleaning lady in the bank in *Prénom: Carmen*) toil to maintain the gym's spotless, antiseptic image. At once prosaic and inspired, and breathtakingly simple in execution, this brief section demonstrates once again that Godard harvests his most compelling images from the most mundane aspects of contemporary existence. But both the *Aria* segment and *J.L.G. Meets W.A.* were mere curtain-raisers to Godard's brilliantly idiosyncratic production of *King Lear*, one of his most successful and original films of the late 1980s.

King Lear's origins as a film are a sort of a modern legend at this point; the project was first conceived as a star-studded deal between Godard, and Menahem Golan and Yoram Globus, the two CEOs of Cannon Films. Golan and Globus, then known as the "Go Go Boys" for their aggressive marketing and production program as the heads of Cannon, proposed a film to Godard that would include a script by Norman Mailer, in which Mailer would also star as Lear, and his daughter, Kate, would play Cordelia. Budgeted at $1.4 million, the film would be shot in English, in Switzerland. The deal was sketched out on a napkin during a luncheon between Godard, Golan, and Globus at the Cannes Film Festival in 1985, but never really got off the ground until 1986, and almost immediately fell apart. Mailer and Godard were uneasy collaborators. As conceived by Mailer, Lear is seen in the film as an aging Mafia Kingpin, Don Learo, a point both men agreed on. But Mailer's script was apparently too linear for Godard, and after one half-day of shooting (which Godard incorporated into the final film), both the Mailers departed for America, leaving Godard to recast the film from scratch. Cannon hastily arranged for Burgess Meredith and Molly Ringwald to take over their respective roles; Woody Allen (in a very minor role) and theatrical director Peter Sellars also signed on to the project.

Godard's *Lear* uses Shakespeare's play as a point of departure for a series of ruminations on the nature of life, cinema, fame, and canonization; plot and characterization are almost nonexistent. At the same time, there is a continuing fluidity to Godard's imagistic/thematic structure in the film. Burgess Meredith is not only Lear; he is also Meredith himself, a veteran of the golden age of classical Hollywood cinema. Molly Ringwald is not only Lear's daughter, Cordelia, but also the "daughter of the cinema," inextricably intertwined in the public's consciousness with the many roles she played in more conventional films of the 1980s as daughter, high school student, and debutante. Godard as Pluggy is transparently Godard, the lionized darling of the avant garde. As Godard's visuals become increasingly sparse and naturalistic (the use of artificial interior light, for one example, is almost absent in the film; rather, silhouettes and window-lit shots document the interior world of *Lear*) and his soundtracks move complicated and free-associational, Godard has concomitantly abandoned any peripheral interest he may once have had in any sort of conventional narrative structure.

With *À bout de souffle*, Godard stuck to a fairly organized narrative, although he broke it up into fragments of shots; in *Week-end*, he mixes the flimsiest outline of a murder plot with political skits and direct acknowledgment of the camera's presence. By the time of *King Lear*, Godard has done away with narrative, characterization, most sets, costumes and props, and manipulates music and dialogue at various speeds and volume levels as a counterpoint to his stripped-down image track. The Godard of the late 1980s composes films as personal treatises rather than audience entertainments, and scripts them from an outline as production progresses. In doing so, he neatly disposes all of those elements which usually draw an audience to the cinema theater, yet this is precisely his intention. Godard as Pluggy is Godard as Lear, the aging fool with more than a little introspective wisdom regarding his position in the cinematic firmament. Pluggy's grim jests and incomprehensible outbursts make him a figure of weakness and strength: the filmmaker as idiot savant.

Lear is, by any measure, a brilliant and groundbreaking film for Godard, but it did not receive the wide-ranging distribution of his earlier works, despite the impressive cast the film boasts, and so its influence was not as pervasive as it might have been otherwise. Cannon, for their part, were not particularly pleased with the finished product. At the premiere at Cannes, Godard pre-

174

FIGURE 41. Peter Sellars (William Shakespeare Jr. V) and Jean-Luc Godard (Pluggy) in *King Lear* (1987). Courtesy Jerry Ohlinger Archives.

sented the film in a state of near-exhaustion after a marathon all-night editing session to balance the stereo soundtrack correctly, but Menahem Golan would say only that he was "satisfied" with the project, and that he had seen an earlier rough cut of the film containing additional footage with Woody Allen. He hoped to persuade Godard to incorporate this material into the final cut, but nothing came of this. Distributed in the United States and Europe in English (with subtitles in foreign territories), the film was a modest "art circuit" success, but soon vanished into the then-rising ranks of VHS videocassette releases, and never received a widespread U.S. theatrical release.

The film remains better known for its somewhat bizarre casting, and the fugitive involvement of the Mailers, than for what the film itself attempted to accomplish. Compromised from the beginning, yet the beneficiary of several luminous talents (Meredith, Ringwald, Sellars—Allen's role is so nominal as to be nonexistent), *King Lear* may be "A FILM SHOT IN THE BACK" (as a Godardian intertitle indicates), but it is also a fully realized meditation on faith, mortality, the decline of one's mental and artistic acuity, and the continuing compromise that is feature film production in the latter half of the twentieth century. At $1.4 million, the film still looks modest and careful in its expenditures; long gone are the days when $100,000 could finance an *Alphaville* or a *Masculin Féminin*. And yet, in the midst of what some might term despair, Godard has found in *King Lear* and *Je vous salue, Marie* a new kind of faith, not only in the immortality of images, but also in the lasting resonance of the human spirit. The effects of his serious accident in the early 1970s, and his long convalescence, have made him both serious and playful in his late work. He no longer lives for the movies, although it is the only work he knows how to do.

Godard in the late 1980s functions as a cultural monitor of the state of our internal existence, of our values, our collective memory, our spiritual and artistic heritage. As he finished *King Lear* and prepared for the work of the 1990s, Jean-Luc Godard was beginning to take stock of his life and accomplishments, to please himself and Anne-Marie Miéville before any other audience, and to create an inventory of images for a proposed history of the cinema, which would consume all his energies to the present day. With *Je vous salue, Marie* and *King Lear*, Godard seemed to be saying goodbye to one style of filmmaking—dispensing with plot, characterization, narrative drive, ordinary structures of aural and visual montage, sets, camera movement; in short, most of the functions of classical cinema—to create a series of cinematic meditations for his own edification and spiritual survival, increasingly immersed not in pop culture, as he was in his early films, but rather in the classical culture of his childhood. *King Lear* might arguably be considered Godard's farewell to conventional feature film production, but in the next seven years, particularly with *Hélas pour moi* and *Allemagne année 90 neuf zéro* (*Germany Year 90 Nine Zero*), he would create some of his most intriguing and inventive *ciné-essais*, following no one's example but his own.

CHAPTER FIVE

———————— ◉ ————————

Fin de Cinéma

"When I made [*À bout de souffle*]" Godard observed, "I was a child in the movies. Now I am becoming an adult. I feel I can be better. I think that artists, as they grow older, discover what they can do." In response to the query, "Were you ever really a Maoist?" Godard responded: "I was too young. I developed slowly. I had my youth very late. I discovered revolution, social questions, after everyone else. . . . I loved Mao as I loved Goethe. It was political romanticism" (Riding 11). Now freed to a large degree from the burden of his celebrity through age and isolation, ensconced in his house in Rolle, Switzerland, Godard turned to more deeply meditational works, with ever greater detail and multilayered complexity. Nor did he care much about commercial or critical acclaim anymore. "After my first film, I never had another success. I was too corrupted by being Godard myself," the director observed (Riding, 11). But Godard had now taken back his life in a thorough and systematic manner, and was ready for new challenges in his life and work. Visiting him at his home, *New York Times* reporter Alan Riding found Godard "quite used to living on the periphery, both physically and artistically . . . he was unshaven, his hair unkempt. . . . [I]t seemed natural [for Godard to] return to Switzerland. He set up a video studio . . . and cut himself off from the world of politics and producers. He recovered control over his day. He enjoyed the chance to swim in the lake, to walk in the hills, to play tennis. He left the other Godard in Paris" (Riding, 11).

The "other" Godard had experienced, despite his disclaimer to the contrary, lasting international success with a string of commercial and critical hits in the 1960s; *Je vous salue, Marie* had marked a return to a degree of notoriety. But rather than assiduously courting continued controversy, Godard seemed intent on creating, more than ever before, a series of highly personal film and video productions centering on the themes of loss, old age, memory, and the archival history of the cinema. His passion for the medium of the cinematograph was unabated. "Movies are so close to reality" he told Riding. "That's how life is made. . . . I think it's why the public still likes films. It's because there's a very archaic image that survives like a flame of human society" (Riding, 11).

Nor had he lost faith in his abilities as a filmmaker, even as he metaphysically contemplated the origin of his gifts as an artist. Puckishly, Godard suggested to Riding that

> I believe I come from elsewhere, let's say, space. I have a need to go to Earth. There's something of mine. There's an image I have to uncover, and cinema allows me to do so. Movies are like clouds that sit over reality: if I do cinema well, I can uncover what is beneath, my friends, my allies, what I am, where I come from. Others can't do it. It's too heavy for them. But it's not too heavy for me, because I come from elsewhere. . . . There you are. I've said everything. (Riding, 11)

But Godard, on the contrary, still had a great deal to say as an artist and *auteur*, although his vision was becoming increasingly idiosyncratic.

Godard followed *King Lear* with the production of *Soigne ta droite* (known by a number of other titles in English translation, the most common being *Keep Up Your Right*), released in 1987, and screened in competition at the Tokyo Film Festival in October of that year. Photographed by Caroline Champetier in 35mm, with a cast headed by Godard himself (as the Idiot/the Prince) and featuring Jacques Villeret as "the Individual" and Jane Birkin as "the Cricket," the film was a return to small-scale, noncommercial filmmaking for Godard after the trying experiences of *King Lear*. The film was shot quickly, almost immediately after the conclusion of the *King Lear* shoot, and centers around three different, fragmented narratives.

In one thread, a group of musicians (the techno pop group Rita Mitsouko) in a recording studio tries to capture some finished material, but never seems to complete a satisfactory take (this strategy, as we have seen in *One Plus One* and *Prénom: Carmen*, is not new for Godard). In another story, a worker interacts with several couples, trying to create some rapport, without much success. In the funniest section of the film (all three stories are intercut with each other, in the usually fragmented fashion one has come to expect from Godard), a group of airplane passengers try to reach their flight destination on a plane captained by a suicidal pilot, who reads an instructional manual on the finer points of suicide, much to his passengers' dismay. Godard emerges in this film as something of a comic figure, with a certain air of courtly truculence in his manner, playing his part for slapstick in the manner of Keaton or Chaplin, with a touch of Jacques Tati thrown in.

Described even by *Cahiers du Cinéma* as "very experimental" in its construction, mixing an air of "nihilism" with strains of "derisive" comedy (*Cahiers* 437, 127), *Soigne ta droite* is at once brutally comic and sadly poetic, replete with a running commentary by the filmmaker on the images we are seeing, and recurring montage patterns in which specific images ("a sky with a jetstream, a little girl getting a glass door slammed in her face, a corpse with a big knife in its belly, a man dancing with the same woman in various stages of undress" ["Cart," 24]) repeat in a flow of sensual violence both seductive and disconcerting. The film is also something of a return to earlier concerns for the director (the recurrent images of the musicians, the worker who wants his concerns shared by members of other social classes, the presence of Godard himself within the film as an "Idiot/Prince" philosopher), and seems a diversion for Godard rather than an attempt to break new ground. Is humankind bound for an ill-defined destination on a plane manned by a suicidal pilot, or created as part of a divine intelligence, as opposed to an unaccountable accident? Godard, in *Soigne ta droite*, may have been seeking personal reassurance that his quirky, iconoclastic spirit had not entirely deserted him, and that perhaps not all matters need to be subjected to sustained, impassioned scrutiny.

On s'est tous défilé was Godard's next project, a thirteen-minute videotape created in early 1988. The videotape was commissioned by Marithé and François Girbaud, the manufacturers of blue jeans for whom Godard had created commercials in the past. The videotape is a mélange of scraps of sound and image, mixing music, slow-motion images of bodies and sounds from the streets into a highly experimental collage of manipulated and fragmented hyperreality. Compact and brief, the tape resembles a music video more than anything else. Godard doesn't seem to be particularly involved in this project, which seems created to please the commercial requirements of the Girbauds above all other considerations. In this brief tape, Godard fulfills his assigned commission, but the video seems perfunctory, unfinished, made-to-order, and lacking any real artistic passion.

Godard's next videotape was *Puissance de la parole* (1988), literally *The Power of Speech*, a 25-minute videotape made at the request of Télécom, the French telecommunications giant. In this tape, Godard again confronts a question which has concerned him since the days of *Le Gai Savoir*, namely, how does one bring into conjunction the image and the word? Godard breaks down the association between the word and the image in his usually insouciant manner, insisting on the primacy of the image (and the image/object), and the inadequacy of any word to describe or delimit the object. Far from being about *The Power of Speech*, the video is highly critical of the illusory nature of aural signification, and shows Godard once again criticizing the corporate sponsors who clamor to underwrite his work. As described in *Cahiers* 437, "the telephone, the emblem of the film's sponsor, which extends speech to the four corners of the world, remains itself empty of sense, and is seen as totally pathetic, ridiculed as a prewar apparatus" (127). In view of Godard's lack of respect for his corporate backers, one is continually surprised that there never seems to be any shortage of companies willing to commission the filmmaker to "extol" the virtues of their various products and for services. There is humor in *Puissance de la parole*, but it is mirth of a peculiarly mordant nature, suspicious of power, and determined to disassociate itself from the shadow of the corporate monolith.

Le Dernier Mot, literally *The Last Word*, is a thirteen-minute videotape created to celebrate the tenth anniversary of *Figaro* magazine. As described in *Cahiers* 437, Godard in this video invents a series of fictitious French celebrities, who have dedicated themselves to creating, "with their last breath," the ultimate *'bon mots'* (or last words) before dying (127). But this sardonic opening sequence is soon abandoned in favor of a more deeply felt narrative, suffused with gorgeous imagery and devoid of sarcasm. As synopsized by Akira Lippit, at the end of World War II, a German officer and his female French companion leave their house with a sense of regret, having lived through the war together. In a subsequent scene, a group of German soldiers capture five civilians, who are in all probability members of the French Resistance. The soldiers, lacking ammunition, draw lots to see whom they will execute, and select a young philosopher, Valentin Feldman. Dying, Feldman addresses the Germans with his own "last words": "Imbeciles, it is for you that I die."

Forty years later, the son of the German officer comes back to visit the places where he had spoken with his father. He is accompanied by a mute violinist who is the son of Valentin Feldman. Shifting between the present and the past, a voiceover explains to the viewer the outlines of this complex, epigrammatic scenario. In this brief exercise, Godard breaks with the studied cynicism which has informed the creation of many of his recent paid commissions, to create a work about collaboration and resistance, the aftermath of the war, and the relationship between those whom fate has placed in opposing camps. It is a film about the destruction of innocence, the end of childhood, pictorially indebted to Fra Angelico. It is a moving still life that ranks as one of Godard's least seen and most compelling late works. As a muted consideration of the twin issues of moral responsibility and conscience, the film is a serious work of genuine depth and sincerity, astonishingly detailed for a thirteen-minute videotape, and a refreshing respite from the relative emptiness of *On s'est tous défilé* (*Cahiers*, 437, 127–28). Above all, it is a consideration of man's apparent need to create wars. As

Godard told Alan Riding, "Men are not real. Women are real because they produce children. Men who can't have children are jealous and avenge themselves by making things like politics, war, social systems" (11). In describing war as a necessarily gendered act, Godard locates the desire for destruction, the will to apocalypse, which dominates the dreams of men. Because men cannot create, they wish to destroy. Only in destruction can men find peace, in the ceasing-to-be of nihilist conflict. As the self is expunged from the domain of real through the agency of mechanized warfare, man regains a tragic sense of personal dimension in the isolated landscape of oblivion.

It was also during this period that Godard began his series of videotapes entitled *Histoire(s) du cinéma*, an anthology of meditations of the past, present, and future of the cinematographic process. The video considers not only film, but also television, the mechanism of cinema/video, the hierarchy and iconic structures of the star system, Hollywood, World War II, and indeed the entire apparatus of memory and image recall. Sweeping, chaotic, and entirely personal, *Histoire(s) du cinéma* is not only about the history of the cinema, but also about Godard's own life within film, and his enduring fascination with the film/video medium.

As described by Katherine Dieckmann, the first two sections (1a and 1b) of Godard's *Histoire(s) du cinéma*, "Toutes les histoires" ("All the Stories"), and "Une Histoire Seule" ("One Single Story"), begun in 1989 and still very much an ongoing project, is

> an expansive, densely layered, elegiac treatise on the fate of cinema. The two . . . episodes of this ongoing project shown at [the Museum of Modern Art in New York] proved the high point of Godard's video retrospective. At once an idiosyncratic version of film history and a brooding autopsy of it, *Histoire(s)* is an imaginative collage of old movie clips, soundtracks, newsreels, film stills, snips of dialogue, reproductions from paintings and words that gradually accumulate to form full, suggestive phrases. Using video to both anoint and indict the intrinsic showiness of cinema, Godard rearranges his collection of filmic elements into a fast-paced work that is every bit as eye-grabbing. . . .

> Shards of music and dialogue snitched from movies (some profoundly moving, some fantastically trite) overlap to the point of near-chaos, swell, then halt abruptly, creating a dislocating sound track that both nudges and grates against the images. There is a desire here to force the components of moviemaking to speak again—or cry out for salvation—by both distorting and dismantling them. (65)

This whirling cacophony of imagery is, as we have seen, nothing new for Godard, but with this project, Godard's obsessive collection and juxtaposition of found and manipulated images from cinema's past reaches a new zenith. It is not enough that Godard has the entire history of cinema in his head, that he is a walking reference library of the cinema. For Godard, all is *simultaneous*, endlessly overlapping, one image and another swirling together to create a hybrid construct which deconstructs both original images and adds something new to them. All is context, history, archival research, and speculation here. Godard uses the Sonimage workshop in *Histoire(s)* to create an endless meshing of word and image that goes far beyond the synthetic falsely proscribed boundaries of conventional cinema history. Godard is immersed in his images, which become phantoms haunting our combinatory consciousness. Eschewing strict categories and taxonomic structures employed by pedestrian historians, Godard shows us too much at once, in an attempt to replicate the overwhelming legacy of cinema's past. The very act of seeing a movie (based as it is on the phenomenon of persistence of vision) is "overload assimilation"; we cannot forget one still image before it is replaced by another, projected on the darkened screen of the cinema auditorium. In his *Histoire(s)*, Godard tries to go beyond mere representationalism (or even collagism) to open up the essence of an object to be viewed and inventoried. "To pry an object from its shell, to destroy its aura, is the mark of a perception whose 'sense of the universal equality of things' has increased to such a degree that it extracts it even from a unique object by means of reproduction" (Benjamin, 225). In *Histoire(s)*, Godard gives us cinema's past as an endless and inexhaustible supply of icons, narrative structures, superimpositions and cross-references that assault the viewer, shaking her/him out of the artificial stupor most examples of dominant cinema create for the intended audiences. There is no one history of the cinema, Godard is telling us, no single track that we can follow through the past. All is present and future, all is mutable and unstable, all images and sounds exist to be related to each other. *Histoire(s)*, another ambitious project for Godard, will no doubt stretch far into the filmmaker's future, and the collagist strategies employed here present themselves again in the later films, particularly *Allemagne année 90 neuf zéro*. As Godard told the late Serge Daney in an interview, "the greatest history is the history of the cinema" (cited in Hoberman 1992, 53). For once, with *Histoire(s) du cinéma*, we are given a director who is more than up to the task of chronicling the tale(s) told by the cinematographic machine.

Le Rapport Darty, made in 1989, is a fifty-minute video which seems almost to be a return to the issues and events of the 1970s, the period in which Godard and Gorin created *Tout va bien*. Co-directed by Godard and Miéville, the film's narrative centers on a large store called Darty. Throughout the film, the offscreen voice of "Mamzelle Clio" (provided by Anne-Marie Miéville) offers a running commentary on the images we see, depicting daily life in the huge store. Mamzelle Clio's ruminations on the video's soundtrack are supplemented by the additional voice of Nathanael, a 2,000-year-old robot, whose voice is that of Godard himself. These two voiceover monologues are mixed with direct sound from scenes of the store during a typical work day. There are citations from Rousseau, Marcel Mauss, Georges Bataille, and Pierre Clastres. The videotape becomes a "spontaneous history of property, work and commerce" (*Cahiers* 437, 128), much in the manner of the earlier Godard/Gorin political films, complemented by a soundtrack of breathtaking complexity. The voice of Léo Ferré, the French pop singer, is also heard on the soundtrack. The video's second section concerns itself with Darty France, the manager of the store, who is unhappy because the store's relationship with the police is being thrown into disarray. Darty corresponds with the police, and the two entities exchange letters detailing the breakdown of their mutual rapport. An examination of internal and cultural politics, the videotape analyzes the concerns of the mainstream workplace, and demonstrates that issues of commercial ownership and labor relations, not to mention the question of one's association with or opposition to the police, are never far from Godard's consciousness.

Before discussing Godard's major project of 1990, *Nouvelle Vague* (*New Wave*), I will touch here briefly on a minor short project which Godard and Miéville created for Unicef, entitled "L'Enfance de l'art" (literally "The Childhood of Art"), a sequence from the film *Comment vont les enfants* (*How Are the Kids?*). This eight-minute project, shot in 35mm, was co-scripted and co-directed by Godard and Miéville. The film deals with "the rights of children" (*Cahiers* 437, 129). A woman reads a text to a young man, questioning insurrections, revolts, and the nature of authority. Outside, in a desolate landscape, groups of men are engaged in a random series of confrontations, the motives for which remain unclear. Children play soccer "while the bullets whistle past them" (*Cahiers* 437, 129). In this short film, Godard and Miéville assert the right of children to live in a society dedicated to the maintenance of social structures, rather than their destruction. The project is no more than a brief sketch, replete with Godard's usual allusions to classical literature and painting, but it offers reassuring evidence of the director's continued political commitment, despite the relative calm of his current Swiss domestic life. As Godard notes near the film's conclusion, "of all tyrannies, the most terrible is the tyranny of ideas" (*Cahiers* 437, 129) or ideologies, which constitutes a break from the dogmatism of Godard's political past, as evidenced in *La Chinoise* and *Vent d'est*.

With *Nouvelle Vague*, Godard returned both to his own past in Switzerland, but also to cinema's past, in the casting of Alain Delon, the great French film star, in the leading role of the film. The film is set on the Swiss estate of a fabulously wealthy woman (Domiziana Giordano), who, out for a spin one day, accidentally runs into a drifter (Alain Delon), and, tending to his minor injuries, takes him back to her enormous mansion as a semi-permanent house guest, something like Jean Renoir as Octave in Renoir's *Règle du jeu* (1939). However, in *Nouvelle Vague*, what transpires between the two is an endless series of philosophical confrontations, pitting Delon's macho yet depressed purity against Giordano's endless wealth. Godard indulges in sev-

eral intriguing tracking shots in the film to suggest the comparative uselessness of these worldly endowments; once past a group
of expensive automobiles in an outdoor parking lot, shaded by a
group of trees; and late in the film, a sweeping tracking shot to
the right, and then returning to the left, to show a series of lights
being turned on and off in the cold, palatial precincts of Giordano's house at night. Indeed, the tracking shot is the dominant
formal element of *Nouvelle Vague*, all the more noticeable
because camera movement has been conspicuously lacking in
many of Godard's films of the late 1980s. What is most prominently displayed in *Nouvelle Vague* is the often-unappreciated
beauty of the Swiss countryside, as stunningly photographed by
William Lubtchansky.

Dressed in a borrowed suit, Delon is uneasily integrated
into Giordano's hypercapitalist domain, looking dourly suspicious and altogether unimpressed by Giordano's consumption-
ist colleagues. Looking haggard and projecting merely a shadow of
his former matinee-idol glory, Delon exerts a considerable degree
of passive effort in *Nouvelle Vague*, and appears to have fallen in
quite well with Godard's world-weary agenda for the film. In the
exquisite world of light and shadow, verdant summer landscapes
and cold factory interiors created by Godard for *Nouvelle Vague*,
Delon functions as a faded moral barometer by which the others'
actions are judged. Although cradled and surrounded by the carefully tended grounds of Giordano's estate, the woman and her
associates pay little attention to the efforts of the full-time gar-
dener who keeps the estate in trim. As with his other films of the
1990s, Godard prefers to use natural light for illumination both
for his interior and exterior shots, but here he carefully positions
his protagonists in the sunlight, even inside the house, so that
their faces, hands, and external features are not obscured. As we
have come to expect from Godard, intertitles continually inter-
rupt the film's narrative; early on, a title advises us that in the
world of *Nouvelle Vague*, it is "THINGS, NOT WORDS" that
count. Conspicuous consumption is all that these people know,
and even then, they seem to take very little pleasure in their consumer culture.

Much is made in the film of class positions, and the back-
stairs roles of the servants and maids who keep the estate run-

ning. There is no privacy for the supposed masters in the world of *Nouvelle Vague*; someone is always listening. Regular tracking shots from the living room of the estate to the exterior staircase reveal the butler and several maids listening in on Giordano's attempted seduction of Delon; the scene is intercut with a sweeping overhead tracking shot over the placid waters of a nearby lake. Even books are seen as objects to be possessed rather than read; stacked neatly in a bookstore, their spines uncracked, they are objects to be purchased rather than the written testimony of their respective authors.

As Giordano contemplates a corporate takeover, she gathers around her a large number of anonymous, bored executives to help her in setting her plan into motion, but everyone seems bored with both business and life. The businessmen treat their wives with contempt and cultivate, in a desultory manner, a number of mistresses who drift through the hallways of the estate like the lost figures of Alain Resnais's *L'Année dernière à Marienbad* (1961). Everyone reads business publications but very little else, trying to outdo each other in predicting stock market fluctuations and the values of various competing currencies. The corporate capitalists are obsessed with beating the Japanese at world financial domination, leaving the maid to recite Schiller, and Delon to berate Giordano for her shallow self-absorption. "You don't understand my silence," Delon tells her. "You talk, you talk . . . how could you understand that there are others? Others who exist. Who think, who suffer, who live. You think only of you." But as much as she might like to be moved by Delon's criticism, Giordano can't give up her games of consumer capitalism at any price. Perhaps she knows that Delon is right, but she is unable to change. Lacking this ability, she tries to change Delon, who correctly notes that if he changes, he will not be who he now is. Delon is an exhausted agent of moral urgency within the stillborn world of *Nouvelle Vague*, and although he can do nothing to alter the views of those around him, he keeps his own integrity intact.

In the end, the territory surveyed by *Nouvelle Vague* is seen by Godard as simultaneously barren and corrupt, even as it blooms with ferocious intensity in the full heat of summer. There are references to the cinema of the past, as is usual for Godard; in one sequence strongly echoing John M. Stahl's *Leave Her to Heaven* (1945), Delon's character nearly drowns in a lake, while Giordano impassively watches him struggle from the safety of her boat. Another intertitle states simply, "THE LONG GOOD-BYE," an obvious reference to Raymond Chandler's celebrate "tough guy" novel. In this context, one is reminded of Fredric Jameson's assertion that

> Godard's [films] are . . . resolutely postmodernist in that they conceive of themselves as sheer text, as a process of production of representations that have no truth content, [and] are, in this sense, sheer surface or superficiality. It is this conviction which accounts for the reflexivity of the Godard film, its resolution to use representation against itself to destroy the binding or absolute status of any representation. (1990, 75)

But these joking, reflexive references are very much at the periphery of *Nouvelle Vague*, which depicts a world of private jets and limousines, a world where a Degas painting is simply a commodity to be bought and/or sold, a place where beauty is only worthwhile if it can be possessed, or transferred to another, for a price. Godard in *Nouvelle Vague* deftly sketches the chasm between the worlds of art and commerce, and aided by the ceaselessly, luxuriantly craning and tracking camera of Lubtchansky, paints a world devoid of emotion of genuine longing, located in the most externally verdant of landscapes. Yet, in the final images of the film, Godard suggests that some sort of rapprochement between Delon and Giordano's characters might be possible, as the two drive off smiling in her sports car together to an unspecified destination, complete with a joking reference to *To Have and Have Not* (Howard Hawks, 1944) ("Was you ever stung by a dead bee?"). As with most late Godard, the end seems abrupt and slightly arbitrary to some viewers, and there is no question that the "dark heart" of *Nouvelle Vague* is the world of weary sadness it so elegantly limns. But Godard is unwilling to rule out hope, even in a world as morally arid as this, and so the film's final moments are positive and evanescently transcendent, in sharp contrast to uncompromising angst of the greater part of the work.

In his later films, Godard, like Nietzsche, adopts a variety of masks and identities to allow himself freer reign within his works, and thus

> advances behind a plurality of masks or names that, like any mask and even any theory of the simulacrum, can propose and produce themselves only by returning a constant yield of protection, a surplus value in which one may still recognize the ruse of life. However, the ruse starts incurring losses as soon as the surplus value does not return again to the living, but to and in the name of names, the community of masks. (Derrida 1985, 7)

This work set the stage for the hour-long *Allemagne année 90 neuf zéro* (*Germany year 90 Nine Zero*), a telefilm that began production in November 1990 in Germany and wrapped in the spring of 1991. The completed film was shown in competition at the Venice Film Festival in September 1991, and broadcast in France on the Antenne 2 network (one of the film's producers) on November 8, 1991, thus bypassing the traditional mechanism of theatrical film distribution. At a precise running time of sixty-two minutes, the film was an odd length for a standard theatrical release, and so Godard had to wait until January 1995 for an American theatrical screening at the Shakespeare Festival Public Theatre in New York City, when the film was "double-billed" with Godard's 1994 self-examination of his life and work, *JLG/JLG—Autoportrait de décembre*.

Allemagne année 90 neuf zéro is a double return for Godard; once again, he works with actor Eddie Constantine, who starred in *Alphaville*, and once again, Godard returns to Constantine's most famous fictive alter ego, secret agent *Lemmy Caution*. In *Alphaville*, Lemmy had been sent on a search-and-destroy mission, to shut down Alpha 60, the giant computer, and assassinate Dr. von Braun. Lemmy Caution was, as befits the role of the secret agent, a person of action. Now, aging and exhausted (Constantine died shortly after making the film), Lemmy Caution, "the last of the secret agents," stumbles forlornly through the desolate landscape of East Germany, a civilization in ruins, surveyed by Godard's camera in a series of cold, contemplative *tableaux*.

190

FIGURE 42. Eddie Constantine (Lemmy Caution) in *Allemagne année 90 neuf zéro* (1991). Courtesy Noon Pictures.

Count Zelten (Hanns Zischler) searches for Lemmy, "the last secret agent" in the ruins of East Germany. This pretense at plot is almost immediately abandoned for a barrage of intertitles (SOLITUDES: A STATE AND VARIATIONS; OH SORROW, HAVE I DREAMT MY LIFE?) and a series of cinematic quotations—stock footage from famous and/or infamous films to illustrate the themes of the collapse of communism, the uneasy reunification of Germany into a congruent whole, and the collapse of individual consciousness in the face of industrial capitalism. Clips from "classical" canonized films are intermingled with sequences from Naziesque "exploitation" films.

The first "cinematic quotation" in the film, a highly stylized and manipulated video image of a fancy dress ball in the era of the Third Reich, is not documentary material, but rather a scene from a fictionalized recreation of Hitler's Germany. This "found" material is manipulated through the medium of video playback, to run forward, then freeze, then move forward frame-by-frame in excruciating slow motion. Quotations from Hegel are mixed with the piano music, as video-manipulated images of a Hitler youth rally fill the screen. Intervals of complete blackness punctuate these scenes. Other shots pass by in rapid succession: a large, bare tree in a springtime field; a hand pulling a hard cover "History of the Führer" off a bookshelf, a black-and-white image of a female German SS guard, framed by the barbed-wire fence of a concentration camp. An intertitle appears: HISTORY OF SOLITUDE. Godard hastily restages a sequence in which a young woman (Dora, played by Claudia Michelsen) metaphorically escapes from a Nazi concentration camp. Moments later, in a rundown section of East Germany, Lemmy comes across a street-peddler hawking "souvenirs of the Reich," including a book that Dora once owned. An intertitle reminds us that "ALL IS ECSTASY, ALL IS AGONY." Scraps of handwriting, still photographs, and droll intertitles ("LOOK, KAFKA'S IN THE GARDEN WITH A GIRL") are intercut with a video-manipulated clip from Leontine Sagan's *Mädchen in Uniform* (1932), followed by the punning intertitle, "YOUNG GIRLS WITHOUT UNIFORM." In *Allemagne année 90 neuf zéro*, Godard becomes more and more the anthologist, and stages his contemporary live action sequences with almost off-hand simplicity. In contrast to *Nou-*

velle Vague, there are no tracking shots in the film; the sunlit splendor of the Swiss countryside has been replaced by the drab brown of the ruined East German state. Christophe Pollock's camerawork is both minimalist and forbidding; faces are never highlighted, much of the action takes place in half-light. There is no attempt here (and quite rightly) at conventional glamor. An intertitle, "THE DEATH OF DEATH," is followed by video-manipulated imagery appropriated from Sergei Eisenstein's *Alexander Nevsky* (1938). Lemmy is seen in a church, praying. The only light comes from a stained-glass window above him. He takes off his hat, looking at once terribly vulnerable and old, deprived of the "armor" of the secret agent's trade. The repeated intertitle "DEATH AND TRANSFIGURATION" signals another return to the faith for Godard, who now more than ever seems preoccupied with the cessation of his corporeal being. The bells of requiem toll on the soundtrack; an intertitle declares that we are witnessing the "END OF GERMANY."

Lemmy sits on a heap of discarded tractor tires, exhausted by his endless odyssey. A man pushing a car appears on the road nearby, followed by Don Quixote (Robert Wittmers) astride a donkey. Lemmy walks over and demands repeatedly, "Hey, you! Which way is the West?," but no answer is forthcoming. Don Quixote merely stares at Lemmy, saying nothing. In the background of the shot stands a forlorn windmill. A clip of the blow-torch torture sequence from Roberto Rossellini's *Roma Città aperta* (1945) is shown, again manipulated for maximum horrific effect through the use of slow-motion video. Other images culled from contemporary existence fill the screen. The deserted playground of a former state school for children; an electric tram snaking its way through the gray city streets in the afternoon; a woman stands on a bridge, staring at the waters below.

Footage of the victims of German concentration camps slowed down into an interminable video frame-by-frame agony of remembrance is intercut with staged color footage of an aging Adolf Hitler and Eva Braun. Shots of the East German subway system in 1990 are intercut with newsreel footage of the same locations during World War II. A soliloquy on the "murder of music" by contemporary culture ("It's only heard in elevators") is punctuated with scenes of swastika banners being thrown unceremoniously into a heap. In perhaps the film's most brutal editorial juxtaposition, the title "UFA presents," taken from the beginning of an actual UFA production (UFA, or Universum Film Aktien Gesellschaft, was the giant film corporation that dominated German film production), is followed by footage of a young Jewish woman in the freezing winter cold, obviously a victim of Hitler's war machine, followed by a brief clip from Fritz Lang's *Siegfried* (1924), in which Siegfried is struck down by a spear. A clip of Rossellini's 1947 film *Germania Anno Zero* (*Germany Year Zero*, the film which gives Godard's work its punning title) shows a young boy walking listlessly through the ruined streets of postwar Germany.

A clip from Lang's *Metropolis* (1927)—Maria with the children of the poor—is intercut with shots of a ravaged urban landscape. Heroic views of nineteenth-century statues give way to a shot of a young woman photographing a Courbet painting hanging on a museum wall; Godard immediately cuts to an old cinema image of a crashing wave that directly corresponds to Courbet's vision. In a house, a group of musicians, silhouetted against the winter light of several windows, practice a string quartet by Bach. Lemmy reappears, still demanding "Which way to the West?," as a close-up of Bach's signature briefly fills the screen.

In the final scene of the film, Lemmy is at last in the heart of the West, ensconced in a luxurious room of the Inter-Continental Berlin hotel. As he gazes out into the city from the balcony, a chorus of hotel workers greets him with military precision, chanting "Welcome to the West, Mr. Caution" in perfect unison. Lemmy turns to face them, and a female concierge abruptly blows her whistle several times. The chambermaids scurry off to make the bed and clean the bathroom, while Lemmy asks the bellboy for his suitcase.

But, as in *Alphaville*, no one will do anything without a tip. In 1965, Lemmy simply told the staff of the luxury hotel in *Alphaville* to "get lost" when they demanded a gratuity; now, he pays. One of the chambermaids helps Lemmy with his overcoat, as an old American film flickers on the television in the back of the shot. Another woman prepares Lemmy's bed, placing two volumes on the history of the Gestapo at the foot of the bed to elevate Lemmy's

194

FIGURE 43. Eddie Constantine (Lemmy Caution) and Claudia Michelson (Dora) in *Allemagne année 90 neuf zéro* (1991). Courtesy Noon Pictures.

feet, to help the aging secret agent's faltering blood circulation.

"So you, too, chose freedom?," Lemmy asks the young woman, as she tucks in the sheets of his bed. The woman looks up from her work, and stares at Lemmy impassively. "Work makes you free," she tells him, reciting the text inscribed on the entrance gates of the Nazi death camps. Then, with a slight smile of resignation, she returns to her task.

Allemagne année 90 neuf zéro is a film about loss, about the death of cinema, a film starring a relic of an earlier age who still pursues an outmoded profession. The same might be said of Godard. In recent interviews, Godard has prophesied the "death of cinema" with an air of neutral resignation, stating on one occasion that "the [cinema] projector will soon disappear" (Hartley, 17), and on another that "when [William Butler] Yeats said the center cannot hold, he was talking for himself, but it was true for the rest of us as well" (Sarris 1994, 89). Except for big-budget films, the cinema, as defined by more than one hundred years of production and exhibition, is undergoing a complete revolution. Theater attendance is down, even among the young. Video games and CD-ROM interactive programs proliferate. Sixteen millimeter film is all but dead as a production medium; universities, which used to depend on 16mm as the backbone of their film screening and production offerings, have switched to VHS video. The resultant degradation of the image (2,000 theoretical lines for the film frame versus 525 lines in conventional American television) is no longer an issue of concern for most academics, but Godard, although he works now in film and video, is unconvinced. "About every two or three years I like to see an old John Ford movie, and even on video you get some idea of what it *was* [emphasis mine], but if you look too closely, you begin to miss the real thing" (Sarris 1994, 88). The "real thing" is large screen theatrical film, but theatrical projection, as Godard has long recognized, is a thing of the past; in *Alphaville*, Godard parenthetically inserted a line which referred to the "cinema museums" of the future, where old films were still shown on a screen. In 1997, the future of 1965 has become the present.

The extraordinary complexity of *Allemagne année 90 neuf zéro* demonstrates that Godard in the 1990s is working toward a new vision of personal cinema, a cinema based co-equally on the

FIGURE 44. Eddie Constantine (Lemmy Caution) meets Don Quixote (Robert Wittmers) in *Allemagne année 90 neuf zéro* (1991). Courtesy Noon Pictures.

image and the word. Ever since his work in the late 1960s and early 1970s with Gorin and the other tangential members of the Dziga Vertov group, Godard has been obsessed with the contest between image and sound in film and video production. In *Allemagne année 90 neuf zéro*, Godard has hit upon a new strategy, creating a visual montage of stunning complexity, using his own material and an anthology of clips from the classical cinema, in juxtaposition with an equally dense soundtrack, composed of natural sound, voiceovers, scripts of old recordings (Dietrich, the Nazi "pop" songs), and classical music. Further, he has smoothly integrated film and video technology to create a visual fabric of dazzling richness and intensity. While *Je vous salue, Marie* is a remarkable achievement, the visuals for the film are resolutely simple, and the film relies on the intricate suture provided by the soundtrack's mix of disparate aural materials for much of its impact. With a brief "feature" length of sixty-two minutes, *Allemagne année 90 neuf zéro* is one of the most compact of Godard's later films, although surely its running time was at least in part dictated by the practical considerations of commercial broadcasting's rigidly defined time slots. Despite the numerous "quotations" of the film's visual track, giving *Allemagne année 90 neuf zéro* a visual density that resists multiple viewings, Godard refused to simplify the film's soundtrack, and this revolutionary blend of sounds won the Osello d'Oro award for achievement in sound at the 1991 Venice Film Festival.

If *Allemagne année 90 neuf zéro* represents a return to the principles of Eisensteinian/Vertovian dialectical montage, it also demonstrates that Godard has lost none of his political commitment as a filmmaker with the passing of the years. He is more subtle in his recent films, and less direct, preferring to provide a series of cultural allusions and cross-references to buttress his assertions, rather than resorting to the mere repetition of slogans, as he was wont to do in the days of *La Chinoise*. Godard remains profoundly suspicious of capitalism and all commercial enterprises, and even when he accepts a commission to do a film (as with *Puissance de la parole* or *Le Dernier Mot*), his vision remains entirely personal, and beyond compromise.

Proof of this was Godard and Miéville's brief sketch for *Contre l'oubli* (*Lest We Forget*), an anthology of politically committed shorts for Amnesty International, produced in 1992. Some thirty French filmmakers contributed to the project, including Chantal Akerman, Constantin Costa-Gavras, Claire Denis, René Allio, and many others in a group effort reminiscent of Godard's involvement with *Loin du Viêtnam* in 1967. The film decrees the use of torture and/or imprisonment to suppress political freedom of speech, an issue which is at the core of Godard's life as an artist.

Most recently, Godard has created a series of ambitious narratives, including *Hélas pour moi* (*Woe is Me*) (1993), based on the play *Amphitryon 38* by Jean Girardoux, and starring French film idol Gérard Depardieu. As discussed in the first chapter of this volume, Depardieu walked out on the project after three weeks of shooting on a six-week schedule (Sarris 1994, 89), leaving Godard to complete the film as best he could, but for a director who had survived the rigors of the *King Lear* shoot, even a major defection such as this was not an insurmountable obstacle. Nevertheless, the film has a fragmentary, hesitant air about it, and Depardieu seems distinctly uncomfortable in his role as Simon Donnadieu. No doubt Godard's improvisational working techniques posed something of a problem for Depardieu, who is much more at home in the narrative-dominated French commercial cinema. And Depardieu does not seem to be giving his entire energy to the project, nor does he seem willing to simply follow Godard's instructions, as Alain Delon did in *Nouvelle Vague*. *Hélas pour moi* looks lovely, thanks to Caroline Champetier's sumptuous cinematography, but ultimately fails to involve the audience.

Calling the film "gorgeous but dead-ended," Amy Taubin wrote that

> *Hélas pour moi* opens with an evocation of the father as the essence of history: "When my father's father's father had a difficult task to accomplish." This mock-commercial venture shot in and around a picturesque Swiss lakefront café stars Gérard Depardieu, who walks through his part, such as it is, looking as miserable as a beached whale. (1994a, 58)

while fellow *Village Voice* critic Jim Hoberman found the film

> inordinately male supremacist—although not without its humorous aspects. God, whose divine consciousness is rep-

FIGURE 45. *Hélas pour moi* (1993). Courtesy Cinema Parallel.

resented by the vomit-voiced croak of the computer from
Alphaville, crassly manifests himself amidst the placid
beauty of a perfect Europe. . . . Although blatantly producing
a movie about the ineffable, Godard has no compunction
about stopping short to ponder the way (for example) a bicy-
cle falls to earth. . . . Stately and fragmented, given to all
manner of sudden emotional outbursts, TV inserts and F-
stop flickers, *Hélas pour moi* is at once fast and slow, beautiful and infuriating, stupid and smart. (1994, 43)

And yet, *Hélas pour moi* has numerous adherents who find
the film both adventurous and sumptuously beautiful. Armond
White, in an essay in *Film Comment*, finds "*Hélas Pour Moi* . . .
concerned with making sense of the world, both the way an artist
will and an audience must. [In a key] f-stop scene . . . [the film's]
two plots—the playful modernization of the Amphitryon legend
and the filmmaker's parallel reconstruction of it—[. . .] converge,
like narratives in an epic poem, to produce one definitive, illu-
minating passage . . . we see a shot of blurred, out-of-focus points
of light slowly coming into focus, followed by a medium closeup
of a woman looking off screen, a lake behind her . . . as [cine-
matographer] Caroline Champetier's f-stop changes, this portrait
shot takes on a poetic quality that is determined solely by the
light" (White, 28). For White, the film is one of Godard's most
accomplished late works, and an essential and integral part of
the director's *ouevre*.
    With *JLG/JLG—autoportrait de décembre*, shot in 35mm
color, Godard created another hour-long television program, in
this instance a sort of autobiography of his life and work as a film
and video artist. In a number of respects, *JLG/JLG* resembles *Allemagne année 90 neuf zéro*, particularly in its use of clips from
other films, intercut with footage shot in and around Godard's
home in Switzerland in the winter of 1993. As Jim Hoberman
wrote in *The Village Voice*, "a goodly portion of *JLG/JLG* is
charged with death, absence, silence. . . . [H]oled up in his tidy
house in Rolle, Switzerland, Godard himself is his own elder, put-
tering with tapes, bent over his notebooks" ("His Life to Live,"
58); Godard's home has become a fortress of books and videotapes,
"a prison in which the caged artist feels at liberty" (Krauss, 160).

Not only the cinema but philosophical discourse itself has become hyperextended, overdetermined, exhausted by the repetition of its efforts to make the social grid intelligible or even tolerable. To quote Habermas, "At the end of the twentieth century too, philosophical thought appears withdrawn, cocooned in esotericism" (1994, 188). As Terrence Rafferty wrote, in *JLG/JLG*,

> The filmmaker, looking like a dishevelled, distracted old crank, rattles around in his dimly lit apartment and goes for solitary, bundled-up walks in the wintry landscape, with no apparent purpose except to sort through his mind's jumbled inventory of words and images and music. Everything he sees or hears seems to call up something from the past— a snippet of dialogue from a Nicholas Ray film, a few sentences of Dostoyevski, a snatch of melody from a Beethoven symphony. The memories bob unpredictably, almost randomly, to the surface of his consciousness, and vanish just as abruptly. Notebook entries flash past, just a word or two per page, and they have a similar wistful quality: each of the terse, allusive phrases, surrounded by whiteness, looks rather forlorn, like an island glimpsed briefly from the air and then left behind. (92)

There is something both ominous and melancholic about the misanthropic manner in which Godard presents himself in *JLG/JLG*, as a cinematic recluse cut off from contemporary society, at home only in the past.

Yet the wintry inner landscape of *JLG/JLG* did not occupy all of Godard's energy; at the same time that Godard was working on that project he also completed the next two sections of his ongoing *Histoire(s) Du Cinéma*, 2a and 2b. Screened on May 6, 1994 at the Museum of Modern Art in New York, the videotapes are a continuation of Godard's open-ended contemplation on the cinema/video process, mixing (in 2A) an interview with Godard by Serge Daney, along with a kaleidoscopic avalanche of archival material, blended together in a cacophonous and overpowering assault of image and sound.

In creating the chaotic continuity of the *Histoire(s)*, Godard seems to be echoing Bataille's profound anxiety when faced with

FIGURE 46. Jean-Luc Godard in *JLG/JLG* (1994). Courtesy Cinema Parallel.

the creation of a text, a text which cannot be new, but can only echo, all in which all order is arbitrary. "From one hour to the next, I become sick at the idea that I am writing, that I must pursue. Never do I have security, certainty. Continuity horrifies me. I persevere in disorder, loyal to the passions of which I really know nothing, which upset me in every sense" (117). Throughout the *Histoire(s)*, however, it is the power of the imagistic/iconic system created by the dominant Hollywood cinema that is most pervasive and powerful, because it constitutes an alternative reality complete unto itself, neither needing nor seeking outside referents. It possesses what Deleuze calls "the power of the false" (1989b, 21), the triumph of the quiescently manufactured image over the domain of the real. Most recently, Godard has continued the *Histoire(s)* videotapes with two additional episodes screened at numerous festivals throughout the world. Working on videotape as he does with this series of sound/image constructs, production costs are relatively inexpensive, and the resultant videos can be re-edited and/or re-structured at will as Godard sees fit.

In 1994, Godard created a 63-minute project for Aaron Spelling's World Vision production unit, *Les Enfants jouent à la russie* (*The Children Play Russian*), which was screened in the fall of 1994 as part of the third New York Video Festival at the Walter Reade Theater, a "side-bar" to the 32nd New York Film Festival. As described by Amy Taubin, in *Les enfants jouent à la russie*, "Godard sends up the actual situation [of the production]—a famous French director is hired by Hollywood to make a television program about Russia—by casting himself as Dostoyevsky's Idiot and refusing to set foot outside of France" (Taubin 1994b, 62). This iconoclastic effort was followed by the creation of an even more audacious project, *2 X 50 ans de cinéma français* (*2 X 50 Years of French Cinema*, 1995), conceived as a commission to create a film/video celebrating the centenary of French cinema, and the enduring heritage of France's contribution to the literature of film. Godard, seemingly unable to turn any new project down, so torrid is the current pace of his film/video production, accepted the invitation to contribute to the series, and the resulting hour-long videotape was co-directed by Godard and Anne-Marie Miéville, starring Michel Piccoli.

In a lecture on April 8, 1995, at Yale University, Colin Mac-Cabe, who executive-produced the program for the British Film Institute along with Bob Last, described the finished project as being entirely devoid of clips from classic French films (unlike the other films in the series), but rather centering on actor Michel Piccoli conducting interviews in a modern French hotel, asking various hotel staff members why the cinema is, in fact, dead. As the film progresses, Piccoli asks the hotel staff if they've ever heard of Arletty, or Jean Gabin, or other major figures from the Golden Age of French Cinema, but in every case, the employees profess complete ignorance. At length, Piccoli asks one staff member to name his favorite films. "*Beverly Hills Cop* and *Pulp Fiction*" the employee replies, thus effectively illustrating the video's despairing contention: cinema *is* dead. This program, produced by the British Film Institute as part of a series of television specials celebrating one hundred years of cinema (1895–1995), also features (among other programs) contributions by Nagisa Oshima on Japanese film, Stephen Frears on British cinema, and Martin Scorsese on the United States, but their individual programs are all fairly straightforward attempts to encapsulate various national cinemas. It is left to Godard to demonstrate that we are, in 1997, moving into a new era beyond the cinema; that, as Antonin Artaud has suggested, "masterpieces of the past are good for the past; they are not good for us" (1958, 74). Indeed, the very concept of theatrical projection may soon serve impracticable for a variety of security and/or societal reasons. As an anonymous writer in *The New York Times Magazine* commented on August 20, 1995,

> With theaters like this, who needs movies? The Sunrise Multiplex in Valley Stream, L.I., may be the movie house of the future. It has metal detectors and armed guards who search patrons. A recording reminds moviegoers that they are being filmed on closed-circuit TV. (15)

In light of this panopticonic theater of the future, Godard and Miéville's apocalyptic assertion in *2x50 ans de cinéma* is not far off the mark. As Amy Taubin summarized the video's position, the 100th anniversary of cinema is "nothing to celebrate because cinema is already dead" (1995, 54). Godard has become part of the past of cinema, part of its shared history, rather than part of whatever future the cinema (or CD-ROMs, interactive videos, the Internet, and other televisual products) might potentially possess. As such, Godard has become an archivist and historian, a collector of images and sounds from the literature of film, decrying the cultural loss that the death of cinema represents, but resigned, it seems, to the totality of this fact.

Asked recently how he would like to be remembered, Godard replied, "I haven't started thinking about that. . . . I don't think I've succeeded in making any really good films. There are moments, scenes, whole movements that sing. It has all added up to a cinema of sorts, even though I'm still learning my art" (Sarris 1994, 89). In January 1995, when the New York Film Critics Circle awarded Jean-Luc Godard the society's first ever career-achievement award. Unable to attend, Godard faxed his regrets to NYFCC chairman Armond White, noting that he had "too little good health, too big snow to the airport, and too few banknotes saved for the ticket" (Hoberman 1995c, 49), and suggesting that the award be sent "to the Bleecker Street Cinema" (which no longer exists), one of the pioneer film revival houses of New York City in the 1960s. In the late 1950s and early 1960s, Godard's black-and-white 35mm features cost approximately $100,000 each to produce; now, with the same four-to-six week schedule, using color, he spends an average of $1 million per film (Riding, 18). He remains as dedicated to the art of improvisation on the set as he does to the craft of image manipulation in the cutting room.

Looking to the future, Godard described his current method of production. "As in war, you have to improvise, but not in any old way. First you have to be aware what you're doing. You look at what you're doing, and you listen to what you're saying. Or perhaps you listen to what you see, and look at what you're hearing. . . . [T]hat's the New Wave" (Riding, 18). It's heartening to hear Godard use this term in such a relatively recent conversation; perhaps it is true, that for him, the cinema, while paradoxically dead, is still in its infancy. And characteristically, Godard remains suspicious of any attempts at canonization, insisting that "that's a perversion of the New Wave's idea of an auteur. Today, anyone is an auteur [which is certainly true in an era

when nearly everyone owns their own device for the instanta-
neous recording of sound and images, the Camcorder. It's society,
the producer, the distributor. They're the *auteur*. I am just the
worker, the builder" (Riding, 18). Godard also continues to be a
caustic moralist. In his statement to the New York Film Critics
Circle, Godard enumerated a number of regrets concerning his
career as a film and video artist, among them that:

> JLG was never able through his whole movie
>   maker/goer career to:
> Prevent M. Spielberg from rebuilding Auschwitz,
> Convince Mr. Ted Turner not to colorize past and
>   dear funny faces,
> To sentence M. Bill Gates for naming his bug's office
>   Rosebud,
> To compel New York Film Critics Circle not to forget
>   Shirley Clarke,
> To oblige Sony ex-Columbia Pictures to imitate Dan
>   Talbot/New Yorker Films when delivering
>   accounts.
> To force Oscar people to reward Abbas Kiarostami
>   instead of Kieslowski,
> To persuade M. Kubrick to screen Santiago Alvarez
>   shorts on Vietnam,
> To beg Ms. Keaton to read Bugsy Siegel's biography.
> To shoot *Contempt* with Sinatra and Novak,
> etc., etc. (Hoberman 1995c, 49)

He also remains deeply suspicious of attempts to canonize his
work or person, or to pay him undue homage. In his interview
with filmmaker Hal Hartley, Godard is both modest and
approachable, sympathizing with Hartley's miniscule budget on
his 1990 film *Trust*, and advising Hartley to build his living
expenses into the budget of his films, as he does ("[b]ecause my
movies are not successful, they are not shown. So I make a living
from the budget" [16]), and treating Hartley with respect (albeit
paternally) as a fellow filmmaker. When dealing with professional
financiers, critics, producers or interviewers, Godard is much
less obliging;

For a long time, I tried to make a film in the United States but never succeeded. I'd meet people, and they'd say, "Very honored," and shake my hand; that's all. So I'd say, "If that's true, at least give me $10." The only one who did was Mel Brooks. "Oh, yes," he said, and gave me $10. (Riding, 18)

It seems significant to me that Brooks is the only one who got the gist of Godard's practical joke: fame is worthless without money when one is a filmmaker, as the last years of Orson Welles so tragically proved.

For the history of cinema is ultimately a tragedy, because "for all its splendor, this imperial road of the movies 'leads nowhere'" (Klawans, 644). Cinema is dead, television is dying, the internet promises us an endless inventory of facts, lies, names, dates, notions, theories, images and sounds; we can now create *Histoire(s)* of our own. Perhaps what Godard bemoans more than anything else in his latest work is not only the death of cinema, and his own mortality, but also the death of the concept of *auteurism* as a privileged discourse, in which the spectator passively watches constructs created by an other for an unknown and unknowable audience.

As Stuart Klawans writes, one has "to watch *Histoire(s) du cinéma* as if it were a film, letting it wash over you, leaving you frustrated and rapt, dazzled and impatient . . . [the] good old days are gone, and they were bad, anyway. . . . [Godard has] failed to revolutionize either the real world or the movie world" (644). I'd agree with all of Klawans's words except his final hypothesis, for it seems to me that Godard, Miéville, and Gorin, working alone and/or together over the span of the past four decades, have pushed the cinema past the point of exhaustion to collapse, to decay, to the realm of the undead, the iridescent half-life of telegenic visual debris. All narratives have been told, all yet remain to be told; all images have been recorded, and yet still seek to be entombed within the cinema/video sarcophagus. All that remains is trench work, the juxtaposition of sound and image to create new self-referential building-blocks leading to a bridge across the *mise en abyme* of time and memory. Loss is the domain of the cinema, and death. Cocteau held that "film documents death at work," and this, finally, is the "accursed share" of the cinema.

Godard and his collaborators started out to create a new world of image signs and systems, and to an extent, they succeeded. Their works span a narrow band of consciousness, and reach an ever-more-limited audience, but Godard has revolutionized the cinema nevertheless, by moving it past the realm of the living into the zone of the living dead.

Godard now reanimates images from the past, slows them down or speeds them up, freezes them, fragments them, splinters the shards of their significatory burden in front of our eyes into a language of maximum access, maximum overload. Artificially jump-started, these sounds and images of the past sweep past our eyes and ears to create a void of overdetermined space, in direct contrast to the pared-down essentialism of *British Sounds*. Godard once wanted to make everything simple, to strip away or pare down until his discourse was simultaneously unavoidable and unmistakable. Now, Godard jumbles as much as he possibly can into every frame, like a manic collagist with a remote control TV selector firmly in the grip of his hand. If we are, as Godard suggests, in the last days of cinema, it may be because the cinema has lived out (and outlived) its role as the dominant image replicator of waking dreams for those who choose to sleep when they are awake.

Now, perhaps, we are overtaking the control of the cinema with our own library of words, sounds, and images (if we care to), as the corporate monolith of the televised signifier (Disney purchases ABC; Westinghouse purchases CBS—vertical and horizontal integration strategies of the 1990s) becomes larger and larger until, perhaps, it collapses back in on itself, crushed under the unbearable weight of its own stranglehold on those wholly passive viewers who persist in staring at the theater or television screen, leaving a black hole in the universe of image production/distribution/exhibition, with only the films and tapes of the past century to mark their absence. The cinema is dead, yet it lives, and indeed the archival retrieval now goes on at an unprecedented pace, fueled by the ceaseless empty space of cable television, the hours in the day, the channel capability of fiber optic television systems, the need for diversion in a collapsing society. Godard, in his films and videos, has now become the custodian of our shared dream of the cinema, where once he had sought the destruction of the old, and the concomitant creation of the new. The new has become the old, and yet it remains ever new, repackaged, scanned, transferred to tape or disseminated through the Internet, available to all without a context, without a past. There is no past, no present, and only a future for any system of image encoding that teaches us to embrace the flickering film/video frame, hang on to every succeeding image until it fades from consciousness, to live in the eternal moment when an image is re-presented to the viewer, without knowledge of origin or originator. Perhaps this is the work that Godard set out to do after all.

Perhaps only when our words and deeds are finite and comprehensible within the domain of a medium that will not let us rest will we understand the scope of Godard's accomplishment. He has transformed the cinema from a bourgeois medium of popular entertainment into a zone of study, reflection, and renewal. It is this "eternal return" that we always seek in the cinema, a harbor from the actual into the world of the constructed, a place of stasis amid constant change. It is this domain in which Jean-Luc Godard has worked, either as theoretician or artist (often simultaneously) for most of his life, and he knows the borders of his chosen territory instinctively and intuitively. As Godard enters the final phase of his life and work, there can be no doubt that he has discharged the duties of his domain brilliantly. He has reconfigured our concept of the cinema, just as he set out to do, from his earliest reviews in *Cahiers du Cinéma*. "Godard's importance," according to Peter Brook, "is that he gives cinema not just mobility of camera but mobility of thought" (in Perez, 210). Godard has created a cinema that offers us the spectacle of ourselves, our actions and their consequences, our vanities, naive assumptions, and our continual quest for a correlation between the deed and the word in our lives. If the sweep and range of his accomplishment are breathtaking, the intensity of his attack (particularly in his recent works) is proof that Godard will continue to create new images, and recycle old ones, as long as the cinematic apparatus survives. As his constructs become ever more involved and complicated, Godard anticipates the collapse of the cinema by hurriedly surveying the ruins that remain. This is the work with which he began, and the work with which he concludes his career. We have been liberated from the tyranny of the moving image by the onslaught of Godard's assault on our senses.

Our perception of the cinema, and of our corporeal existence, has been materially, and permanently, altered because of this.

As Laura Mulvey recently observed,

> the Hollywood studio system film . . . is really a thing of the past—I mean, it's like studying the Renaissance. But at the same time I think perhaps like the Renaissance, it's something that doesn't go away and still stays a source of imagery and myths and motifs. . . .
>
> Although we could say that the studio system is dead and buried, and that Hollywood cinema, however very powerful it is today, works from very different economic and production structures, at the same time, our culture—MTV images, advertising images, or to take a big obvious example, Madonna—all recycle the images of the old Hollywood cinema, all of which have become points of reference, almost as though they've become myths in their own right, which are then taken over, absorbed, and recycled every day in the different media. (Suárez and Manglis, 7)

Godard thus belongs to both the old and the new, the living and the dead, the sign and the signifier, the domain of the creator and the realm of the museum-guide. Godard cannot stop reevaluating the images that shaped his existence, and shape ours, because if "philosophy is a discourse and all discourse is a response to a call or invitation from something other, then philosophy dies/ends only with the death, or end, of the other" (Oliver, 198). The "other" of the cinema has died, and yet it can still be called forth, if only to remember the fact of its previous existence. As long as the muse of cinema can be summoned, even as a phantom, Godard will continue his work. Perhaps Foucault best summarizes Godard's current quest when he states that "the dispersion of language is linked, in fact, in a fundamental way, with the archaeological event we may designate as the disappearance of Discourse. To discover the vast play of language contained once more within a single space might be just as decisive a leap towards a wholly new form of thought as to draw to a close a mode of knowing constituted during the previous century" (1973, 307).

FILMOGRAPHY,
1954–1995

●

1. **OPÉRATION BÉTON** (Actua-Films, Geneva, 1954)
Producer: Jean-Luc Godard
Director: Jean-Luc Godard
Script: Jean-Luc Godard
Director of Photography: Adrien Porchet
Editing: Jean-Luc Godard
Music: Handel
       Bach
Format: B/W, 35mm
Running Time: 17 minutes

2. **UNE FEMME COQUETTE** (Jean-Luc Godard, Geneva, 1955)
Producer: Jean-Luc Godard
Director: Jean-Luc Godard
Script: Hans Lucas (Jean-Luc Godard), based on the story *Le Signe*
       by Guy de Maupassant
Director of Photography: Hans Lucas (Jean-Luc Godard)
Editing: Hans Lucas (Jean-Luc Godard)
Music: Bach
Cast: Maria Lysandre (The Woman)
      Roland Tolma (The Man)
      Jean-Luc Godard (The Client)
Format: B/W, 16mm
Running Time: 10 minutes

3. **TOUS LES GARÇONS S'APPELLENT PATRICK**
Alternative Title: Charlotte et Véronique (Les Films de la Pléiade,
      Paris, 1957)

American Title: *Every Boy Is Called Patrick*
British Title: *All Boys Are Called Patrick*
Producer: Pierre Braunberger
Director: Jean-Luc Godard
Script: Eric Rohmer
Director of Photography: Michel Latouche
Editing: Cécile Decugis
Music: Beethoven
　　　　Pierre Monsigny
Sound: Jacques Maumont
Cast: Jean-Claude Brialy (Patrick)
　　　Nicole Berger (Véronique)
　　　Anne Colette (Charlotte)
Format: B/W, 35mm
Running Time: 21 minutes

4. **UNE HISTOIRE D'EAU** (Les Films de la Pléiade, Paris, 1958)
English Title: *A Story of Water*
Producer: Pierre Braunberger
Production Manager: Roger Fleytoux
Directors: François Truffaut
　　　　　Jean-Luc Godard
Script: Jean-Luc Godard
Director of Photography: Michel Latouche
Editing: Jean-Luc Godard
Sound: Jacques Maumont
Cast: Jean-Claude Brialy (The Young Man)
　　　Caroline Dim (The Girl)
　　　Jean-Luc Godard (Narrator)
Format: B/W, 35mm
Running Time: 18 minutes

5. **CHARLOTTE ET SON JULES** (Les Films de la Pléiade, Paris, 1959)
British Title: *Charlotte and Her Boy Friend*
Producer: Pierre Braunberger
Director: Jean-Luc Godard
Script: Jean-Luc Godard
Director of Photography: Michel Latouche
Editing: Cécile Decugis
Music: Pierre Monsigny

Sound: Jacques Maumont
Cast: Jean-Paul Belmondo [voice dubbed by Jean-Luc Godard]
(Jean)
Anne Colette (Charlotte)
Gérard Blain (Charlotte's Friend)
Format: B/W, 35mm
Running Time: 20 minutes

6. À BOUT DE SOUFFLE (Georges de Beauregard/Société Nouvelle
de Cinéma, Paris, 1959)
English Title: *Breathless*
Producer: Georges de Beauregard
Director: Jean-Luc Godard
Assistant Director: Pierre Rissient
Script: Jean-Luc Godard. Based on an idea by François Truffaut
Director of Photography: Raoul Coutard
Camera Operator: Claude Beausoleil
Editing: Cécile Decugis
Lila Herman
Music: Martial Solal
Mozart
Sound: Jacques Maumont
Cast: Jean-Paul Belmondo (Michel Poiccard alias Laszlo Kovacs)
Jean Seberg (Patricia Franchini)
Daniel Boulanger (Police Inspector)
Jean-Pierre Melville (Parvulesco)
Liliane Robin (Minouche)
Henri-Jacques Huet (Antonio Berrutti)
Van Doude (The Journalist)
Claude Mansard (Claudius Mansard)
Michel Fabre (Plain-clothes Policeman)
Jean-Luc Godard (An Informer)
Jean Domarchi (A Drunk)
Richard Balducci (Tolmatchoff)
Roger Hanin (Carl Zumbach)
Jean-Louis Richard (A Journalist)
André-S. Labarth
Jacques Siclier
Michel Mourlet
Jean Douchet
Philippe de Broca

Guido Orlando
Jacques Serguine
Louiguy
Virginie Ullmann
Émile Villion
José Bénazéraf
Madame Paul
Raymond Ravanbaz
Format: B/W, 35mm
Running Time: 90 minutes

7. **LE PETIT SOLDAT** (Georges de Beauregard/Société Nouvelle de
   Cinéma, Paris, 1960)
English Title: *The Little Soldier*
Producer: Georges de Beauregard
Director: Jean-Luc Godard
Assistant Director: Francis Cognany
Script: Jean-Luc Godard
Director of Photography: Raoul Coutard
Camera Operator: Michel Latouche
Editing: Agnès Guillemot
        Nadine Marquand
        Lila Herman
Music: Maurice Leroux
Sound: Jacques Maumont
Cast: Michel Subor (Bruno Forestier)
       Anna Karina (Véronica Dreyer)
       Henri-Jacques Huet (Jacques)
       Paul Beauvais (Paul)
       Laszlo Szabo (Laszlo)
       Georges de Beauregard (Activist Leader)
       Jean-Luc Godard (Bystander at railway station)
       Gilbert Edard
Format: B/W, 35mm
Running Time: 88 minutes

8. **UNE FEMME EST UNE FEMME** (Rome-Paris Films, Paris, 1961)
English Title: *A Woman Is a Woman*
Producers: Georges de Beauregard
           Carlo Ponti
Production Manager: Philippe Dussart

Director: Jean-Luc Godard
Assistant Director: Francis Cognany
Script: Jean-Luc Godard. Based on an idea by Geneviève Cluny
Director of Photography: Raoul Coutard (Techniscope) (35mm)
Color Process: Eastman Color
Editing: Agnès Guillemot
        Lila Herman
Music: Michel Legrand
Song "Chanson d'Angéla": Michel Legrand
                        Jean-Luc Godard
Sound: Guy Villette
Cast: Jean-Paul Belmondo (Alfred Lubitsch)
      Anna Karina (Angéla)
      Jean-Claude Brialy (Émile Récamier)
      Marie Dubois (Suzanne)
      Nicole Paquin (1st Prostitute)
      Marion Sarraut (2nd Prostitute)
      Jeanne Moreau (Woman in bar)
      Catherine Demongeot
Format: Color, Techniscope, 35mm
Running Time: 84 minutes

9. **LA PARESSE** (sketch in *Les Sept Péchés capitaux*) (Les Films
   Gibe/Franco-London Films, Paris/Titanus, Rome, 1961)
English Title: *Sloth* (in *The Seven Capital Sins*)
Production Manager: Jean Lavie
Director: Jean-Luc Godard
Assistant Director: Marin Karmitz
Script: Jean-Luc Godard
Director of Photography: Henri Decaë (Dyaliscope)
Camera Operator: Jean-Paul Schwartz
Editing: Jacques Gaillard
Music: Michel Legrand
Sound: Jean-Claude Marchetti
       Jean Labussière
Cast: Eddie Constantine (Himself)
      Nicole Mirel (The Starlet)
Format: B/W, 35mm
Running Time: 15 minutes

10. **VIVRE SA VIE** (Films de la Pléiade, Paris, 1962)
British Title: *It's My Life/My Life to Live*

Producer: Pierre Braunberger
Production Manager: Roger Fleytoux
Director: Jean-Luc Godard
Assistant Directors: Bernard Toublanc-Michel
                    Jean-Paul Savignac
Script: Jean-Luc Godard. Documentation from *Où en est la
    prostitution?* by Marcel Sacotte
Director of Photography: Raoul Coutard
Camera Operators: Claude Beausoleil
                 Charles Bitsch
Editing: Agnès Guillemot
     Lila Lakshmanan
Music: Michel Legrand
Song "Ma môme, elle joue pas les starlettes": Jean Ferrat
                                 Pierre Frachet
Sound: Guy Villette
      Jacques Maumont
Cast: Anna Karina (Nana Kleinfrankenheim)
     Sady Rebbot (Raoul)
     André-S. Labarthe (Paul)
     Guylaine Schlumberger (Yvette)
     Brice Parain (The Philosopher)
     Peter Kassowitz [voice dubbed by Jean-Luc Godard]
        (Young Man)
     Dimitri Dinoff (Dimitri)
     Monique Messine (Elizabeth)
     Gérard Hoffmann (Man to whom Nana is sold)
     Gilles Quéant (Client)
     Paul Pavel (The Photographer)
     Eric Schlumberger (Luigi)
     Marcel Charton (Policeman at typewriter)
     Laszlo Szabo (Wounded man who enters bar)
     Gisèle Hauchecorne (Concierge)
     Odile Geoffroy (Barmaid)
     Jacques Florency (Man in cinema)
     Jean Ferrat (Man at jukebox who watches Nana)
     Henri Atal (Arthur)
     Jean-Paul Savignac (Young Soldier in bar)
     Mario Botti (The Italian)
Format: B/W, 35mm
Running Time: 85 minutes

11. **LE NOUVEAU MONDE** (sketch in *RoGoPaG*) (Arco
    Film/Cineriz, Rome, Lyre Film, Paris, 1962)
Producer: Alfredo Bini
Production Manager: Yves Laplache
Director: Jean-Luc Godard
Script: Jean-Luc Godard
Director of Photography: Jean Rabier
Editing: Agnès Guillemot
          Lila Lakshmanan
Music: Beethoven
Sound: Hérvé
Cast: Alexandra Stewart (Alexandra)
      Jean-Marc Bory (The Narrator)
      Jean-André Fieschi
      Michel Delahaye
Format: B/W, 35mm
Running Time: 20 minutes

12. **LES CARABINIERS** (Rome-Paris Films, Paris/Laetitia, Rome,
    1963)
American Title: *The Riflemen*
British Title: *The Soldiers*
Producers: Georges de Beauregard
           Carlo Ponti
Director: Jean-Luc Godard
Assistant Directors: Charles Bitsch
                     Jean-Paul Savignac
Script: Jean-Luc Godard
        Jean Gruault
        Roberto Rossellini. Based on the play *I Carabinieri* by
            Benjamino Joppolo, adapted into French by Jacques
            Audiberti.
Director of Photography: Raoul Coutard
Camera Operator: Claude Beausoleil
Editing: Agnès Guillemot
         Lila Lakshmanan
Art Director: Jean-Jacques Fabre
Music: Philippe Arthuys
Sound: Jacques Maumont, Hortion
Cast: Marino Masé (Ulysse)
      Albert Juross (Michel-Ange)

Geneviève Galéa (Vénus)
Catherine Ribéro (Cléopâtre)
Gérard Poirot (1st Carabinier)
Jean Brassat (2nd Carabinier)
Alvaro Gheri (3rd Carabinier)
Barbet Schroeder (Car Salesman)
Odile Geoffroy (Young Communist Girl)
Roger Coggio and Pascale Audret (The Couple in the car)
Catherine Durante (Heroine of film-within-film)
Jean Gruault ("Bébé's" Father)
Jean-Louis Comolli (Soldier with the fish)
Wladimir Faters (Revolutionary)
Jean Monsigny (Soldier)
Gilbert Servien (Soldier)
Format: B/W, 35mm
Running Time: 80 minutes

13. **LE GRAND ESCROC** (sketch for *Les Plus Belles Escroqueries du monde*) (Ulysse Productions, Paris/Primex Films, Marseille/Vides, Rome/Toho, Tokyo Caesar Film, Amsterdam, 1963)
Producer: Pierre Roustang
Production Manager: Philippe Dussart
Director: Jean-Luc Godard
Assistant Director: Charles Bitsch
Script: Jean-Luc Godard
Director of Photography: Raoul Coutard (FranScope)
Editing: Agnès Guillemot
        Lila Lakshmanan
Music: Michel Legrand
Sound: Hervé
Narrator: Jean-Luc Godard
Cast: Jean Seberg (Patricia Leacock)
      Charles Denner (The Swindler)
      Laszlo Szabo (Police Inspector)
Format: B/W, 35mm
Running Time: 25 minutes

14. **LE MÉPRIS** (Rome-Paris Films/Films Concordia, Paris/Compagnia Cinematografica Champion, Rome, 1963)
English Title: *Contempt*

Italian Title: *Il Meprezzo* ("mistrust")
Producers: Georges de Beauregard
              Carlo Ponti
              Joseph E. Levine
Production Managers: Philippe Dussart
                        Carlo Lastricati
Director: Jean-Luc Godard
Assistant Director: Charles Bitsch
Script: Jean-Luc Godard. Based on the novel *Il Disprezzo* by
     Alberto Moravia
Director of Photography: Raoul Coutard (FranScope)
Color Process: Technicolor
Editing: Agnès Guillemot
         Lila Lakshmanan
Music: Georges Delerue (Italian version: Piero Piccioni)
Costumes: Janine Autre
Sound: William Sivel
Cast: Brigitte Bardot (Camille Javal)
      Michel Piccoli (Paul Javal)
      Jack Palance (Jeremy Prokosch)
      Fritz Lang (Himself)
      Giorgia Moll (Francesca Vanini)
      Jean-Luc Godard (Assistant Director)
      Linda Veras (A Siren)
Format: Color, 35mm
Running Time: 103 minutes (U.S.); 100 minutes (France); 84
     minutes (Italy)

15. **BANDE À PART** (Anouchka Films/Orsay Films, Paris, 1964)
British Title: *The Outsiders*
American Title: *Band of Outsiders*
Production Manager: Philippe Dussart
Director: Jean-Luc Godard
Assistant Director: Jean-Paul Savignac
Script: Jean-Luc Godard. Based on the novel *Fool's Gold* by
     Dolores and Bert Hitchens
Director of Photography: Raoul Coutard
Camera Operator: Georges Liron
Editing: Agnès Guillemot
         Françoise Collin
Music: Michel Legrand

Sound: René Levert
    Antoine Bonfanti
Narrator: Jean-Luc Godard
Cast: Anna Karina (Odile)
      Claude Brasseur (Arthur)
      Sami Frey (Franz)
      Louisa Colpeyn (Madame Victoria)
      Danièle Girard (English Teacher)
      Ernest Menzer (Arthur's Uncle)
      Chantal Darget (Arthur's Aunt)
      Michèle Seghers (Pupil)
      Claude Makovski (Pupil)
      Georges Staquet (Légionnaire)
      Michel Delahaye (Doorman at language school)
Format: B/W, 35mm
Running Time: 95 minutes

16. **UNE FEMME MARIÉE** (Anouchka Films/Orsay Films, Paris, 1964)
American Title: *The Married Woman*
British Title: *A Married Woman*
Production Manager: Philippe Dussart
Director: Jean-Luc Godard
Assistant Directors: Claude Othin-Girard
                     Jean-Pierre Léaud
                     Hélène Kalouguine
Script: Jean-Luc Godard
Director of Photography: Raoul Coutard
Camera Operator: Georges Liron
Editing: Agnès Guillemot
      Françoise Collin
Art Director: Henri Nogaret
Music: Extracts from Beethoven's quartets nos. 7, 9, 10, 14, and 15
Jazz Music: Claude Nougaro
Song "Quand le film est trist": J. D. Loudermilk
                              G. Aber
                              L. Morisse
Sung by: Sylvie Vartan
Sound: Antoine Bonfanti
      René Levert
      Jacques Maumont

Cast: Macha Méril (Charlotte Giraud)
       Bernard Noël (Robert, the Lover)
       Philippe Leroy (Pierre, the Husband)
       Roger Leenhardt (Himself)
       Rita Maiden (Madame Céline)
       Chris Tophe (Nicolas)
       Margaret Le-Van and Véronique Duval (Two girls in
           swimming-pool bar)
Format: B/W, 35mm
Running Time: 95 minutes

17. ALPHAVILLE, UNE ÉTRANGE AVENTURE DE LEMMY CAUTION (Chaumiane, Paris/Filmstudio, Rome, 1965)

Producer: André Michelin
Production Manager: Philippe Dussart
Director: Jean-Luc Godard
Assistant Directors: Charles Bitsch
                    Jean-Paul Savignac
                    Hélène Kalouguine
Script: Jean-Luc Godard
Director of Photography: Raoul Coutard
Camera Operator: Georges Liron
Editing: Agnès Guillemot
Music: Paul Misraki
Sound: René Levert
Cast: Eddie Constantine (Lemmy Caution)
       Anna Karina (Natacha von Braun)
       Akim Tamiroff (Henri Dickson)
       Howard Vernon (Professor Léonard Nosferatu, alias von
           Braun)
       Laszlo Szabo (Chief Engineer)
       Michel Delahaye (von Braun's Assistant)
       Jean-André Fieschi (Professor Heckell)
       Jean-Louis Comolli (Professor Jeckell)
Format: B/W, 35mm
Running Time: 98 minutes

18. MONTPARNASSE-LEVALLOIS (sketch in *Paris vu par . . .*)
(Les Films du Losange/Barbet Schroeder, Paris, 1965)
British Title: *Six in Paris*
Producer: Barbet Schroeder

Associate Producer: Patrick Bauchau
Director: Jean-Luc Godard
Script: Jean-Luc Godard
Director of Photography: Albert Maysles
Color Process: 16mm Ektachrome, blown up to Eastman Color
        35mm print
Editing: Jacqueline Raynal
Sound: René Levert
Cast: Johanna Shimkus (Monika)
     Philippe Hiquily (Ivan)
     Serge Davri (Roger)
Format: Color, 35mm
Running Time: 18 minutes

19. **PIERROT LE FOU** (Rome-Paris Films, Paris/Dino de Laurentiis
   Cinematografica, Rome, 1965)
Producer: Georges de Beauregard
Production Manager: René Demoulin
Director: Jean-Luc Godard
Assistant Directors: Philippe Fourastié
                   Jean-Pierre Léaud
Script: Jean-Luc Godard. Based on the novel *Obsession* by Lionel
   White
Director of Photography: Raoul Coutard (Techniscope)
Color Process: Eastman Color
Camera Operator: Georges Liron
Editing: Françoise Collin
Art Director: Pierre Guffroy
Music: Antoine Duhamel
Songs "Ma Ligne de Chance" and "Jamais je ne t'ai dit que je
   t'aimerai toujours": Antoine Duhamel, Bassiak
Sound: René Levert
Cast: Jean-Paul Belmondo (Ferdinand)
     Anna Karina (Marianne)
     Dirk Sanders (Marianne's Brother)
     Raymond Devos (The Man on the pier)
     Graziella Galvani (Ferdinand's Wife)
     Roger Dutoit (Gangster)
     Hans Meyer (Gangster)
     Jimmy Karoubi (Dwarf)
     Christa Nell (Mme. Staquet)

Pascal Aubier (2nd Brother)
Pierre Hanin (3rd Brother)
Princess Aicha Abidir (Herself)
Samuel Fuller (Himself)
Alexis Poliakoff (Sailor)
Laszlo Szabo (Political Exile from Santo Domingo)
Jean-Pierre Léaud (Young Man in cinema)
Format: Color, 35mm
Running Time: 110 minutes

20. **MASCULIN FÉMININ** (Anouchka Films/Argos-Films,
    Paris/Svensk Filmindustri/Sandrews, Stockholm, 1966)
English Title: *Masculine Feminine*
Production Manager: Philippe Dussart
Director: Jean-Luc Godard
Assistant Directors: Bernard Toublanc-Michel
                    Jacques Barratier
Script: Jean-Luc Godard. Based on two stories, *La Femme de Paul*
    and *Le Signe* by Guy de Maupassant.
Director of Photography: Willy Kurant
Editing: Agnès Guillemot
Music: Francis Lai
Sound: René Levert
Cast: Jean-Pierre Léaud (Paul)
      Chantal Goya (Madeleine)
      Catherine-Isabelle Dupont (Catherine)
      Marlène Jobert (Elizabeth)
      Michel Debord (Robert)
      Birger Malmsten (The Man in film-within-the-film)
      Eva Britt Strandberg (The Woman in film-within-the-film)
      Brigitte Bardot and Antoine Bourseiller (Couple rehearsing
          play in café)
      Chantal Darget (Woman in Métro)
      Elsa Leroy ("Mademoiselle 19 Ans")
      Françoise Hardy (Friend of American officer in car)
Format: B/W, 35mm
Running Time: 110 minutes

21. **MADE IN U.S.A.** (Rome-Paris Films/Anouchka
    Films/S.E.P.I.C., Paris, 1966)
Producer: Georges de Beauregard

Production Manager: René Demoulin
Director: Jean-Luc Godard
Assistant Directors: Charles Bitsch
       Claude Bakka
       Jean-Pierre Léaud
       Philippe Pouzenc
Script: Jean-Luc Godard, based on the novel *The Jugger* (*Rien dans le coffre*) by Richard Stark
Director of Photography: Raoul Coutard (Techniscope)
Color Process: Eastman Color
Camera Operator: Georges Liron
Editing: Agnès Guillemot
Music: Beethoven
   Schumann
Sound: René Levert
   Jacques Maumont
Cast: Anna Karina (Paula Nelson)
   Laszlo Szabo (Richard Widmark)
   Jean-Pierre Léaud (Donald Siegel)
   Yves Alfonso (David Goodis)
   Ernest Menzer (Edgar Typhus)
   Jean-Claude Bouillon (Inspector Aldrich)
   Kyoko Kosaka (Doris Mizoguchi)
   Marianne Faithfull (Herself)
   Claude Bakka (Man with Marianne Faithfull)
   Philippe Labro (Himself)
   Rémo Forlani (Workman in bar)
   Marc Dudicourt (Barman)
   Jean-Pierre Biesse (Richard Nixon)
   Sylvain Godet (Robert MacNamara)
   Alexis Poliakoff (Man with notebook and red telephone)
   Eliane Giovagnoli (Dentist's Assistant)
   Roger Scipion (Dr. Korvo)
   Danièle Palmero (Hotel Chambermaid)
   Rita Maiden (Woman who gives Paula information)
   Isabelle Pons (Provincial Journalist)
   Philippe Pouzenc (Policeman)
   Fernand Coquet (Billposter)
   Miguel (Dentist)
   Annie Guégan (Girl in bandages)
   Marika Perioli (Girl with dog)

Jean-Philippe Nierman (Note-taking policeman)
Charles Bitsch (Taxi-driver)
Daniel Bart (Policeman)
Jean-Luc Godard (Voice of Richard Politzer)
Format: Color, 35mm
Running Time: 90 minutes

22. **DEUX OU TROIS CHOSES QUE JE SAIS D'ELLE** (Anouchka
    Films/Argos-Films/Les Films du Carrosse/Parc Film, Paris,
    1966)
Production Manager: Philippe Senné
English Title: *Two or Three Things I Know about Her*
Director: Jean-Luc Godard
Assistant Directors: Charles Bitsch
                     Isabelle Pons
Script: Jean-Luc Godard. Suggested by an investigative report by
        Catherine Vimenet published in *Le Nouvel Observateur*
Director of Photography: Raoul Coutard (Techniscope)
Color Process: Eastman Color
Camera Operator: Georges Liron
Editing: Françoise Collin
         Chantal Delattre
Music: Beethoven
Sound: René Levert
       Antoine Bonfanti
Narrator: Jean-Luc Godard
Cast: Marina Vlady (Juliette Janson)
       Anny Duperey (Marianne)
       Roger Montsoret (Robert Janson)
       Jean Narboni (Roger)
       Christophe Bourseiller (Christophe)
       Marie Bourseiller (Solange)
       Raoul Lévy (John Bogus)
       Joseph Gehrard (Monsieur Gérard)
       Helena Bielicic (Girl in bath)
       Robert Chevassu (Electricity Meter-reader)
       Yves Beneyton (Long-haired Youth)
       Jean-Pierre Laverne (The Writer)
       Blandine Jeanson (The Student)
       Claude Miler (Bouvard)
       Jean-Patrick Lebel (Pécuchet)

Juliet Berto (Girl who talks to Robert)
Anna Manga (Woman in basement)
Benjamin Rosette (Man in basement)
Helen Scott (Woman at pin-ball machine)
Format: Color, 35mm
Running Time: 95 minutes

23. **ANTICIPATION, OU L'AMOUR EN L'AN 2,000** (Sketch in *Le
Plus Vieux Métier du monde, ou l'amour à travers les âges*)
(Francoriz Films/Les Films Gibé, Paris/Rialto Films,
Berlin/Rizzoli Films, Rome, 1967)
English Title: *The Oldest Profession*
Producer: Joseph Bergholz
Director: Jean-Luc Godard
Assistant Director: Charles Bitsch
Script: Jean-Luc Godard
Director of Photography: Pierre Lhomme
Color Process: Eastman Color
Editing: Agnès Guillemot
Music: Michel Legrand
Cast: Jacques Charrier (John Dmitrios)
      Marilù Tolo (1st Prostitute—Physical Love)
      Anna Karina (Eléonor Roméovitch—Sentimental Love)
      Jean-Pierre Léaud (Bellboy)
      Daniel Bart
      Jean-Patrick Lebel
Format: Color, 35mm
Running Time: 20 minutes

24. **CAMÉRA-OEIL** (Sequence in *Loin du Viêtnam*) (S.L.O.N.,
1967)
English Title of Godard's Episode: *Film Eye*
Directors of *Loin du Vietnam*: Alain Resnais
                                William Klein
                                Joris Ivens
                                Agnès Varda [episode not
                                    included]
                                Claude Lelouch
                                Jean-Luc Godard
Organisers: Jacqueline Meppiel
            Andrea Haran

Principal Collaborators
on *Loin du Viêtnam*:   Michèle Ray
                           Roger Pic
                           K. S. Karol
                           Marceline Loriday
                           François Maspero
                           Chris Marker
                           Jacques Sternberg
                           Jean Lacoutre
                           Willy Kurant
                           Jean Bosty
                           Kieu Tham
                           Denis Clairval
                           Ghislain Cloquet
                           Bernard Zitzerman
                           Alain Levent
                           Théo Robichet
                           Antoine Bonfanti
                           Harold Maury
                           Claire Grunstein
                           Alain Franchet
                           Didier Beaudet
                           Florence Malraux
                           Marie-Louise Guinet
                           Roger de Menestrol
                           Ragnar
                           Jean Ravel
                           Colette Leloup
                           Eric Pluet
                           Albert Jurgenson
                           Ethel Blum
                           Michèle Bouder
                           Christian Quinson
                           Jean Larivière
                           Maurice Carrel
                           Bernard Fresson
                           Karen Blanguernon
                           Anne Bellec
                           Valérie Mayoux
Color Process: Eastman Color (in part only)
Uncredited Supervisory Editor: Chris Marker

Format: Color, 35mm, 16mm (16mm blown up to 35mm)
Running Time: 115 minutes; Godard's segment, 15 minutes

25. **LA CHINOISE, OU PLUTÔT À LA CHINOISE** (Productions
   de la Guéville/Parc Films/Simar Films/Anouchka Films/Athos-
   Films, 1967)
Subtitle: *Ou plutôt à la Chinoise*
English Title: *La Chinoise, Or, More Actually, After the Fashion of
   the Chinese*
Production Manager: Philippe Dussart
Director: Jean-Luc Godard
Assistant Director: Charles Bitsch
Script: Jean-Luc Godard
Director of Photography: Raoul Coutard
Color Process: Eastman Color
Camera Operator: Georges Liron
Editing: Agnès Guillemot
        Delphine Desfons
Music: Karl-Heinz Stockhausen
Sound: René Levert
Cast: Anne Wiazemsky (Véronique)
       Jean-Pierre Léaud (Guillaume)
       Michel Sémeniako (Henri)
       Lex de Bruïjn (Kirilov)
       Juliet Berto (Yvonne)
       Omar Diop (Comrade X)
       Francis Jeanson (Himself)
Format: Color, 35mm
Running Time: 90 minutes

26. **L'ALLER ET RETOUR ANDATE E RITORNO DES ENFANTS
   PRODIGUES DEI FIGLI PRODIGHI** (Sketch in *Amore e
   rabbia/Vangelo 70*) (Anouchka Films/Castoro Film, 1967)
Director: Jean-Luc Godard
Assistant Director: Charles Bitsch
Script: Jean-Luc Godard
Director of Photography: Alain Levent (Techniscope, Eastman
        color)
Editing: Agnès Guillemot
Sound: Guy Villette
Art Director: Mimmo Scavia

Music: Giovanni Fusco
Cast: Nino Castelnuovo (Him)
       Catherine Jourdan (Female Witness)
       Christine Guého (Her)
       Paolo Pozzesi (Male Witness)
Format: Color, 35mm
Running Time: 26 minutes

27. **LE WEEK-END** (Comacico/Les Films Copernic/LIRA Films,
    Paris/Ascot Cineraid, Rome, 1967)
U.S./British Title: *Week-end*
Production Managers: Ralph Baum
                  Philippe Senné
Director: Jean-Luc Godard
Assistant Director: Claude Miler
Script: Jean-Luc Godard
Director of Photography: Raoul Coutard
Color Process: Eastman Color
Editing: Agnès Guillemot
Music: Antoine Duhamel
      Mozart's Piano Sonata K. 576
Song: "Allô, tu m'entends": Guy Béart
Sound: René Levert
Cast: Mireille Darc (Corinne)
       Jean Yanne (Roland)
       Jean-Pierre Kalfon (Leader of the F.L.S.O.)
       Valérie Lagrange (His Moll)
       Jean-Pierre Léaud (Saint-Just/Man in Phone Booth)
       Yves Beneyton (Member of the F.L.S.O.)
       Paul Gégauff (Pianist)
       Daniel Pommereulle (Joseph Balsamo)
       Yves Afonso (Gros Poucet)
       Blandine Jeanson (Emily Brontë/Girl in Farmyard)
       Ernest Menzer (Cook)
       Georges Staquet (Tractor Driver)
       Juliet Berto (Girl in car crash/Member of the F.L.S.O.)
       Anne Wiazemsky (Girl in farmyard/Member of the
          F.L.S.O.)
       Virginie Vignon (Marie-Madeleine)
       Monsieur Jojot
       Isabelle Pons

Format: Color, 35mm
Running Time: 95 minutes

28. **LE GAI SAVOIR** (O.R.T.F., Anouchka Films, Paris/Bavaria Atelier, Munich, 1968)
American Title: *The Joyful Wisdom*
Director: Jean-Luc Godard
Script: Jean-Luc Godard
Director of Photography: Jean Leclerc
Color Process: Eastman Color
Cast: Juliet Berto (Patricia)
         Jean-Pierre Léaud (Émile Rousseau)
Format: Color, 35mm
Running Time: 91 minutes

29. **CINÉ-TRACTS** (Series of 2 to 4 minute shorts) (1968)
Producer: Jean-Luc Godard
Director: Jean-Luc Godard
Script: Jean-Luc Godard
Editing: Jean-Luc Godard and others
Format: B/W, 16mm

30. **UN FILM COMME LES AUTRES** (1968)
English Title: *A Film Like All the Others*
Directors: Groupe Dziga Vertov
                  (Jean-Luc Godard, Jean-Pierre Gorin)
Producer: Jean-Luc Godard, Jean-Pierre Gorin)
Script: Jean-Luc Godard, Jean-Pierre Gorin)
Cast: "Students from Vincennes and workers from the Renault plant at Flins" (Monaco 1988, 398).
Color Process: Eastman Color
Format: Color, 16mm
Running Time: 100 minutes

31. **ONE PLUS ONE** (Cupid Productions, 1968)
Distributor's Title: *Sympathy for the Devil*
Executive Producer: Eleni Collard
Producers: Michael Pearson
                  Iain Quarrier

Production Managers: Clive Freedman
　　　　　　　　　　Paul de Burgh
Director: Jean-Luc Godard
Script: Jean-Luc Godard
Director of Photography: Tony Richmond
Color Process: Eastman Color
Camera Operator: Colin Corby
Editing: Ken Rowles
Music: The Rolling Stones
Sound: Arthur Bradburn
Narrator: Sean Lynch
Cast: The Rolling Stones (Mick Jagger, Keith Richards, Brian
　　　　Jones, Charlie Watts, Bill Wyman)
　　　Anne Wiazemsky (Eve Democracy)
　　　Iain Quarrier
　　　Frankie Dymon, Jr.
　　　Danny Daniels
　　　Illario Pedro
　　　Roy Stewart
　　　Limbert Spencer
　　　Tommy Ansar
　　　Michael McKay
　　　Rudi Patterson
　　　Mark Matthew
　　　Karl Lewis
　　　Bernard Boston
　　　Niké Arrighi
　　　Françoise Pascal
　　　Joanna David
　　　Monica Walters
　　　Glenna Forster Jones
　　　Elizabeth Long
　　　Jeanette Wild
　　　Harry Douglas
　　　Colin Cunningham
　　　Graham Peet
　　　Matthew Knox
　　　Barbara Coleridge
Format: Color, 35mm
Running Time: 99 minutes

32. **ONE AMERICAN MOVIE (1 A.M.).** Abandoned by
Godard/Gorin during production. See entry Number 39, **ONE
P.M.**, below.

33. **BRITISH SOUNDS** (Kestrel Productions, for London Weekend
Television, 1969)
Producers: Irving Teitelbaum
          Kenith Trodd
Director: Jean-Luc Godard
Script: Jean-Luc Godard
Director of Photography: Charles Stewart
Color Process: Eastman Color
Editing: Elizabeth Kozmian
Sound: Fred Sharp
Researcher: Mo Teitelbaum
Format: Color, 16mm
Running Time: 52 minutes

34. **PRAVDA** (Centre Européen Cinéma Radio Télévision, 1969)
English Title: *Truth*
Producer: Claude Nedjar
Directors: Groupe Dziga Vertov (Jean-Luc Godard, Jean-Henri
     Roger, Paul Burron)
Script: Groupe Dziga Vertov (Jean-Luc Godard, Jean-Henri Roger,
     Paul Burron)
Director of Photography: Groupe Dziga Vertov (Jean-Luc Godard,
                 Jean-Henri Roger, Paul Burron)
Color Process: Eastman Color
Editing: Groupe Dziga Vertov (Jean-Luc Godard, Jean-Henri Roger,
     Paul Burron)
Sound: Groupe Dziga Vertov (Jean-Luc Godard, Jean-Henri Roger,
     Paul Burron)
Cast: Vera Chytilova (Herself)
      Other natives of the CSR
Format: Color, 16mm
Running Time: 58 minutes

35. **LE VENT D'EST** (Poli Film/Anouchka Films/Kuntz Film, 1969)
English Title: *Wind from the East*
Director: Groupe Dziga Vertov (Jean-Luc Godard, Jean-Pierre
     Gorin, Gérard Martin)

Script: Jean-Luc Godard
    Daniel Cohn-Bendit
    Sergio Bazzini
Director of Photography: Mario Vulpiani
Color Process: Eastman Color
Editing: Jean-Luc Godard
    Jean-Pierre Gorin
Sound: Antonio Ventura
    Carlo Diotalleri
Cast: Gian Maria Volonté (Cavalry Officer)
    Anne Wiazemsky (The Girl)
    Paolo Pozzesi
    Christiana Tullio Altan
Format: Color, 16mm
Running Time: 100 minutes

36. **LOTTE IN ITALIA / LUTTES EN ITALIE** (Cosmoseion for RAI, 1969)
English Title: *Struggle in Italy*
Director: Groupe Dziga Vertov (Jean-Luc Godard, Jean-Pierre Gorin)
Script: Groupe Dziga Vertov (Jean-Luc Godard, Jean-Pierre Gorin)
Cast: Christiana Tullio Altan
    Anne Wiazemsky
    Jérôme Hinstin
    Paolo Pozzesi
Color Process: Eastman Color
Format: Color, 16mm
Running Time: 76 minutes

37. **VLADIMIR ET ROSA** (Grove Press Evergreen Films/Telepool, 1971)
Director: Groupe Dziga Vertov (Jean-Luc Godard, Jean-Pierre Gorin)
Script: Groupe Dziga Vertov (Jean-Luc Godard, Jean-Pierre Gorin)
Director of Photography: Groupe Dziga Vertov (Jean-Luc Godard, Jean-Pierre Gorin)
Cast: Anne Wiazemsky (Herself)
    Jean-Pierre Gorin (Vladimir)
    Juliet Berto (Herself)

Jean-Luc Godard (Rosa)
Ernest Menzer (Judge Julius Hoffman)
Claude Nedjar (Dave Dellinger)
Color Process: Eastman Color
Format: Color, 16mm
Running Time: 106 minutes

38. JUSQU'À LA VICTOIRE (Groupe Dziga Vertov, 1970)
English Title: *Till Victory*
Directors: Groupe Dziga Vertov (Jean-Luc Godard, Jean-Pierre
    Gorin)
Never completed; editing interrupted by Godard's accident in
    1971.
Footage used in *Ici et ailleurs* (1974); see entry 42 below.

39. 1 P.M./ONE PARALLEL MOVIE (Leacock-Pennebaker, Inc.,
    1968–71)
Incorporates footage from: *1 P.M./One Parallel Movie*, abandoned
    by Godard/Gorin (see entry 32)
Directors: Jean-Luc Godard/Jean-Pierre Gorin/D. A. Pennebaker
Script: Jean-Luc Godard/Jean-Pierre Gorin/D. A. Pennebaker
Color Process: Eastman Color
Directors of Photography: D. A. Pennebaker
                          Richard Leacock
Cast: Rip Torn (Himself)
       The Jefferson Airplane (Themselves)
       Eldridge Cleaver (Himself)
       Tom Hayden (Himself)
       Tom Luddy (Himself)
       Paula Madder (Herself)
       Anne Wiazemsky (Herself)
       Jean-Luc Godard (Himself)
       Richard Leacock (Himself)
       LeRoi Jones (Himself)
Format: Color, 16mm
Running Time: 90 minutes
The film was begun in Fall, 1968, but Godard and Gorin quit the
project in March of 1970. Leacock-Pennebaker supervised final
editing of the film, which was finally released in 1971 as *1 P.M.*, or
One Parallel Movie.

40. **TOUT VA BIEN** (Anouchka Films/Vicco Films/Empire
   Film/Belstan Productions, 1972)
English Titles: *Everything's O.K./Just Great/All is Well*
Producers: Alain Coiffier
          J. P. Rassam
          Jean-Luc Godard
Directors: Jean-Luc Godard
          Jean-Pierre Gorin
Script: Jean-Luc Godard
          Jean-Pierre Gorin
Director of Photography: Armand Marco
Editing: Kenout Peltier
Sound: Bernard Ortion
          Armand Bonfanti
Art Director: Jacques Dugied
Music: Eric Charden
          Thomas Rivat
          Paul Beuscher
Cast: Yves Montand (Jacques)
          Jane Fonda (Susan)
          Anne Wiazemsky (Leftist)
          Vittorio Caprioli (Factory Manager)
          Jean Pignol (CGT Relegate)
          Pierre Oudry (Frédérick)
          Elizabeth Chauvin (Geneviève)
          Eric Chartier (Lucien)
          Yves Gabrielli (Leon)
          Bugette (Georges)
          Castel Casti (Jacques)
          Michel Marot (Communist Party Representative)
          Huguette Miéville (Georgette)
          Marcel Gassouk (2nd CGT Delegate)
          Jean-René Defleurieu (Leftist)
Color Process: Eastman Color
Format: Color, 35mm
Running Time: 95 minutes

41. **LETTRE À JANE:** *Investigation of a Still Photograph* (Jean-Luc
   Godard and Jean-Pierre Gorin, 1972)
Producer: Sonimage

Directors: Jean-Luc Godard
    Jean-Pierre Gorin
Script: Jean-Luc Godard
    Jean-Pierre Gorin
Cast: A still of Jane Fonda in Vietnam, along with stills from *The Magnificent Ambersons* and other films.
Narrators: Jean-Luc Godard, Jean-Pierre Gorin
Color Process: Eastman Color
Format: Color, 16mm
Running Time: 52 minutes

42. **ICI ET AILLEURS** (Sonimage/I.N.A., 1974)
English Title: *Here and Elsewhere*
Producer: Coralie International and JR Films
Directors: Jean-Luc Godard
    Anne-Marie Miéville
    Jean-Pierre Gorin
Script: Jean-Luc Godard
    Anne-Marie Miéville
    Jean-Pierre Gorin
Director of Photography: William Lubtchansky
Color Process: Eastman Color
Editing: Anne-Marie Miéville (from footage shot in 1970 by
    Groupe Dziga Vertov as *Jusqu'à la victoire*)
Format: Color, 16mm
Running Time: 55 minutes

43. **NUMÉRO DEUX** (Sonimage/Bela Prod./S.N.C., 1975)
Subtitle: *À bout de souffle (Out of Breath Again)*
English Title: *Number Two*
Producers: Jean-Luc Godard
    Anne-Marie Miéville
Director: Jean-Luc Godard
Script: Jean-Luc Godard
    Anne-Marie Miéville
Director of Photography: William Lubtchansky
Video: Gérard Teissedre
Technical Collaboration: Milka Assaf
         Gérard Martin
Sound: Jean-Pierre Ruh
Music: Leo Ferré

Cast: Sandrine Battistella (Sandrine, the wife)
   Pierre Oudry (Husband)
   Alexandre Rignault (Grandpa)
   Rachel Stefanopoli (Grandma)
   Jean-Luc Godard (Himself)
Format: Color, 35mm, using video elements
Running Time: 88 minutes

44. **COMMENT ÇA VA** (Sonimage/I.N.A./Bela Prod./S.N.C., 1976)
Directors: Jean-Luc Godard
      Anne-Marie Miéville
Script: Jean-Luc Godard
      Anne-Marie Miéville
Director of Photography: William Lubtchansky
Music: Jean Schwartz
Cast: Anne-Marie Miéville (Master Narrator)
   M. Marot
Color Process: Eastman Color
Format: Color, 16mm
Running Time: 78 minutes
Note: Released in 1978

45. **SIX FOIS DEUX/SUR ET SOUS LA COMMUNICATION.** Part
   1: Ya personne/Louison. Part 2: Leçons de choses/Jean-Luc.
   Part 3: Photo et cie/Marcel. Part 4: Pas d'histoires/Nanas. Part
   5: Nous trois/René(e)s. Part 6: Avant et après/Jacqueline et
   Ludovic. (Sonimage/I.N.A., 1976)
English Title: *6 x 2*
Directors: Jean-Luc Godard
      Anne-Marie Miéville
Script: Jean-Luc Godard
      Anne-Marie Miéville
Editing: Jean-Luc Godard
      Anne-Marie Miéville
Directors of Photography: William Lubtchansky
               Gérard Teissedre
Technical Collaboration: Dominique Champuis
               Philippe Rony
               Henri False
               Joël Mellier
               Louisette Neil

Format: Color, video
Running Time: 100 minutes each part

46. FRANCE/TOUR/DÉTOUR/DEUX/ENFANTS. Program 1:
Obscur/Chimie. Program 2: Lumière/Physique. Program 3:
Connu/Géométrie/Géographie. Program 4:
Inconnu/Technique. Program 5: Inpression/Dictée. Program 6:
Expression/Français. Program 9: Pouvoir/Musique. Program 10:
Roman/Économie. Program 11: Réalité/Logique. Program 12:
Rêve/Morale. (I.N.A. for Antenne 2/Sonimage, Grenoble,
1977–78)
Directors: Jean-Luc Godard
           Anne-Marie Miéville
Script: Jean-Luc Godard
        Anne-Marie Miéville
Directors of Photography: Pierre Binggeli
                          William Lubtchansky
                          Dominique Chapuis
                          Philippe Rony
Cast: Camille Virolleud
      Arnaud Martin
      Betty Berr
      Albert Dray
Format: Color, video
Running Time: 26 minutes per episode; twelve episodes

47. SCÉNARIO DE SAUVE QUI PEUT (LA VIE) (1979)
Producer: JLG Films
Director: Jean-Luc Godard
Format: Color, video
Running Time: 20 minutes

48. SAUVE QUI PEUT (LA VIE) (Sara Films/MK2/Saga
Production/Sonimage/ C.N.C./ Z.D.F./S.S.R./O.R.F., 1979)
English Titles: *Every Man For Himself; Slow Motion*
Producers: Alain Sarde
           Jean-Luc Godard
Director: Jean-Luc Godard
Script: Anne-Marie Miéville
        Jean-Claude Carrière

Directors of Photography: William Lubtchansky
                          Renato Berta
                          Jean-Bernard Menoud
Color Process: Eastman Color
Editing: Jean-Luc Godard
         Anne-Marie Miéville
Sound: Jacques Maumont
       Luc Yersin
       Oscar Stellavox
Music: Gabriel Yared
Cast: Isabelle Huppert (Isabella Rivière)
      Jacques Dutronc (Paul Godard)
      Nathalie Baye (Denise Rimbaud)
      Cécile Tanner (Paul's Daughter)
      Roland Amstutz (2nd Client)
      Anna Baldaccini (Isabella's Sister)
      Fred Personne (2nd Client)
      Nicole Jacquet (Woman)
      Dore DeRosa (Life Attendant)
      Monique Barshaca (Opera Singer)
      Paule Muret (Paul's Ex-Wife)
      Michel Cassagne (Piaget)
      Marguerite Duras (Her Own Voice)
Format: Color, 35mm
Running Time: 87 minutes

49. **LETTRE À FREDDY BUACHE** (Film et Vidéo Productions, 1981)
Director: Jean-Luc Godard in collaboration with Pierre Binggeli and Gérard Rucy
Script: Jean-Luc Godard
Director of Photography: Jean-Bernard Menoud
Editing: Jean-Luc Godard
Sound: François Musy.
Music: Ravel
Format: Video transferred to 35mm Eastman Color
Running Time: 11 minutes

50. **CHANGER D'IMAGE** (sequence for the broadcast Le Changement a plus d'un titre) (1982)
Director: Jean-Luc Godard

Cast: Jean-Luc Godard
Format: Color, video
Running Time: 9 minutes

51. **PASSION** (Sara Films/Sonimage/Films A2/Film et Vidéo
    Production SA/S.S.R., 1982)
Producer: Alain Sarde
Director: Jean-Luc Godard
Script: Jean-Luc Godard
Editing: Jean-Luc Godard
Director of Photography: Raoul Coutard
Sound: François Musy
Music: Mozart
       Dvorak
       Ravel
       Beethoven
       Fauré
Cast: Isabelle Huppert (Isabelle)
       Hanna Schygulla (Hanna)
       Michel Piccoli (Michel Gulla)
       Jerzy Radziwilowicz (Jerzy)
       Laszlo Szabo (Lazlo)
Color Process: Eastman Color
Format: Color, 35 mm
Running Time: 87 minutes

52. **SCÉNARIO DU FILM PASSION** (JLG Films/Studio
    TransVidéo/Télévision Suisse Romande, 1982)
Directors: Jean-Luc Godard in collaboration with Jean-Bernard
       Menoud, Anne-Marie Miéville, and Pierre Binggeli
Format: Color, video
Running Time: 54 minutes

53. **PRÉNOM: CARMEN** (Sara Films/Jean-Luc Godard Films, 1983)
English Title: *First Name Carmen*
Producer: Alain Sarde
Director: Jean-Luc Godard
Script: Anne-Marie Miéville
Color Process: Eastman Color
Directors of Photography: Raoul Coutard
                   Jean Garcenot

Editing: Suzanne Lang-Villar
          Jean-Luc Godard
Sound: François Musy
Music: Beethoven (Quartets Nos. 9, 10, 14, 15, and 16)
          Tom Waits ("Ruby's Arms")
Cast: Maruschka Detmers (Carmen X)
          Jacques Bonaffé (Joseph Bonaffe)
          Myriem Roussel (Claire)
          Christophe Odent (Gang Leader)
          Jean-Luc Godard (Uncle Jean)
          Hippolyte Girardot (Fred)
          Bertrand Liebert (Carmen's Bodyguard)
Format: Color, 35mm
Running Time: 85 minutes

54. PETITES NOTES À PROPOS DU FILM JE VOUS SALUE, MARIE (1983)
Producer: JLG Films
Director: Jean-Luc Godard
Cast: Jean-Luc Godard
          Myriem Roussel
          Thierry Rode
          Anne-Marie Miéville
Format: Color, video
Running Time: 25 minutes

55. JE VOUS SALUE, MARIE (Pégase Films/S.S.R./JLG Films/Sara Films/Channel 4, 1985)
English Title: *Hail Mary*
Director: Jean-Luc Godard
Script: Jean-Luc Godard
Directors of Photography: Jean-Bernard Menoud
                                         Jacques Firmann
Color Process: Eastman Color
Editing: Anne-Marie Miéville
Sound: François Musy
Music: Bach
          Dvorak
          Coltrane
Cast: Anne Gauthier (Eva)
          Johan Leysen (Professor)

Myriem Roussel (Marie)
Thierry Rode (Joseph)
Philippe Lacoste (Angel Gabriel)
Juliette Binoche (Juliette)
Manon Anderson (Little Girl)
Malachi Jara Kohan (Little Boy Jesus)
Format: Color, 35mm
Running Time: 72 minutes

56. **DÉTECTIVE** (Sara Films/JLG Films, 1985)
Director: Jean-Luc Godard
Assistant Director: Rénald Calcagni
Script: Jean-Luc Godard
        Alain Sarde
        Philippe Setbon
        Anne-Marie Miéville
Director of Photography: Bruno Nuytten
Color Process: Eastman Color
Editing: Marilyne Dubreuil
Sound: Pierre Gamet
        François Musy
Music: Schubert
        Wagner
        Chopin
        Liszt
        Honegger
        Chabrier
        Ornette Coleman
        Jean Schwarz
Cast: Nathalie Baye (Françoise Chenal)
        Claude Brasseur (Émile Chenal)
        Stéphane Ferrara (Tiger Jones)
        Johnny Hallyday (Jim Fox-Warner/Impresario)
        Jean-Pierre Léaud (Inspector Neveu)
        Alain Cuny (Old Mafioso)
        Laurent Terzieff (Uncle William Prospero, Detective)
        Cyril Autin (Punk Groupie)
        Eugene Berthier (Eugene)
        Emmanuelle Seigner (Grace Kelly)
        Julie Delpy (Wise Young Girl)
        Xavier Saint-Marcary (Accountant/Body Guard)

Anne Gisele Glass (Anne)
Aurelle Doazan (Ariel)
Pierre Bertin (Young Son)
Alexandra Garijo (Young Daughter)
Format: Color, 35mm
Running Time: 95 minutes

57. **GRANDEUR ET DÉCADENCE D'UN PETIT COMMERCE DE
    CINÉMA** (TFI, "Série Noire"/Hamster Prod./JLG Films, 1986)
Director: Jean-Luc Godard
Producer: Pierre Grimblat
English Titles: *The Grandeur and Decadence of a Small-Time
               Filmmaker/The Rise and Fall of a Small Film
               Company*
Script: Jean-Luc Godard, from a novel by James Hadley Chase
Assistant Directors: Rénald Calcagni
                     Richard Debuisne
                     Marie-Christine Barrière
Directors of Photography: Caroline Champetier
                          Serge Le François
Color Process: Eastman Color
Sound: François Musy
       Pierre-Alain Besse
Music: Béla Bartók
       Leonard Cohen
       Bob Dylan
       Janis Joplin
       Joni Mitchell
Cast: Jean-Pierre Léaud (Gaspard Bazin)
      Jean-Pierre Mocky (Jean Almereyda)
      Marie Valera
      Jean-Luc Godard
Format: Color, 16mm
Running Time: 52 minutes

58. **SOFT AND HARD (A Soft Conversation between Two Friends
    on a Hard Subject)** (JLG Films/Channel 4, 1986)
Directors: Jean-Luc Godard
           Anne-Marie Miéville
Cast: Jean-Luc Godard
      Anne-Marie Miéville

Format: Color, video
Running Time: 48 minutes

59. **J.L.G. MEETS W.A. (Meetin' WA)** (Jean-Luc Godard, 1986)
Director: Jean-Luc Godard
Cast: Woody Allen
        Jean-Luc Godard
Format: Color, video
Running Time: 26 minutes

60. **ARMIDE** (sequence for *Aria*) (Lightyear Entertainment/Virgin
        Vision, 1987)
Producer: Don Boyd
Associate Producer: François Hamel
Director: Jean-Luc Godard
Assistant Directors: Rénald Calcagni
                            Jacques Lobeleux
Director of Photography: Caroline Champetier
Color Process: Eastman Color
Editing: Jean-Luc Godard
Music: Jean-Baptiste Lully (aria "Enfin, il est en ma puissance")
        sung by Rachel Yakar, Zeger Wandersteene, Danièle Borst
Cast: Marion Peterson
        Valérie Allain
        Jacques Neuville
        Luke Corre
Format: Color, 35mm
Running Time: 12 minutes

61. **KING LEAR** (Cannon Films, Golan-Globus, 1987)
Producers: Menahem Golan
                Yoram Globus
Director: Jean-Luc Godard
Script: Jean-Luc Godard, from the play *King Lear*, by William
        Shakespeare
Director of Photography: Sophie Maintigneux
Color Process: Eastman Color
Editing: Jean-Luc Godard
Sound: François Musy
Cast: Burgess Meredith (Don Learo/King Lear)
        Peter Sellars (William Shakespeare Jr. V)

Molly Ringwald (Cordelia)
Woody Allen (Mr. Alien)
Norman Mailer (the First Don Learo)
Kate Mailer (the First Cordelia)
Jean-Luc Godard (Pluggy)
Michele Halberstadt
Léos Carax
Julie Delpy
Format: Color, 35mm
Running Time: 90 minutes

62. **SOIGNE TA DROITE** (Gaumont/JLG Films/Xanadu Films, 1987)
English Titles: *Keep Your Right Up, Keep Up Your Right, Watch Your Right, Look Out for Your Right.*
Producer: Philippe DeChaise Martin
Director: Jean-Luc Godard
Script: Jean-Luc Godard
Assistant Director: Richard Debuisne
Camera Operator: Jean-Bernard Menoud
With the Assistance of: Marie-Christine Barrière
                        Rénald Calcagni
                        Hervé Duhamel
Director of Photography: Caroline Champetier
Color Process: Eastman Color
Editing: Christine Benoît
Sound: François Musy
Music: Rita Mitsouko
Cast: Jean-Luc Godard (The Idiot/The Prince)
      Jacques Villeret (The Individual)
      François Périer (The Man)
      Jane Birkin (The Cricket)
      Michel Galabru (The Admiral)
      Dominique Lavanant (The Admiral's Wife)
      Jacques Rufus (The Policeman)
      Pauline Lafont (The Golfer)
Format: Color, 35mm
Running Time: 82 minutes

63. **ON S'EST TOUS DÉFILÉ** (1988)
Producer: JLG Films

Director: Jean-Luc Godard
Format: Color, video
Running Time: 13 minutes

64. **PUISSANCE DE LA PAROLE** (Gaumont/JLG Films/France
Télécom, 1988)
English Title: *The Power of Speech*
Director: Jean-Luc Godard
Directors of Photography: Caroline Champetier
                          Pierre-Alain Besse
Sound: François Musy
        Pierre-Alain Besse
        Marc-Antoine Beldent
Music: Bach
        Bob Dylan
        Beethoven
        Cage
        Richard Strauss
        Franck
        Ravel
        Leonard Cohen
Cast: Jean Bouise
        Laurence Cote
        Lydia Andrei
        Michel Iribarren
Format: Color, video
Running Time: 25 minutes

65. **LE DERNIER MOT/LES FRANÇAIS ENTENDUS PAR** (for the
broadcast series *Les Français vus par*) (1988)
English Title: *The Last Word*
Producers: Anne-Marie Miéville
            Hervé Duhamel
            Marie-Christine Barrière/Erato Films/Socpresse/Le
            Figaro/JLG Films
Director: Jean-Luc Godard
Director of Photography: Pierre Bingelli
Sound: Pierre Camus
        Raoul Fruhauf
        François Musy
Music: Bach

Cast: André Marcon
        Catherine Aymerie
        Pierre Amoyal
Format: Color, video
Running Time: 13 minutes

66. **HISTOIRE(S) DU CINÉMA** (1989–   ). 1a: "Toutes les
histoires" ("All the Stories"). 1b: "Une Histoire seule" ("One
Single Story"). (Gaumont/JLG Films/La Sept/FR 3/Centre
National de la Cinématographie/Radio Télévision Suisse
Romande/Véga Films)
Director: Jean-Luc Godard
Script: Jean-Luc Godard
Editing: Jean-Luc Godard
Format: Color, video
Running Time: Total 100 minutes; 50 minutes per episode

67. **LE RAPPORT DARTY** (1989)
Directors: Jean-Luc Godard
          Anne-Marie Miéville
Cast: Jean-Luc Godard (Nathanael, the 2,000 Year-Old Robot)
      Anne-Marie Miéville ("Mamzelle Clio")
Format: Color, video
Running Time: 50 minutes

68. **NOUVELLE VAGUE** (Sara Films/Périphéria/Canal +/Véga
Films/Berne/Télévision Suisse Romande/Films
A2/C.N.C./Sofia Investimage/Sofia Créations, 1990)
English Title: *New Wave*
Producers: Alain Sarde
          Ruth Waldburger
Director: Jean-Luc Godard
Script: Jean-Luc Godard
Director of Photography: William Lubtchansky
Costume Designer: Ingebord Dietsche
Editing: Jean-Luc Godard
Production Managers: Hervé Duhamel
                    Emmanuel Finkiel
Sound: François Musy
Color Process: Eastman Color
Art Direction: Anne-Marie Miéville

Cast: Alain Delon (The Man)
     Domiziana Giordano (The Woman)
     Roland Amstutz (The Gardener)
     Laurence Cote (The Housekeeper)
     Jacques Dacqmine (The Chairman of the Board)
     Christophe Odent (The Lawyer)
     Lawrence Guerre (The Secretary)
     Joseph Lisbona (The Doctor)
     Laure Killing (The Doctor's Wife)
     Veronique Muller (1st Friend)
     Maria Pitarresti (2nd Friend)
Format: Color, 35mm
Running Time: 89 minutes

69. **L'ENFANCE DE L'ART** (sequence for the film *Comment vont les enfants*) (1990)
Producer: JLG Films/UNICEF
Directors: Jean-Luc Godard
     Anne-Marie Miéville
Script: Jean-Luc Godard
     Anne-Marie Miéville
Color Process: Eastman Color
Format: Color, 35mm
Running Time: 8 minutes

70. **ALLEMAGNE ANNÉE 90 NEUF ZÉRO** (Antenne 2/Brainstorm Productions, 1991)
English Title: *Germany Year 90 Nine Zero*
Producer: Nicole Ruelle
Director: Jean-Luc Godard
Script: Jean-Luc Godard, based on *Nos Solitudes* by Michel Hanoun (éditions du Seuil), 1991
Directors of Photography: Christophe Pollock
Camera Assistants: Andréas Erben
     Stépan Benda
Sound: Pierre-Alain Besse
     François Musy
Costumers: Alexandra Pitz
     Julia Griep
Production Management: Frederick Jardin
     Mark Schlichter

Magda Gressman
Regine Provvedi-Wedekind
Titus Fischer-Fels
Unit Production Manager/Art Director: Romain Goupil
Music: Bryars
Scelsi
Liszt
Mozart
Bach
Stravinsky
Hindemith
Beethoven
Shostakovitch
Cast: Eddie Constantine (Lemmy Caution)
Hanns Zischler (Count Zelten)
Claudia Michelsen (Charlotte Kestner/Dora)
André Labarthe (Narrator)
Nathalie Kadem (Delphine de Stael)
Robert Wittmers (Don Quixote)
Kim Kashkashian (Concert Performer)
Anton Mossine (Dimitri)
Format: Color, 35mm
Running Time: 62 minutes

71. **CONTRE L'OUBLI** (Les Films du Paradoxe/PRV/Amnesty
International, 1992)
English Title: *Lest We Forget*
Thirty directors collaborated on this film made to mark the 30th
anniversary of Amnesty International; each director appears briefly
on camera to speak out against a single instance of imprisonment
and/or torture to suppress political opposition.
Directors include: Chantal Akerman, René Allio, Constantin
Costa-Gavras, Claire Denis, Alain Resnais,
Jean-Luc Godard, Anne-Marie Miéville and
others.
Music: Mino Cinelli
Cast: Catherine Deneuve
Jane Birkin
Sami Frey
Isabelle Huppert
Marie Trintignant

Henri Cartier-Bresson
Philippe Noiret
(all as themselves)
Color Process: Eastman Color
Format: Color, 35mm
Running Time: 110 minutes

72. HÉLAS POUR MOI (Les Films Alain Sarde/Véga Films, 1993)
English Title: *Woe is Me*
Producer: Ruth Waldburger
Director: Jean-Luc Godard
Script: Jean-Luc Godard, from the play *Amphitryon 38* by Jean
       Giraudoux
Director of Photography: Caroline Champetier
Art Director: Stéphane Levy
1st Assistant Director: Frédéric Jardin
Production Managers: Catherine Mazières
                    Pierre-Alain Schatzmann
Unit Manager: Claudia Sontheim
Music: Bach
       Shostakovich
       Beethoven
       Tchaikovsky
       Honegger
Sound: François Musy
Cast: Gérard Depardieu (Simon Donnadieu)
      Laurence Masliah (Rachel Donnadieu)
      Bernard Verley (Abraham Klimt)
      Jean-Louis Loca (Max Mercure)
      François Germond (The Pastor)
      Jean-Pierre Miquel (The Other Pastor)
      Anny Romand (Drawing Instructor)
      Marc Betton (Doctor)
Color Process: Eastman Color
Format: Color, 35mm
Running Time: 85 minutes

73. JLG/JLG—Autoportrait de décembre (Gaumont/Périphéria,
    1994)
English Title: *JLG/JLG—Self-Portrait in December*
Producer: Jean-Luc Godard

Direction/Script: Jean-Luc Godard
Directors of Photography: Yves Pouliquen
                          Christian Jaquenod
Editor: Catherine Cormon
Cast: Jean-Luc Godard
       Denis Jadót
Color Process: Eastman Color
Format: Color, 35mm
Running Time: 63 minutes

74. **HISTOIRE(S) DU CINEMA** (Gaumont/JLG Films/La Sept/Fr
    3/Centre National de la Cinématographie/Radio Télévision
    Suisse Romande/Vega Films, 1994)

NB: As confirmed by Charles Silver of the Museum of Modern Art,
the exact taxonomy of these latest episodes seems subject to change.
It is important to note that these videos have been screened at various festivals and museums with alternative titles, as well as differing
segment numbers and subdivisions.
    Armond White (1996, 29) offers this taxonomy:

> So far there are two two-part videos: the first pair, made in
> 1989 and subtitled "Toutes les histoires" ("All the Stories")
> and "Une histoire seule" ("One Single Story"); the second,
> 1994's "Beauté fatale" ("Deadly Beauty") and "La Réponse des
> ténèbres" ("Darkness Answers").

However, at the 25th International Film Festival in Rotterdam
in 1996, the two new sections were divided into four parts, and presented as:

> A video project about the history of film, in which the history of
> our century is also told. Godard worked on this project for years:
> the first part was premiered in [1989] and after an apparently
> stationary period he has now added another four parts. The
> largest part of the various episodes is made up of fragments from
> historic films, from stills and aphorisms projected on screen . . .
> [in which] the pictures, the sounds and the texts often tell [asy-
> chronous] stories. A much smaller part of the material com-
> prises footage shot by Godard himself, e.g., with people like
> Serge Daney, actor/director Alain Cuny (both now dead) and

actresses such as Sabine Azéma and Julie Delpy. The four new parts, each just under half an hour (26 minutes) long are referred to as parts 2 and 3, each split up into an A and B part. Part 2A, "Seul le cinéma," consists of a kind of interview with, or rather a monologue by, Serge Daney; part 3B, "Une vague nouvelle," provides an atmospheric, even melancholy homage to post-war Italian cinema. (Program notes, 25th Rotterdam Film Festival)

So in view of these varying titles and subdivisions of the later segments of *Histoire(s) de cinéma*, the exact or final form of these episodes seems yet to be firmly established.

Director: Jean-Luc Godard
Script: Jean-Luc Godard
Editing: Jean-Luc Godard
Format: Color, video
Running Time: Total 104 minutes; 26 minutes per episode (see NB
        above)

75. **LES ENFANTS JOUENT À LA RUSSIE** (JLG Films, 1994)
English Title: *The Children Play Russian/The Kids Play Russian*
Direction/Script/Editing: Jean-Luc Godard
Producer: Ruth Waldburger
Camera: Christophe Pollock
Cast: Laszlo Szabo
        Bernard Eisenschitz
        Jean-Luc Godard
        André S. Labarthe
Running Time: 63 minutes
Format: Color, video
Distribution: Momentous Films

76. **2 X 50 ANS DE CINÉMA FRANÇAIS** (Périphéria/BFI TV/La
    Sept/ARTE, 1995)
English Title: *2 X 50 Years of French Cinema*
Direction/Script: Anne-Marie Miéville
                Jean-Luc Godard.
Camera: Anne-Marie Miéville
        Jean-Luc Godard
Editors: Jean-Luc Godard
        Anne-Marie Miéville

Production Company: France Périphéria Suisse
Executive Producers: Colin MacCabe
                     Bob Last
Executive Production Manager for the BFI: Esther Johnson
With thanks to: Mary Lea Bandy, Celeste Bartos, John Labadie,
               Gérard Vaugeois; the Museum of Modern Art;
               Pinewood Foundation.
Series Consultant: Tony Rayns
Cast: Michel Piccoli (Himself, President of the First Century of
      Cinema Association)
    C. Reigher
    E. Grynspan
    D. Jacquet
    P. Gillieron
    F. Dierx-Bernard
    X. Jougleux
Format: Color, video
Running Time: 51 minutes

WORKS CITED
AND CONSULTED

———————————— ◉ ————————————

Adair, Gilbert. 1981. "Gilbert Adair from London." *Film Comment* 17.3 (May/June): 4, 6.

Albrecht, Thomas. 1991. "Sauve qui peut (l'image): Reading for a Double Life." *Cinema Journal* 30.2 (Winter): 61–73.

Anderegg, Michael. 1982. "A Documentary Fantasy: Jean-Luc Godard's *La Chinoise*." *North Dakota Quarterly* 50.2 (Spring): 31–40.

Armes, Roy. 1966a. *French Cinema Since 1946*. Vol. 1: *The Great Tradition*. New York: A. S. Barnes.

———. 1966b. *French Cinema Since 1946*. Vol. 2: *The Personal Style*. New York: A. S. Barnes.

———. 1970. *French Film*. London: Studio Vista.

Artaud, Antonin. 1958. *The Theatre and Its Double*. Trans. Mary Caroline Richards. New York: Grove.

———. 1972a. *Antonin Artaud: Collected Works*. Vol. 3. Trans. Alastair Hamilton. London: Calder and Boyars.

———. 1972b. "Distinction between Fundamental and Formal Avant-Garde." *Collected Works*. Vol. 3. Trans. Alastair Hamilton. London: Calder and Boyars, 68.

———. 1972c. "Plan for Setting up a Company for the Production of Short Films Which Will Pay Off Quickly and Surely." *Collected Works*. Vol. 3. Trans. Alastair Hamilton. London: Calder and Boyars, 69.

Aumont, Jacques. 1985. "Godard: The View and the Voice." *Discourse* 7 (Spring): 42–65.

———. 1990. "The Fall of the Gods: Jean-Luc Godard's *Le Mépris*." Trans. Peter Graham. *French Film: Texts and Contexts*. Eds. Susan Hayward and Ginette Vincendeau. London: Routledge, 217–29.

Bachmann, Gideon. 1983. "In the Cinema, It is Never Monday." *Sight and Sound* 52.2 (Spring): 118–20.

———. 1984. "The Carrots are Cooked: A Conversation with Jean-Luc Godard." *Film Quarterly* 27.3 (Spring): 13–19.

Baecque, Antoine de. 1990. "Dans le regard de Cannes: la catastrophe." *Cahiers du Cinéma* 433 (June): 68–71.

Ball, Edward. 1986. "Thinking Out Loud." *Afterimage* 14 (October), 22.

Baron, Anne-Marie and Sylvain Garel. 1990. "*Nouvelle Vague*." *Cinéma* 468 (June): 8–10.

Barrowclough, Susan. 1985. "Godard's Marie: The Virgin Birth and a Flurry of Protest." *Sight and Sound* 54.2 (Spring): 80.

Bataille, Georges. 1988. *Inner Experience*. Trans. Leslie Anne Boldt. Albany: State U of New York P.

Bates, Robin. 1985. "Holes in the Sausage of History: May '68 as Absent Center in Three European Films." *Cinema Journal* 24.3 (Spring): 24–42.

Bellour, Raymond. 1990. *L'Entre - Images: Photo. Cinéma. Vidéo*. Paris: La Différence.

———. 1992. "(Not) Just an Other Filmmaker." *Jean-Luc Godard: Son + Image, 1974–1991*. Eds. Raymond Bellour and Mary Lea Bandy. New York: Abrams/Museum of Modern Art, 215–31.

Bellour, Raymond and Mary Lea Bandy, eds. 1992. *Jean-Luc Godard: Son + Image, 1974–1991*. New York: Abrams/Museum of Modern Art.

Benjamin, Walter. 1968. *Illuminations*. New York: Harcourt, Brace.

Benoît, Laurent. 1987. "*King Lear.*" *Cahiers du Cinéma* 399 (September): 399.

Bergala, Alain. 1979. "Enfants: Ralentir." *Cahiers du Cinéma* 301 (June): 28–33.

———. 1986a. "La beauté du geste: Serie noire de Jean-Luc Godard sur TF1." *Cahiers du Cinéma* 385 (June): 57–58.

———. 1986b. "Godard en colloque." *Cahiers du Cinéma* 386 (July/August): xii.

———. 1994. "*Hélas pour moi*: du présent comme passé légèrement corrigé." *Cinematheque* 5 (Spring): 19–27.

Bergala, Alain and Léos Carax. 1979. "Jean-Luc Godard: *Sauve qui peut (la vie)*: une journée de tournage." *Cahiers du Cinéma* 306 (December): 32–37.

Bergala, Alain, Pascal Bonitzer, and Serge Toubiana. 1985. "La guerre et la paix." *Cahiers du Cinéma* 373 (June): 60–65.

Bergala, Alain and Serge Toubiana. 1982. "En attendant *Passion*: Le chemin vers la parole." *Cahiers du Cinéma* 336 (May): 5–14, 57–60, 62–63.

———. 1988. "L'Art de (dé)montrer." *Cahiers du Cinéma* 403 (January): 50–57.

Bergstrom, Janet. 1982. "Violence and Enunciation." *Camera Obscura* 8–10 (Fall): 21–30.

Bhabha, Homi K. 1987. "Of Mimicry and Man: The Ambivalence of Colonial Discourse." *October: The First Decade, 1976–1986.* Eds. Annette Michelson, Rosalind Krauss, Douglas Crimp, and Joan Copjec. Cambridge, MA: MIT P, 317–25.

Biette, Jean-Claude. 1981. "Godard et son histoire du cinéma." *Cahiers du Cinéma* 327 (September): v–vi.

———. 1985. "L'Encrier de la modernité." *Cahiers du Cinéma* 375 (September): x–xi.

Bilodeau, François. 1988. "Godard, Wenders et Scott: L'Odysée ici-bas." *Liberte* 175 (February): 82–88.

Bogdanovich, Peter. 1967. *Fritz Lang in America*. New York: Praeger.

Bonitzer, Pascal. 1976. "Jean-Marie Straub et Jean-Luc Godard," *Cahiers du Cinéma* 264 (February): 5–10.

———. 1989. "*Sauve Qui Peut (la vie):* peur et commerce." *Cahiers du Cinéma* 316 (October): 5–7.

Bonnet, J. C., L. Audibert, and M. Devillers. 1983. "*Prénom: Carmen*." *Cinématographe* 95 (December): 8–11.

Bougut, M. 1984. "Voir un scénario." *Avant-Scène du Cinema* 323/324 (March): 77–89.

Bourdain, G. S. 1986. "Television by Godard." *New York Times* (April 13): 64.

Brooks, Peter. 1993. *Body Work: Objects of Desire in Modern Narrative*. Cambridge, MA: Harvard UP.

Braudy, Leo. and M. Dickstein, eds. 1978. *Great Film Directors: A Critical Anthology*. New York: Oxford UP.

Brown, Georgia. 1994. "His Life to Live." *The Village Voice* (May 10): 58.

Brown, Royal S., ed. 1972. *Focus on Godard*. Englewood Cliffs, NJ: Prentice Hall.

Buache, Freddy. 1985. "De Godard à Jean-Luc." *Revue Belge du Cinéma* 14 (Winter): 50–62.

Buchsbaum, Jonathan. 1988. *Cinema Engagé: Film in the Popular Front*. Urbana: U of Illinois P.

Burgoyne, Robert. 1983. "The Political Typology of Montage: The Conflict of Genres in the Films of Godard." *Enclitic* 7.1 (Spring): 14–23.

Cameron, Ian, ed. 1969. *The Films of Jean-Luc Godard*. New York: Praeger.

Canby, Vincent. 1971. "Vladimir and Rosa." *New York Times* (April 30): 45.

———. 1983a. "Proto-Fassbinder: *Letter to Freddy Buache*." *New York Times* (June 24): C8.

———. 1983b. *"Passion." New York Times* (October 4): C13.

———. 1985. "Gumshoe Gaucherie." *New York Times* (August 23): C4.

Carcassonne, Phillippe and Jacques Fieschi. 1981. "Jean-Luc Godard." *Cinématographe* 66 (March/April): 7–12.

"Cart." (pseud.). 1987. *"Soigne ta droite (Keep up Your Right).* Variety 328.11 (October 7): 24.

Caughie, John. 1986. "Popular Culture: Notes and Revisions." *High Theory/Low Culture: Analyzing Popular Television and Film.* Manchester: Manchester UP, 156–71.

Cerisuelo, Marc. 1989. *Jean-Luc Godard.* Paris: Lherminier/Quatre-Vents.

Chadwick, Whitney and Isabelle de Courtviron. 1993. *Significant Others: Creativity and Intimate Partnership.* London: Thames and Hudson.

Christensen, Peter G. 1985. "Jean-Luc Godard's *La Chinoise* and the Work of Paul Nizan." *New Zealand Journal of French Studies* 6.2 (November): 37–53.

Ciment, Michel. 1988. "Je vous salue Godard." *Positif* 324 (February): 31–33.

Clark, John. 1995. "Major League?" *Premiere* 9.1. (September): 74–77.

Collet, Jean. 1970. *Jean-Luc Godard: An Investigation into His Films and Philosophy.* Trans. Ciba Vaughan. New York: Crown, 1970. Trans. of *Jean-Luc Godard: cinéma d'aujourd'hui 18.* Paris: Éditions Séghers, 1963.

———. 1974. *Jean-Luc Godard.* Revised ed. Paris: Éditions Séghers.

Conely, Verena Andermatt. 1990. "A Fraying of Voices: Jean-Luc Godard's *Prénom Carmen." L'Esprit Createur* 39.2 (Summer): 68–80.

Cott, Jonathan. 1980. "Godard: Born-Again Filmmaker." *Rolling Stone* (November 27): 32–36.

Cox, Harvey. 1993. "Mariology, or the Feminine Side of God." *Jean-Luc Godard's "Hail Mary": Women and the Sacred in Film.* Eds. Maryel Locke and Charles Warren. Carbondale: Southern Illinois UP, 86–89.

Cunningham, Stuart and Ross Harley. 1987. "The Logic of the Virgin Mother: A Discussion of *Hail Mary.*" *Screen* 28.1 (Winter): 62–76.

Daney, Serge. 1976. "La Thérrorisé (pédagogie godardienne)." *Cahiers du Cinéma* 262–63 (January): 32–39.

Debord, Guy. 1995. *The Society of the Spectacle.* Trans. Donald Nicholson-Smith. New York: Zone.

Deleuze, Gilles. 1986. *Cinema 1: The Movement-Image.* Trans. Hugh Tomlinson and Barbara Habberjam. Minneapolis: U of Minnesota P.

———. 1989a. *Cinema 2: The Time-Image.* Trans. Hugh Tomlinson and Robert Galeta. Minneapolis: U of Minnesota P.

———. 1989b. "On the 'Crystalline Regime.'" *Art & Text* 34 (Spring): 18–22.

Denby, David. 1985. "Full of Grace." *New York* (October 21): 87–88.

Derrida, Jacques. 1985. *The Ear of the Other: Otobiography, Transference, Translation.* Trans. Peggy Kamuf. Ed. Christie McDonald. Lincoln: U of Nebraska P.

Desbarats, Carole and Jean-Paul Gorce. 1989. *L 'Effet-Godard.* Toulouse: Milan.

Diawara, Manthia. 1992. *African Cinema: Politics and Culture.* Bloomington: Indiana UP.

Dieckmann, Katherine. 1985–86. "Godard in His 'Fifth Period': An Interview." *Film Quarterly* 39.1 (Winter): 2–6.

———. 1993. "Godard's Counter Memory." *Art in America*, 81.10 (October): 65–67.

Dixon, Wheeler Winston. 1993. *The Early Film Criticism of François Truffaut.* Bloomington: Indiana UP.

————. 1995. *It Looks at You: The Returned Gaze of Cinema.* Albany: State University of New York Press.

Douchet, Jean. 1990. "Sur deux ou trois grands." *Cahiers du Cinéma* 434 (July/August): 54–55.

Draper, Ellen. 1993. "An Alternative to Godard's Metaphysics: Cinematic Presence in Miéville's *Le Livre de Marie." Jean-Luc Godard's "Hail Mary": Women and the Sacred in Film.* Eds. Maryel Locke and Charles Warren. Carbondale: Southern Illinois UP, 67–74.

Dubois, P. et al., eds. 1988. "Jean-Luc Godard: Le cinéma." *Revue Belge du Cinéma* 22/23: 1–92.

Duhamel, Georges. 1932. *Scènes de la vie future.* Paris: Mercure de France.

Duras, Marguerite and Jean-Luc Godard. 1987. "Duras-Godard: un dialogue tendre et passionné." *Cinéma* 422 (December): 6–7.

Durgnat, Raymond. 1985. "Jean-Luc Godard: His Crucifixion and Resurrection." *Monthly Film Bulletin* 52.620 (September): 268–71.

Eco, Umberto. 1993. "Do-It-Yourself Godard." *Harper's,* (May): 24–26.

Eisenstein, Sergei. 1987. "Notes for a Film of *Capital.*" Trans. Maciej Sliwowski, Jay Leyda and Annette Michelson. *October: The First Decade, 1976–1986.* Ed. Annette Michelson, Rosalind Krauss, Douglas Crimp, and Joan Copjec. Cambridge, MA: MIT Press, 115–38.

Eisner, Lotte H. 1977. *Fritz Lang.* Ed. David Robinson. New York: Oxford UP.

Eluard, Paul. 1966. *Capitale de la douleur.* Paris: Gallimard.

Erb, Cynthia. 1993. "The Madonna's Reproduction(s): Miéville, Godard, and the Figure of Mary." *Journal of Film and Video* 45.4 (Winter): 40–46.

Estève, Michel, ed. 1967. *Jean-Luc Godard au-delà du récit.* Paris: Lettres Modernes, Collection Etudes Cinématographiques.

Faccini, Dominic. 1990. *"Nouvelle Vague." Sight and Sound* 59.4 (Autumn): 274–75.

Falkenberg, Pamela. 1985. "'Hollywood' and the 'Art Cinema' as a Bipolar Modeling System: *À bout de souffle* and *Breathless.*" *Wide Angle* 7.3: 44–53.

Forbes, J. 1980–81. "Jean-Luc Godard: 2 into 3." *Sight and Sound* 50.1 (Winter): 40–45.

Foss, Paul. 1986. "Eyes, Fetishism and the Gaze." *Art & Text* 20 (February/April): 24–41.

Foucault, Michel. 1973. *The Order of Things: An Archaeology of the Human Sciences.* New York: Random House.

———. 1979. "What Is an Author?" Trans. Kari Hanet. *Screen* 20.1 (Spring): 13–33.

———. 1980. *The History of Sexuality.* Vol. 1: *An Introduction.* Trans. Robert Hurley. New York: Vintage.

———. 1986. *The History of Sexuality.* Vol. 3: *The Care of the Self.* Trans. Robert Hurley. New York: Pantheon.

Fox, T. C. 1977. "Looking for Mr. Godard." *The Village Voice* (October 31): 41.

French, Philip et al. 1967. *The Films of Jean-Luc Godard.* London: Studio Vista.

Geloin, Ghislaine. 1981. "Sartre, les media/le cinema/et le film moderne." *Papers in Romance* 3.2 (Spring): 103–16.

Gervais, Marc. 1985. "Jean-Luc Godard, 1985: These Are Not the Days." *Sight and Sound* 54.4 (Autumn): 278–83.

Ghigo, Rosa Bezzola. 1985. "Un Modello negativo: *Alphaville* di Jean-Luc Godard." *Studi di Letteratura Francese* 11: 258–74.

Giannetti, Louis D. 1975. *Godard and Others—Essays on Film Form.* Rutherford, NJ: Fairleigh Dickinson UP.

Gianvito, John. 1993. "Biographical Sketch and Filmography of Anne-Marie Miéville." *Jean-Luc Godard's "Hail Mary": Women and the Sacred in Film.* Eds. Maryel Locke and Charles Warren. Carbondale: Southern Illinois UP, 125.

Giavarini, Laurence. 1991. "À l'ouest le crépescule." *Cahiers du Cinéma* 449 (November): 82–86.

Giles, D. 1979. "Les Dernières Leçons du conneur." *Cahiers du Cinéma* 300 (May): 60–66.

Godard, Jean-Luc. 1977. *Introduction à une véritable histoire du cinéma*. Paris: Éditions Albatros.

———. 1979. "Les Dernières Leçons du donneur," *Cahiers du Cinéma* 300 (May): 60–66.

———. 1984. "Screenplay for *Week-end*." Trans. Marianne Sinclair. New York: Lorrimer.

———. 1985. *Jean-Luc Godard par Jean-Luc Godard*. Ed. Alain Bergala. Paris: Cahiers du Cinéma/Éditions de L'Étoile.

———. 1986. *Godard on Godard*. Trans. and ed. Tom Milne and Jean Narboni. New York: Da Capo.

———. 1987a. "La 9ème Symphonie," *Cahiers du Cinéma* 400 (October): 28–29.

———. 1987b. "Colles et ciseaux." *Cahiers du Cinéma* 402 (December): 14–19.

———. "Conférence de presse de Jean-Luc Godard (extraits)." 1990. *Cahiers du Cinéma* 433 (June): 10–11.

Goldmann, Annie. 1971. *Cinéma et société moderne*. Paris: Editions Anthropos.

Goodwin, Michael and Greil Marcus. 1972. *Double Feature: Movies and Politics*. New York: Outerbridge and Lazard.

Graham, Peter, ed. 1968. *The New Wave*. New York: Doubleday.

Habermas, Jürgen. 1976. *Communication and the Evolution of Society*. Trans. Thomas McCarthy. Boston: Beacon.

———. 1994. *The Past as Future*. Interviewed by Michael Haller. Trans. and ed. Max Pensky. Lincoln: U of Nebraska P.

Hachem, S. 1981. "Jean-Luc Godard, the Rebel without a Pause, is Searching for a New Cinema Grammar." *Millimeter* 9.9 (September): 187–88, 190–92.

Harcourt, Peter. 1974. *Six European Directors: Essays on the Meaning of Film Style*. Baltimore: Penguin.

Hartley, Hal. 1994. "In Images We Trust: Hal Hartley Interviews Jean-Luc Godard." *Filmmaker* 3.1 (Fall): 14, 16–18, 55–56.

Haskell, Molly. 1985. "Immaculate Deception." *Vogue*, October, p. 92.

Haycock, Joel. 1990. "The Sign of the Sociologist: Show and Anti-Show in Godard's *Masculin Féminin*." *Cinema Journal* 29.4 (Summer): 51–74.

Hedges, Inez. 1993. "Jean-Luc Godard's *Hail Mary*: Cinema's 'Virgin Birth.'" In *Jean-Luc Godard's "Hail Mary": Women and the Sacred in Film*. Ed. Maryel Locke and Charles Warren. Carbondale: Southern Illinois UP, 61–66.

Henderson, Brian. 1974. "Godard on Godard: Notes for a Reading." *Film Quarterly* 27.4 (Summer): 34–46.

————. 1980. *A Critique of Film Theory*. New York: Dutton.

Hoberman, Jim. 1986. "He-e-ere's Jean-ee: TV à la Godard." *Village Voice* (April 28): 45–46.

————. 1988. "Law and Daughter." *Village Voice* (January 26): 53.

————. 1992. "Making History." *Village Voice* (November 3): 53.

————. 1993. "Jean-Luc Godard: Picasso, Marx, and Coca-Cola." *Artnews* 92.2 (February): 57–58.

————. 1994. "The Last Wave." *Village Voice* (March 22): 43.

————. 1995a. "*Germany Year 90 Nine Zero* and *JLG by JGL*." *Village Voice* (January 24): 49.

————. 1995b. "Winter Light." *Village Voice* (January 24): 49.

————. 1995c. "Letter from Jean-Luc." *Village Voice* (February 14): 49.

Hughes, John. 1977. "Atlantic City: John Hughes on Godard's *Made in U.S.A.*" *Film Comment* 13.2 (March/April): 53–55.

Indiana, Gary. "Getting Ready for *The Golden Eighties*: A Conversation with Chantal Akerman." *Artforum* 21.10 (Summer 1983): 55–61.

Jacobson, Harlan. 1985. *"Hail Mary." Film Comment* 21 (November/December): 61–64.

James, Caryn. 1992. "Godard's Video Works." *New York Times* (October 30): C16.

Jameson, Fredric. 1990. *Signatures of the Visible.* New York: Routledge.

———. 1995. *The Geopolitical Aesthetic: Cinema and Space in the World System.* Bloomington: Indiana UP.

"Jagr." (pseudo.). 1984. *"Room 666." Variety* 315.11 (July 11): 17.

Jousse, Thierry. 1990a. "La Splendeur dans l'herbe." *Cahiers du Cinéma* 433 (June): 6–11.

———. 1990b. *"Nouvelle Vague." Cahiers du Cinéma* 433 (June): 6–9.

Jousse, Thierry and Serge Toubiana, eds. 1990a. Numéro Spécial Godard. *Cahiers du Cinéma* 437 (November).

———. 1990b. "Trente ans Depuis." *Cahiers du Cinéma* 437 (November): 4–129.

Kaplan, E. Ann. and J. Halley. 1980. "One Plus One: Ideology and Deconstruction in Godard's *Ici et ailleurs* and *Comment ça va." Millennium Film Journal* 6 (Spring): 98–102.

Katsahnias, Iannis. 1987. "Big Trouble in Little Switzerland (*King Lear* de Jean-Luc Godard)." *Cahiers du Cinéma* 397 (June): 19.

Kawin, Bruce. 1978. F. *Mindscreen: Bergman, Godard and First-Person Film.* Princeton: Princeton UP.

"Kell." (pseud.). 1983. *"Prénom: Carmen." Variety* 312.7 (September 14): 18.

Kiely, Robert. 1993. "One Catholic's View." *Jean-Luc Godard's "Hail Mary": Women and the Sacred in Film.* Eds. Maryel Locke and Charles Warren. Carbondale: Southern Illinois UP, 75–81.

Kiernan, Maureen. 1990. "Making Films Politically: Marxism in Eisenstein and Godard." *Alif: Journal of Comparative Poetics* 10: 93–113.

Kiernan, Thomas. 1973. *Jane: An Intimate Biography of Jane Fonda.* New York: Putnam.

Kinder, Marsha. 1981. "A Thrice-Told Tale: Godard's *Le Mépris.*" *Modern European Filmmakers and the Art of Adaptation.* Eds. Andrew Horton and Joan Magretta. New York: Ungar, 383.

Klawans, Stuart. 1992. "Jean-Luc Godard: Son + Image." *The Nation* 255.17 (November 23): 642–44.

Knight, Deborah. 1995. "Women, Subjectivity and the Rhetoric of Anti-Humanism in Feminist Film Theory." *New Literary History* 26.1: 39–56.

Kolker, Robert Phillip. 1973. "Angle and Reality: Godard and Gorin in America." *Sight and Sound* 42.3 (Summer): 130–33.

Kolker, Robert Phillip and Madeleine Cottenet-Hage. 1987. "Godard's *Le Gai Savoir*: A Filmic Rousseau?" *Eighteenth-Century Life* 11.2 (May): 117–22.

Krauss, Rosalind E. 1985. *The Originality of the Avant-Garde and Other Modernist Myths.* Cambridge, MA: MIT Press.

Kreidl, John. 1980. *Jean-Luc Godard.* Boston: Twayne.

Laing, Stuart. 1992. "The Politics of Culture: Institutional Change." *Cultural Revolution? The Challenge of the Arts in the 1960s.* Eds. Bart Moore-Gilbert and John Seed. London: Routledge, 72–95.

Lesage, Julia. 1974. "Looking at a Film Politically." *Jump Cut* 4 (November/December): 18–21.

———. 1976. "Visual Distancing in Godard." *Wide Angle* 1.3: 4–13.

———. 1979. *Jean-Luc Godard: A Guide to References and Resources.* Boston: G. K. Hall.

Lavaudant, Georges. 1991. "Le Cinéma spectacle." *Cahiers du Cinéma* 439 (January): 46–47.

Lefevre, Raymond. 1983. *Jean-Luc Godard.* Paris: Edilig.

Leutrat, Jean-Louis. 1994. "*Histoire(s) du cinéma*: comment devenir maître d'un souvenir." *Cinémathèque* 5 (Spring): 28–39.

Leutrat, Jean-Louis and Monique Cresci. 1986. "Traces that Resemble Us: Godard's *Passion*." *Substance: A Review of Theory and Literary Theory* 15.3: 36–51.

Leutrat, Jean-Louis and Suzanne Liandrat-Guigues. 1990. "Le Sphinx." *L'Esprit Créateur* 30.2 (Summer): 81–91.

Lev, Peter. 1993. *The Euro-American Cinema*. Austin: U of Texas P.

Locke, Maryel. 1993. "A History of the Public Controversy." *Jean-Luc Godard's "Hail Mary": Women and the Sacred in Film*. Eds. Maryel Locke and Charles Warren. Carbondale: Southern Illinois UP, 1–9.

Locke, Maryel and Charles Warren, eds. 1993. *Jean-Luc Godard's "Hail Mary": Women and the Sacred in Film*. Carbondale: Southern Illinois UP.

Loshitzky, Yosefa. 1992. "More than Style: Bettolucci's Postmodernism versus Godard's Modernism." *Criticism* 34.1 (Winter): 119–42.

———. 1995. *The Radical Faces of Godard and Bertolucci*. Detroit: Wayne State UP.

Lovell, A. 1983. "Epic Theater and Counter Cinema." *Jump Cut* 28 (April): 49–51.

Lyon, Elisabeth. 1982. "*La Passion*, c'est pas ça." *Camera Obscura* 8–10 (Fall): 7–10.

MacBean, James Roy. 1972. "Godard and the Dziga Vertov Group: Film and Dialectics." *Film Quarterly* 34.1 (Fall): 30–44.

———. 1975. *Film and Revolution*. Bloomington: Indiana UP.

———. 1984. "Filming the Inside of His Own Head: Godard's Cerebral *Passion*." *Film Quarterly* 38.1 (Fall): 16–24.

———. 1986. "*Every Man for Himself*: An Open Letter to Godard." *Jump Cut* 31 (March): 8–12.

MacCabe, Colin Myles. 1980. *Godard: Images, Sounds, Politics*. Bloomington: Indiana UP.

———. 1984. "*Every Man for Himself*." *American Film* 9.8 (June): 30–35, 71, 73.

———. 1985. "Betaville: Jean-Luc Godard Turned Film Inside Out—Now He's Doing the Same to Video." *American Film* 10.10 (September): 61–63.

———. 1992. "Jean-Luc Godard: A Life in Seven Episodes (to date)." *Jean-Luc Godard: Son + Image 1974–1991*. Eds. Raymond Bellour and Mary Lea Bandy. New York: Abrams/Museum of Modern Art, 13–21.

MacCabe, Colin and Laura Mulvey. 1980. "Images of Woman, Images of Sexuality." *Godard: Images, Sounds, Politics*. Eds. Colin MacCabe, Mick Eaton, and Laura Mulvey. Bloomington: Indiana UP, 79–104.

MacCabe, Colin, Mick Eaton and Laura Mulvey. 1980. *Godard: Images, Sounds, Politics*. Indiana UP: Bloomington.

Mahieu, Jose A. 1981. "Godard Ahora." *Cuadernos Hispanoamericanos: Revista Mensual de Cultura Hispanica* 374 (August): 373–84.

Mancini, Michelle. 1969. *Godard*. Rome: Trevi.

Marie, Michel. 1990. "'It really makes you sick!': Jean-Luc Godard's *À bout de souffle*." Trans. Carrie Tarr. *French Film: Texts and Contexts*. Eds. Susan Hayward and Ginette Vincendeau. London: Routledge, 201–15.

Martin, John W. 1983. *The Golden Age of French Cinema 1929–1939*. Boston: Twayne.

Mazabrard, Colette. 1989. "Godard Revigorant." *Cahiers du Cinéma* 419/420 (May): vi–vii.

McDonald, Boyd. 1986. "Art from the Post-Heterosexual Age." *Art & Text* 20 (February/April): 18–23.

Meisel, Myron. S. 1981. "An Interview Composed by Jean-Luc Godard." *Los Angeles Reader* (January 23): 9–11.

Mellen, Joan. 1970–71. "Vladimir and Rosa." *Cinéaste* 4.3 (Winter): 39.

Merrill, Martha. 1972. "Black Panthers in the New Wave." *Film Culture* 53/54/55 (Spring): 134–45.

Milne, Tom and Jean Narboni, eds. and trans. 1986. *Godard on Godard*. New York: Da Capo.

Minh-ha, Trinh T. *Framer Framed*. New York: Routledge, 1992.

Monaco, James. 1976. *The New Wave: Truffaut, Godard, Chabrol, Rohmer, Rivette*. New York: Oxford UP.

————. 1988. "Godard, Jean-Luc." *World Film Directors, Volume Two: 1945–1985*. Ed. John Wakeman. New York: H. W. Wilson, 392–400.

Moore, Kevin Z. 1994. "Reincarnating the Radical: Godard's *Je vous salue, Marie*," *Cinema Journal* 34.1 (Fall): 18–30.

"Mosk." (pseud.) 1975. "*Numéro Deux (Number Two)*." *Variety* 280.9 (October 8): 20.

————. 1980. "*Sauve qui peut (la vie) (Everyone for Himself in Life)*. *Variety* 299.4 (May 28): 15.

————. 1982. "*Passion*." *Variety* 307.5 (June 2): 15.

Moulds, Michael, ed. 1972–93. *International Index to Film Periodicals: An Annotated Guide*. London: International Federation of Film Archives.

Mulvey, Laura. 1993. "Marie/Eve: Continuity and Discontinuity in J-L Godard's Iconography of Women." *Jean-Luc Godard's "Hail Mary": Women and the Sacred in Film*. Ed. Maryel Locke and Charles Warren. Carbondale: Southern Illinois UP, 39–53.

Mussman, Toby, ed. 1968. *Jean-Luc Godard: A Critical Anthology*. New York: Dutton.

Narboni, Jean. 1980. "Jean-Luc Godard à Avignon: 'Laissez rêver la ligne.'" *Cahiers du Cinéma* 316 (October): 8–9.

Narboni, Jean and Tom Milne, eds. 1972. *Godard on Godard*. New York: Viking.

Naremore, James. 1990. "Authorship and the Cultural Politics of Film Criticism." *Film Quarterly* 44.1 (Fall): 14–22.

Neupert, Richard. 1985. "*Je vous salue, Marie*: Godard the Father." *Film Criticism* 10.1 (Fall): 52–56.

——. 1987. "444,000 Images Speak for Themselves." *Wide Angle* 9.1: 50–58.

Newson, Robert. 1994. "Fear of Fictions," *Narrative* 2.2 (May): 140–51.

Nicholls, David. 1979–80. "Godard's *Week-end*: Totem, Taboo, and the Fifth Republic." *Sight and Sound* 49.1 (Winter): 22–24.

Paini, Dominique. 1984. "Cinéma prénom musique." *Cahiers du Cinéma* 356 (February): vi–vii.

Pajaczkowska, Claire. 1990. "Liberté! Egalité! Paternité': Jean-Luc Godard and Anne-Marie Miéville's *Sauve qui peut (la vie)*. *French Film: Texts and Contexts*. Eds. Susan Hayward and Ginette Vincendeau. London: Routledge, 241–55.

Peary, Gerald. 1974. "Jane Fonda on Tour: Answering *Letter to Jane*." *Take One* 4.4 (July): 24–26.

Penley, Constance. 1982. "Les Enfants de la Patrie." *Camera Obscura* 8–10 (Fall): 33–60.

——. 1989. *The Future of an Illusion: Film, Feminism and Psychoanalysis*. Minneapolis: U of Minnesota P.

Perez, Gilberto. 1991. "Bell Bottom Blues." *The Nation*, 252–56 (February 18), 209–12.

Pheterson, Gail. "The Whore Stigma: Female Dishonor and Male Unworthiness." *Social Text* 37: 39–64.

Pieters, John. 1984. "Post-Structuralist 'Reading' and the Post-Modernist Text: Godard's *Two or Three Things I Know about Her*." *Soundings* 67.1 (Spring): 103–21.

Polan, Dana. 1989. "Jack and Gilles: Reflections on Deleuze's Cinema of Ideas." *Art & Text* 34 (Spring): 23–30.

Powrie, Phil. 1995. "Godard's *Prénom: Carmen*, Masochism and the Male Gaze." *Forum for Modern Language Studies* 31.1: 64–73.

Prédal, René. 1977. "La Troisième 'Époque' de Jean-Luc Godard." *Jeune Cinéma* 101 (March): 23–26.

——. 1987. "Godard, la télévision dans le cinéma." *CinémAction* 44 (June): 149–53.

Prieur, Jérôme and Alain Bergala. 1979. "France/tour/détour/deux/ enfants." *Cahiers du Cinéma* 301 (June): 24–33.

Rafferty, Terrence. 1995. "Double Godard." *New Yorker* (February 6): 92–95.

Ranvaud, D. and A. Farassino. 1983. "An Interview with Jean-Luc Godard." *Framework* 21 (Summer): 8–9.

Rawlence, Christopher. 1990. *The Missing Reel: The Untold Story of the Lost Inventor of Motion Pictures.* New York: Atheneum.

"Rich." (pseud.). 1986. "*Grandeur et Décadence d'un Petit Commerce de Cinéma (The Grandeur and Decadence of a Small-Time Filmmaker).*" *Variety* 324.6 (September 3): 20.

———. 1987. "*King Lear.*" *Variety* 328.6 (September 2): 14.

Riding, Alan. 1992. "What's in a Name if the Name is Godard?" *New York Times* (October 25): B11, B18.

Robinson, Marc. 1988. "Resurrected Images: Godard's *King Lear.*" *Performing Arts Journal* 11.1: 20–25.

Rodchenko, H. A. 1987. "Bluejean-Luc Godard." *Film Comment* 23.6 (November/December): 2, 4.

Ropars, Marie-Claire. 1982c. "L'Instance graphique dans l'écriture du film." *Littérature* 46: 59–81.

Rosenbaum, Jonathan. 1979. "Jean-Luc, Chantal, Danièle, Jean-Marie and the Others" *American Film* 4.4 (February): 52–56.

———. 1980. "Bringing Godard Back Home." *Soho News* (September 24): 41–42.

———. 1990–91. "Criticism on Film." *Sight and Sound* 60.1 (Winter): 51–54.

Roud, Richard. 1970. *Jean-Luc Godard.* Bloomington: Indiana UP.

———. 1972. "Godard is Dead, Long Live Godard/Gorin, *Tout va bien!*" *Sight and Sound* 16.3 (Summer): 122–24.

———. 1980. "Jean-Luc Godard." *Cinéma, a Critical Dictionary: The Major Film-makers,* Volume 1. Ed. Richard Roud. New York: Viking, 436–46.

Rowe, Kathleen K. 1990. "Romanticism, Sexuality, and the Canon." *Journal of Film and Video* 42.1 (Spring): 49–65.

Sarris, Andrew. 1970. "Films in Focus: Godard and the Revolution." *Village Voice* (April 30): 53, 61, 63–64.

———. 1994. "Jean-Luc Godard Now." *Interview* 24.7 (July): 84–89.

Schienfeld, Michael. 1988. *"King Lear." Films in Review* 39.5 (May): 301–2.

Schleicher, Harald. 1991. *Film-Reflexionen: autothematische filme von Wim Wenders, Jean-Luc Godard und Federico Fellini*. Tübingen: Niemeyer, 246.

Ségal, Abraham. 1976. "Les Films 'invisibles' 1968–1972." *Avant-Scène* 171–72 (July–September): 46–70.

Seiter, Ellen, et al., eds. 1989. *Remote Control: Television Audiences and Cultural Power*. New York: Routledge.

Seremetakis, C. Nadia. 1994. "The Memory of the Senses, Part II: Still Acts." *The Senses Still: Perception and Memory as Material Culture in Modernity*. Ed. C. Nadia Seremetakis. Boulder: Westview P, 23–43.

Sihvonen, Jukka Veli. 1991. "Exceeding the Limits: On the Poetics and Politics of Audiovisuality." *Dissertation Abstracts International* 52.4 (Winter): 2036C.

Silverman, Kaja. 1992. *Male Subjectivity at the Margins*. New York: Routledge.

Simon, Jean-Paul. 1976. "Les Signes et leur maître." *Ça* 3.9: 27–36.

Smith, Gavin. 1996. "Jean-Luc Godard: An Interview." *Film Comment* 32.2 (March–April): 31–41.

Sobchack, Vivian. 1992. *The Address of the Eye: A Phenomenology of Film Experience*. Princeton: Princeton UP.

Sollers, Phillippe. 1985. "Godard/Sollers: L'Entretien." *Cinéma* 314 (February): 36.

Sontag, Susan. 1996. "The Decay of Cinema." *New York Times Magazine* (February 25): 60–61.

Spivak, Gayatri Chakravorty. 1988. "Can the Subaltern Speak?" *Marxism and the Interpretation of Culture.* Ed. C. Nelson and L. Grossberg. Urbana: U of Illinois P, 271–313.

Staiger, Janet. 1985. "The Politics of Film Canons." *Cinema Journal* 24.3 (Summer): 4–22.

Stam, Robert. 1979. "*Numéro Deux*: Politics, Pornography and the Media." *Millennium Film Journal* 3 (Winter/Spring): 72–78.

——— . 1981–82. "Jean-Luc Godard's *Sauve qui peut (la vie).*" *Millennium Film Journal* 10/11 (Fall/Winter): 194–99.

——— . 1991. "*Nouvelle Vague.*" *Film Comment* 27 (January/February): 63–66.

——— . 1992. *Reflexivity in Film and Literature: From Don Quixote to Jean-Luc Godard.* New York: Columbia UP, 285.

Stein, Elliott. 1985. "*Hail Mary.*" *Film Comment* 21 (November/December): 70–71.

Sterrit, David. 1993. "Miéville and Godard: From Psychology to Spirit." *Jean-Luc Godard's "Hail Mary": Women and the Sacred in Film.* Ed. Maryel Locke and Charles Warren. Carbondale: Southern Illinois UP, 54–60.

Stoneman, Rod. 1993. "Bon Voyage: *Histoire(s) du Cinéma.*" *Sight and Sound* 3.3 (Summer): 29.

"Strat." (pseud.). 1985. "*Detective.*" *Variety* 319.3 (May 15): 14, 20.

Suárez, Juan and Millicent Manglis. 1995. "Cinema, Gender, and the Topography of Enigmas: A Conversation with Laura Mulvey." *Cinefocus* 3: 2–8.

Tarantino, Michael. 1988. "*King Lear.*" *Artforum* 26.8 (April): 141.

Taubin, Amy. 1992. "Death and the Maiden; Jean-Luc Godard at MOMA: the Video Years." *Village Voice* (November 24): 45–46.

——— . 1994a. "All My Sons." *Village Voice* (March 22): 43.

——— . 1994b. "Tapehead." *Village Voice* (September 27): 62.

——— . 1995. "Berlin's Bear Market." *Village Voice* (March 14): 54.

Thiher, Allen. 1979. *The Cinematic Muse: Critical Studies in the History of French Studies in the History of French Cinema.* Columbia: U of Missouri P.

Toffatti, S., ed. 1990. *Jean-Luc Godard.* Turin: Centre Culturel Français de Turin.

Toubiana, Serge. 1987. *"Soigne ta Droite."* *Cahiers du Cinéma* 402 (December): 10–13.

———. 1988. *"Histoire(s) du Cinema."* *Cahiers du Cinéma* 409 (June): 48.

Turner, Dennis. 1983. *"Breathless*: Mirror Stage of *Nouvelle Vague."* *Substance: A Review of Theory and Literary Criticism* 12.4: 50–63.

Vadim, Roger. 1986. *Bardot/Deneuve/Fonda.* Trans. Melinda Camber Porter. New York: Simon & Schuster.

Vincendeau, Ginette. 1992. "France 1945–65 and Hollywood: The *Policier* as International Text." *Screen* 33.1 (Spring): 50–80.

Walsh, Michael. 1976. "Godard and Me: Jean-Pierre Gorin Talks." *Take One* 5.1 (February): 14–17.

———. 1981. "Godard and Me: Jean-Pierre Gorin Talks." *The Brechtian Aspect of Radical Cinema.* Ed. Keith M. Griffiths. London: BFI, 116–28.

Walton, Kendall L. 1990. *Mimesis as Make-Believe: On the Foundations of the Representational Arts.* Cambridge, MA: Harvard UP.

Warren, Charles. 1993. "Whim, God, and the Screen." *Jean-Luc Godard's "Hail Mary": Women and the Sacred in Film.* Ed. Maryel Locke and Charles Warren. Carbondale: Southern Illinois UP, 10–26.

Waters, John. 1986. *"Hail Mary."* *American Film* 11 (January/February): 38–41.

Whalen, Tom. 1992. "The Poetry of Negation: Godard's *Les Carabiniers."* *New Orleans Review* 19.1 (Spring): 62–66.

White, Armond. 1996. "Double Helix: Jean-Luc Godard." *Film Comment* 32.2 (March–April): 26–30.

Will, David. 1986. "Edinburgh Film Festival Notes: 1. Godard's Second Comings." *Framework* 30/31: 158–69.

Williams, Alan. 1992. *Republic of Images: A History of French Filmmaking.* Cambridge, MA: Harvard UP.

Wills, David. 1986. "*Carmen*: Sound/Effect." *Cinema Journal* 25.4 (Summer): 33–43.

"With Theatres Like This, Who Needs Movies?" 1995. *New York Times Magazine* (August 20): 15.

Wollen, Peter. 1982. *Readings and Writings.* London: Verso.

———. 1992. "*L'Eternel Retour.*" *Jean-Luc Godard: Son + Image, 1974– 1991.* Eds. Raymond Bellour and Mary Lea Bandy. New York: Abrams/Museum of Modern Art, 187–95.

Wood, Robin. 1975. "In Defense of Art." *Film Comment* 11.4 (July/August): 44–51.

———. 1990. "Godard, Jean-Luc." *The International Dictionary of Films and Filmmakers. Volume 2, Directors/Filmmakers.* Ed. Christopher Lyon. Chicago: St. James, 215–22.

Woodward, Katherine S. 1984. "European Anti-Melodrama: Godard, Truffaut, and Fassbinder." *Post Script* 3.2 (Winter): 34–47.

Woolf, Virginia. 1957. *A Room of One's Own.* San Diego: Harcourt Brace Jovanovich. First Edition, 1929.

RENTAL SOURCES
FOR FILMS BY
JEAN-LUC GODARD

◉

New Yorker Films
16 West 61st Street
New York, NY 10023
PHONE (212) 247-6110
FAX (212) 307-7855

Noon Pictures
611 Broadway
Suite 742
New York, NY 10012
PHONE (212) 254-4118
FAX (212) 254-3154

Cinema Parallel
601 River Road
Sykesville, MD 21784
PHONE (410) 442-1752
FAX (410) 442-1768

Electronic Arts Intermix
536 Broadway
New York, NY 10012
(212) 966-4605
FAX (212) 941-6118

ABOUT THE AUTHOR

——————————— ◉ ———————————

Wheeler Winston Dixon is the Chairperson of the Film Studies Program at the University of Nebraska, Lincoln, and Editor of the SUNY series, Cultural Studies in Cinema/Video. Dixon is the author of more than fifty articles on film theory, history, and criticism, which have appeared in *Cinéaste, Interview, Literature/Film Quarterly, Films in Review, Post Script, Journal of Film and Video, Film Criticism, New Orleans Review, Classic Images, Film and Philosophy*, and numerous other journals. His next book will be *The Exploding Eye: A Re-Visionary History of 1960s Experimental Cinema* (SUNY Press).

INDEX